D1587347

# BRIDGESCAPE

## THE ART OF DESIGNING BRIDGES

Frederick Gottemoeller

**John Wiley & Sons, Inc.**

New York • Chichester • Weinheim • Brisbane • Singapore • Toronto

This book is printed on acid-free paper.

*Library of Congress Cataloging-in-Publication Data*
Gottemoeller, Frederick.
    Bridgescape: the art of designing bridges/by Frederick Gottemoeller.
        p. cm.
    Includes index.
    ISBN 0-471-29296-6(cloth; acid-free paper)
    1. Bridges—Design and construction. 2. Architecture—Aesthetics.
    I. Title.
    TG300.G67 1997
    725'.98—DC20                        96-8197
                                        CIP

**Printed in the United States of America**

10  9  8  7  6  5  4  3  2  1

# CONTENTS

# FOREWORD

BY DAVID P. BILLINGTON
PRINETON UNIVERSITY

In the United States of the early 1950s, anyone beginning to practice structural engineering faced a society where new construction was growing at an unprecedented rate and yet education in engineering design practically did not exist. In particular, once the interstate system began, bridges suddenly appeared in vast numbers with, sadly, very few attracting attention as anything more than "mere" utilitarian objects. Education in structural analysis and the dimensioning of structural elements took precedence over design—design, that is, in the sense of setting the form and paying attention to appearance. There was almost no literature on bridge design in the United States; post-World War II structural engineers had little knowledge of the great structures in the recent past.

Recently, however, many articles on bridge aesthetics have appeared; but in reality these works, especially those by engineers, are on design. The most complete, annotated bibliography on bridge aesthetics illustrates well the absence of bridge design writings right after World War II. Of the 244 entries, only 65 were written in the 100 years before 1950 and only 8 were written in the 1950s. By contrast 34 appeared in the sixties, 69 in the seventies, and 68 between 1980 and 1990. What all of this writing needed was some work that would organize and focus these diverse ideas into a book which could be used directly by both educators and practicing engineers. Frederick Gottemoeller has done just that in this carefully illustrated volume.

Three features mark off this book.

First, he has organized design around two sets each of five criteria: one primarily structural and having major influences on appearance and the other only secondarily structural and having less influence. Moreover, by putting each of the ten criteria in order of importance, he focuses our attention on priorities and controlling ideas rather than on merely a long checklist. At the same time he does deal with a wide variety of details but in an ordered way.

Second, he has illustrated all of the ideas with clear photos of actual bridges as well as with elegant drawings. The illustrations are not mere decoration, as they are in so many engineering texts, but are linked carefully to the text. As such they not only make clear Mr. Gottemoeller's ideas but overall they fit his central theme that all parts of the structure are to be at once both useful and attractive.

Third, he continually emphasizes the idea that bridge appearance is the province of the structural engineer and that the primary features of bridge are structural. It is *just* those structural ideas that can best lead to more pleasing bridges. The profession is called upon by society to design bridges that will please not only the present population but also posterity. The book thus expands the vision of engineering to include design in its most general sense, which implies, as he makes clear, that engineers become articulate spokespersons for the profession both in their handling of the materials for design and in their interactions with the general public.

I have worked with Fred Gottemoeller on bridge design issues for over 10 years and I know that our profession will welcome his book. It is sorely needed. Together, he and I have collaborated with many forward-looking state bridge engineers—all of whom are wrestling with the problem of responsible design: bridges that will appeal visually to the public while at the same time satisfying the stringent requirements of performance and cost. Bridges are one major example of that central cultural issue in an open society of public accountability.

That feature of accountability represents another aspect of Fred Gottemoeller's talents reflected in this book. He is deeply concerned with the problem of involving local people in the design process such that they can better understand engineering and engineers can better appreciate the need for striking appearance in bridges. Mr. Gottemoeller devotes much of his professional practice to interactions with the public and this book lays a strong groundwork for such activity. The book, being free from the dense jargon of engineering while being beautifully illustrated, will provide common ground for citizen–engineer mutual education.

The author's education in both engineering and architecture allows him to introduce ideas common to one profession that stresses aesthetics and the other profession that centers upon technique. When these two sets of ideas merge, as they do in this book, a new synthesis emerges that opens up opportunities for structural engineers. The general public is aware of the great suspension bridges; this book should make them look again at what they now see as the more mundane works of bridge engineering.

# FOREWORD

BY HAL KASSOFF
FORMER MARYLAND STATE
HIGHWAY ADMINISTRATOR

Architect, engineer, planner, teacher, leader—Fred Gottemoeller's career has been extraordinary in its breadth and commitment to excellence in all things. I've known Fred for 25 years as a colleague who has worked tirelessly to broaden the horizons of those who might otherwise become so mired in the routine trappings of technology that they would fail to seize the moment— to add a touch of character, a touch of style, a touch of class to rise above mere "by-the-book" engineering solutions.

Fred's professional passion has always been bridge architecture. His work in Maryland as highway planning director, deputy administrator of the State Highway Administration (SHA), and later as a consultant and advisor, has helped to transform aesthetic bridge design from rare exception to everyday practice. His pioneering work with SHA's chief bridge engineer, Earle "Jock" Freedman, has led to award-winning designs and national recognition for both. Fred assisted Jock, along with several SHA bridge engineers, in creating a guide to aesthetic bridge design in Maryland (distributed nationally through SHA's bridge office); on seminars for bridge design engineers in Maryland; and, with Jodi Albright (former Governor's Arts and Culture advisor), on a milestone bridge aesthetics conference and an international design competition for one of Maryland's most impressive structures, the award-winning U.S. Naval Academy Bridge over the Severn River in Annapolis.

This book is not about adding expensive gingerbread. This book is not about aesthetics as an afterthought. This book is not by an artist decrying the tyranny of technology. Rather, this book is written by an enlightened practitioner for any professional who is designing even an "everyday" bridge. The message is simply that any bridge deserves, and can be made, to be pleasing to the eye. It's that simple.

With this book, Fred Gottemoeller removes all excuses for unattractive bridges. No one intentionally sets out to design such a structure, but somewhere along the line, the design of too many bridges becomes driven by technical considerations that, for the most part, pay little attention to appearance. What Fred does in this book is direct the designer's attention to a number of key design factors that can profoundly affect the structure's appearance, with little or virtually no impact on cost. This affords every bridge designer the opportunity to experience the pride that can come when the end result meets not only the technical requirements, but also the aesthetic expectations of our customers as well. For this, we owe Fred our serious attention and our heartfelt thanks.

# PREFACE

FREDERICK GOTTEMOELLER
COLUMBIA, MARYLAND

## ENGINEERS AND AESTHETICS

In 30 years of working in, for, and managing engineering organizations I have found that most engineers recognize the importance of good appearance. Most would like to do a better job with the aesthetics of their bridges. They just are not sure how to do it.

"Aesthetics" is a mysterious subject to most engineers, not lending itself to the engineer's usual tools of analysis, and rarely taught in engineering schools. Being both an architect and engineer, I know that it is possible to demystify "aesthetics" in the minds of engineers. The works of engineers like Robert Maillart, Christian Menn, Jean Muller, and others prove that engineers can understand aesthetics. Unfortunately, such examples are too rare. The principles of bridge aesthetics should be made accessible to all engineers.

That is my goal for this book.

Bridge design is an art, an art which uses science and mathematics to support many of its judgments. Other judgments are made during bridge design which science cannot help, such as judgments about appearance. This book will give bridge designers a basis to support those aesthetic judgments, so that their judgments about appearance can be just as definitive as the ones they make about structural members, safety, or cost.

Aesthetic ideas, like any other, change over time as people working in the field bring new insights, respond to new materials and technologies, and learn from their own experiences and those of others. This book will prepare engineers to respond to these developments and contribute aesthetic insights of their own. The book's strategy is to provide engineers with basic principles and tools of analysis which will help them think through questions of appearance and then show how those ideas have been applied to example bridges.

Appearance is a subject which does not benefit from hard and fast rules. Each bridge is unique, and should be treated that way. While this book does present guidelines, rules of thumb, and comparative examples, it also encourages engineers to make their own judgments about what looks good and what doesn't, and which guidelines may apply to a particular structure and which not.

Engineers should take away from this book a permanent commitment to always consider each structure's appearance, starting with the structure's "bones": the girders, piers, and abutments. The aesthetic impact of a bridge is primarily a product of the structural members themselves. Details and color are important, but secondary.

Every year thousands of engineers design thousands of small and medium-sized bridges. These bridges are the "workhorses" of our transportation systems. Because there are so many of them, they dominate the appearance of most of our highways, neighborhoods, towns, and landscapes. Large bridges, because of their size and prominence, often receive more attention. However, smaller bridges, taken together, have the greater total impact. This book focuses on workhorse bridges—bridges with spans below 500 feet.

Most of the examples shown and some of the discussion on perception involve highway bridges and highway conditions. The principles described, however, are equally applicable to transit bridges. The sections on viaducts and ramps, for example, have a clear application to elevated transit structures.

While this book is aimed at engineers, other professionals, such as architects, landscape architects, and artists, and members of the general public concerned about the appearance of bridges should find it a useful introduction to the aesthetic side of bridge engineering.

## ACKNOWLEDGMENTS

This book grew out of observations of bridges in the United States and abroad beginning when I was a student of architecture in the College of Fine Arts at Carnegie Mellon University. Max Bill's book on Robert Maillart[1] had kindled my interest in bridges, and led to my adding civil engineering to my studies at Carnegie Mellon.

I found an intellectual framework for my observations in the work of David P. Billington of Princeton University, particularly in his book *The Tower and the Bridge*[2] and his works on Maillart.[3] David has since become a source of valuable support, a collaborator on various projects, and a friend.

The German engineer Jorg Schlaich's thoughts on conceptual engineering and his pedestrian bridges have been sources of inspiration. Another German engineer, Fritz Leonhardt, through his book *Brucken*[4] has also had a major influence on me. I am particularly indebted for his willingness to allow me the use of several illustrations from his book.

The catalyst for the book was work for the Maryland State Highway Administration (SHA). In 1987, Hal Kassoff, the highway administrator; the deputy chief engineer for bridges, Earle "Jock" Freedman; and the director of the Governor's Office of Art and Culture, Jodi Albright, agreed to a collaborative effort to improve the appearance of Maryland's bridges. David and I were engaged to assist with this effort. The following items resulted:

- Bridgescape, an international conference on bridge aesthetics.
- An international design competition for the Severn River Bridge in Annapolis, Maryland, now completed. (See Figure 1-24 (page 21), now named the new U.S. Naval Academy Bridge.)
- A program of seminars on bridge aesthetics for Maryland's bridge designers.
- *Aesthetics Bridges Users Guide,* the Maryland State Highway Administration's aesthetic design guidelines.

The Maryland Users Guide included many of the observations that I had developed, along with material from other sources, all tailored to meet Maryland conditions and requirements.

I am much indebted to Hal and Jock for permission to use the Maryland material in preparing this book. Others from the SHA Bridge Division who provided ideas and support are Paul Matys, Bob Healey, John Sarikas, Monica Pats and Glenn Vaughn.

This book takes several steps beyond the Maryland guidelines. The additional material establishes the intellectual base for the aesthetic ideas, broadens the examples, and provides guidelines with national application as well as additional detail.

The Maryland experience encouraged me to open a consulting firm specializing in the aesthetics of transportation facilities. The resulting projects have included, in most cases, substantial citizen participation efforts. These efforts have led to new insights in the productive role citizens can play in bridge design. For these I am indebted to many members of the citizen advisory committees that I have worked with.

Marty Burke of Burgess and Niple (Columbus, Ohio) has been the source of inspiration, information, and valuable criticism. His example of indefatigable effort in the preparation of *Bridge Aesthetics Around the World* by the Transportation Research Board has kept me going in the face of the usual distractions. His review of an early draft helped sharpen the sections on cost as well as other elements.

Several state and provincial bridge engineers have provided information, ideas, and inspiration. I include in this group Ed Wasserman of Tennessee;

Roger Dorton of Ontario; Don Flemming of Minnesota; John Smith and Bill Rogers of North Carolina; and Jim Roberts of California. A number of consulting engineers have been similar resources, including Tom Jenkins of Urs Greiner, Inc. (Baltimore); Ken Price of J. Muller International (Chicago); Charles Diver of Diver Brothers (Baltimore); Conrad Bridges, Art Hedgren, and Theun Van der Veen of HDR International (Sacramento, Pittsburgh, and Tampa respectively); John Kulicki of Modjeski & Masters (Harrisburg); David Harvey of Associated Engineers (Vancouver); John Steenberg of Short, Elliot and Hendrickson (St. Paul); and Frank Sears.

Working with Don Hilderbrandt of LDR International (Columbia, Maryland) on the Woodrow Wilson Bridge in Washington, D.C. has made me more aware of the role urban designers and landscape architects can play in assisting bridge design by helping to define the larger environment. Don's insights on color have also been helpful.

My associate Alicia Buchwalter has been a great help in creating, researching and organizing the illustrations.

Cathy Levay, Mary Kay Chadrue, Charlotte Miller, and Sharyn Smith have helped with the preparation of the manuscript and endured with patience and good humor my penchant for second thoughts and revisions.

In the early stages of this endeavor I was also engaged in real estate development. I am indebted to my associate, Jay Winer, for his flexibility during that time.

My good friends Jim Truby and Karl Sattler have been invaluable sources of support. Without their encouragement it is unlikely that I would have undertaken the effort.

The strongest acknowledgment must go to my wife Pat and daughters Megan and Hillary. Their patience with stops for photographs, their tolerance of me spending long nights and weekends at my trusty MacIntosh, and, most of all, their appreciation and enthusiasm made this book possible.

1   Bill, Max, 1969. *Robert Maillart, Bridges and Construction*. Westport, CT: Praeger Publishers, a division of Greenwood Publishers. First edition 1949.

2   Billington, David P., 1983. *The Tower and the Bridge: The New Art of Structural Engineering*. New York, NY: Basic Books, Inc.

3   Billington, David P., 1979. *Robert Maillart's Bridges: The Art of Engineering*. Princeton, NJ: Princeton University Press and Billington, David P., 1989. *Robert Maillart and the Art of Reinforced Concrete*. Cambridge, MA: The MIT Press.

4   Leonhardt, Fritz, 1982. *Brucken*. Cambridge, MA: The MIT Press.

chapter *one*

# INTRODUCTION

*"When the history of our time is written posterity will know us not by a cathedral or temple, but by a bridge."*

—MONTGOMERY SCHUYLER, 1877, WRITING ABOUT
JOHN ROEBLING'S BROOKLYN BRIDGE

## THE AESTHETIC DIMENSION
## OF BRIDGE ENGINEERING

Bridges speak to us.

They speak to us about the places they are or the places they take us. They speak to us about travel: the new wonders to be seen, the money to be made, the time saved, the excitement of the crossing. They speak to us about the skill of their designers and the courage of their builders. Above all, they speak to us about the values and aspirations of the communities, organizations, and persons who build them.

Several years ago United Airlines wanted to make a television commercial which conveyed the message that their services reached consumers coast to coast. Which visual images did they choose to convey that message? They chose the Brooklyn Bridge to represent the East Coast and the Golden Gate Bridge to represent the West Coast.

That's not surprising. Stretching across the Mississippi River or Tampa Bay, bridges can become symbols for whole regions. The recent and widespread familiarity of Tampa's new Sunshine Skyway shows how quickly an

FIGURE 1-1 *Brooklyn Bridge, a symbol of the East Coast.*

FIGURE 1-2 *Sunshine Skyway, a symbol of Tampa and of modern technology.*

attractive bridge can come to symbolize a region. The old Skyway was just as functional, but it never caught people's imagination. The new Skyway, with its golden cables gleaming in the sun, has become a nationally recognized symbol of the Tampa area.

The Skyway has come to symbolize something else as well. It is used to represent the best and most modern of technology. It has appeared in nationally televised commercials for luxury cars and computers. That's not such an unusual role for bridges. In the Skyway's day, Schuyler was one of many who cited the Brooklyn Bridge as the best of nineteenth-century technology.

FIGURE 1-3 *Puente de Alcantara, Spain, c. A.D. 100,[1] a symbol of imperial power.*

FIGURE 1-4 *Pont d'Avignon, France, 1178–1187,[2] a symbol of Divine charity.*

In other times, bridges spoke as well, but with different messages. To the Romans, bridges were psychological as well as physical tools to extend the emperor's control. Their message was, "I, the Emperor Trajan, by the power of Rome, have built this massive bridge; realize the impossibility of revolt."[1] In medieval times, specialized orders of monks built bridges for the benefit of the community and the greater glory of God. Their message was, "We, Les Freres du Pont, by the grace of our Lord, have built this bridge for you; join us in our pilgrimages to His holy shrines." Throughout time rulers have used bridges to control travel and commerce. Their bridges said, "I, the Duke of Cahors, have built this bridge at the edge of my realm; none may pass unless I consent; all who pass must pay my toll."[2]

**FIGURE 1-5** *Pont Valentre, France, c. 1337. A symbol of military control.*

The thousands of "everyday" bridges convey messages, too.

Take the example of the Capital Beltway (I-95/495) around Washington, D.C. There must be at least two hundred bridges on the Capital Beltway. Only two, the Woodrow Wilson and the American Legion Bridges over the Potomac River, can be considered large bridges. The other 198, taken together, cost more to build and maintain than these two. They are seen everyday by hundreds of thousands of people. They are a more prominent part of the everyday lives of these people than any of the world-famous monuments of the capital city. Collectively they have a huge impact on people's perception of their city.

Unfortunately, most everyday bridges convey a message of apathy and mediocrity. Carrying traffic but lacking grace, they are merely functional.

They could be much more. They could be works of civic art which would enliven each day's travels and make everyone's journey more pleasant. Bridges have the ability to arouse emotions like wonder, awe, surprise, or sheer enjoyment of form or color. The bridge in Figure 5-37 (page 157), on I-70 west of Denver, frames the westward traveler's first view of the Continental Divide, and magnifies the traveler's awe. It is an exception. Too many bridges arouse only boredom.

FIGURE 1-6 *A message of apathy and mediocrity, arousing only boredom.*

FIGURE 1-7 *A message of pride and skill, enhancing the traveler's enjoyment of the Virginia countryside along I-66, west of Washington, D.C.*

Today, in most countries, freedom of travel is an accepted right, and bridges are no longer asked to carry the weight (literally) of government propaganda. Bridges are public works, authorized by the voters and paid for by the tax dollars of the entire community. In this democratic age, when bridges are built by cities and states made up of voting taxpayers, everyone in a community feels the pride involved in the accomplishment. The unspoken thought is: "Isn't it great that we were able to assemble the knowledge, money, and skill to build this wonderful bridge? And now we are that much closer to our jobs, our homes, our recreation."

People today first ask that their bridges take advantage of modern technology, make wise use of resources, achieve economic efficiency, and be responsible to the environment. Then they go a step farther. They want their cities and towns to be attractive places to live. They know the truth of what Mark Twain once said, "we take stock of a city like we take stock of a man. The clothes and appearance are the externals by which we judge." They want their bridges to be a positive feature of their city. In short, they want their bridges to be beautiful.

Indeed, they are willing to act personally on their desire. Having seen so many ordinary or even ugly bridges built, they are no longer willing to leave bridge design to the professionals.

Many citizens today are demanding a voice in deciding specifically where their bridges are built and what their bridges look like.

## FIVE FUNDAMENTAL IDEAS

This book is based on five fundamental ideas.

### All Bridges Make an Aesthetic Impact

When an engineer builds a bridge, he or she creates a visible object in the environment. People see it, and they react to what they see. The bridge will make an impression: of excitement, appreciation, repulsion, or perhaps boredom. Whether or not the engineer has thought about this visual impact, the bridge will make an impact.

### People Can Agree on What is Beautiful for Bridges as Well as for Paintings and Concertos

We often hear that "beauty is in the eye of the beholder." If we take this phrase to mean that our emotional reaction to a work of art is personal and individual, then that is certainly true. But, if we take it to mean that two people cannot agree on what is a good piece of art, then it is not true. Two people may have individual reactions to the Mona Lisa, but they and millions of others can agree that the Mona Lisa is a great painting. Similarly, people can agree on which bridges are more attractive than others.

**FIGURE 1-8** *Highway Overcrossing #1.*

**FIGURE 1-9** *Highway Overcrossing #2.*

FIGURE 1-10 *Pedestrian Bridge #1.*                    FIGURE 1-11 *Pedestrian Bridge #2.*

Figures 1-8 to 1-13 show three pairs of bridges that are similar in site requirements but very different in appearance. Study them for a moment and form your own opinion about which bridge of each pair is the more attractive.

Most of us will agree that the second bridge in each pair is the more attractive.

Do the better-looking bridges have characteristics in common? Yes.

- They are "simpler," by which is meant there are fewer individual elements, and that elements which are similar in function (such as girders) are similar in size and shape.

- The girders are relatively thinner (the ratio of depth to span is smaller).

- The lines of the structure are continuous, which usually means the spans are continuous or appear to be continuous.

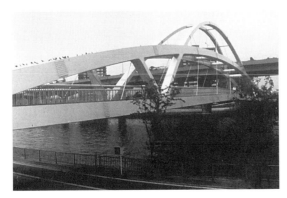

FIGURE 1-12 *River Crossing #1.*

FIGURE 1-13 *River Crossing #2.*

- The shapes of the structural members reflect the forces on them. They are thickest where the forces are the greatest, and thinner elsewhere.

We will discuss these characteristics further in Chapter Two and show how they can be used to develop new designs.

The ability to reach agreement on the characteristics of better-looking bridges is critical in a democratic society. It is only with some degree of agreement that the consensus is created for the expenditure of public funds. That does not mean the appearance of a bridge must be put to a popular vote. It does mean that, through processes of public debate, written criticism of the type prevalent in the other arts, and the example of works by outstanding practitioners, consensus can emerge about what makes a good-looking bridge. Engineers, public works directors, and the public at large can then use this consensus to guide their decisions about the bridges they build.

## Engineers Must Take Responsibility for the Aesthetic Impact of Their Bridges

Engineering is the profession in our society given responsibility for designing bridges. Engineers are used to dealing with issues of performance, efficiency, and cost, but they must also be prepared to deal with the issues of appearance as well: symbolism, appropriateness to the site, and beauty.

Engineers can't avoid the issue by taking care of the structural elements and leaving the visual quality to someone else. The appearance of the bridge is dominated by the shapes and sizes of the structural elements themselves, not by details, color, or surfaces. The Golden Gate Bridge owes its appeal to the graceful shape of its towers and cables, not to its reddish color. If the towers were ugly, painting them red would not make them attractive.

At times it has been suggested that engineers should delegate responsibility for the appearance of bridges to architects or other visually trained professionals such as urban designers, landscape architects, or sculptors. The notion is that this would result in better-looking structures. There have been some cases in which such collaborations have been successful. However, there have also been many cases in which they have resulted in overly elaborate and overly costly structures, without a great improvement in appearance. It is not hard to understand why this is so; there are significant differences between engineers and the visual professions in both approach and experience.

The differences begin with the approach of each professional to form. The visual professionals see form primarily as a tool to control space or evoke an emotion. The engineer sees form primarily as a means to control forces, and thereby costs.

A second difference is that most visual professionals are used to dealing with buildings and their immediate surroundings—but bridges are significantly different from buildings. For one thing, appearance is a matter of perception, and the perceptions of people in and around buildings are different from those perceptions of people around bridges. People in and around buildings are walking, standing, sitting, or even lying down. Most people viewing bridges are moving at 30 to 70 miles per hour and view the bridge through the windows of an automobile. Their perceptions are significantly altered in ways that are not immediately obvious, as will be explained in Chapter Two.

Bridges are also larger than all but the largest buildings, thus they are seen from greater distances and have a greater impact on the landscape and the people around them. Small elements which are important at the scale of a building, such as bricks, can become visually lost when applied to a bridge. Bridge loads are generally larger and more dynamic in character, imposing significantly different requirements on a bridge structure than on a building structure. The thermal and weather exposure of a bridge is more rigorous than that of a building structure, which usually is protected by the building's "skin."

Unless the visual professional understands all of these issues, he or she cannot make a positive contribution to the design.

Even if the engineer gives way to the visual professional, the delegation can never be complete. In the United States engineers have the professional and legal responsibility for bridges. The organizations that commission, finance, and build bridges are usually run by engineers. None of these people is willing or able to delegate complete responsibility for a bridge to a nonengineer, no matter how talented. This usually means that the "important" (structural) aspects of the bridge are reserved for the engineers, while the "window dressing" (surface details, color) is left for the visual professional. Although the details are an important part of a structure's aesthetic impact, it is the structure itself—its spans, proportions, and major elements—that has the largest role in creating its effect. If the engineer does a poor job with these major elements, no amount of architectural add-ons will compensate.

Engineers must control the structural elements—that's their job. However, if the bridge is to be a complete aesthetic success, the details, colors, and surfaces have to be in tune with the structural concept. This means the engineers should control those as well.

Architects and artists who are willing to take the time to understand the special nature of bridges can offer a positive contribution to engineers by advising on the visual aspects of span arrangements, proportions, and the shapes of major elements. Their role is comparable to that of other specialists, such as geologists or hydrologists, whom the engineer may call on for advice. However, it must be clear that the final decisions must be made by the engineer based on performance, cost, and appearance, judged together. An architect or artist can have a positive impact in the role of aesthetic advisor and critic, but the engineer must have the last word.

Engineers have accepted a responsibility to society for bridge design. For that reason, no engineer would knowingly build a bridge that is unsafe. For the same reason, no engineer should knowingly build a bridge that is ugly.

## Engineers Should Consider Good Appearance Co-equal with Strength, Safety and Cost

Bridges must safely carry their loads for a long enough time to repay the investment made in them. This basic fact imposes a hierarchy on design decision making:

- performance: structural capacity, safety, durability and maintainability;
- cost: construction and maintenance;
- appearance.

However, this statement often creates the assumption that the three criteria are necessarily in conflict, that one must be sacrificed for the other. This is not true. For example, many people think improved appearance will automatically add cost. That's because they think good appearance derives from add-ons, like an unusual color, special materials such as stone or brick, or ornamental features. In fact, the greatest aesthetic impact is made by the struc-

FIGURE 1-14 *Bridge designed by engineers of the Tennessee Department of Transportation.*

FIGURE 1-15 *Maryland route 7A over Amtrak, Havre de Grace, Maryland.*

tural members themselves—the cables, girders, and piers. These things have to be there anyway. If they are well-shaped, the bridge will be attractive, without necessarily adding cost.

The works of many of the greatest bridge engineers, men like Thomas Telford, Gustave Eiffel, John Roebling, and Robert Maillart, were able to achieve bridges which are beautiful, structurally sound, and less expensive than any alternative, all at the same time.

In decisions about appearance, as in decisions about strength and durability, the challenge is to achieve an improvement without an increase in cost. It can be done. The California, Tennessee (Figure 1-14), and Washington Department of Transportation, the Ontario Ministry of Transport, and others do this routinely.

Too often, however, some restriction in the "hard" criteria—for example, a tight budget or an unusual span requirement—is used as an excuse to ignore appearance. That shirks responsibility. The better approach is to consider the restriction a challenge and use it to find the inherent beauty contained within the problem.

That is what the engineer did, for the bridge in Figure 1-15, taking an almost impossible span-and-clearance problem and turning it into a bridge of uncommon grace. It could have been an aesthetic disaster, like so many backyard railroad bridges. Instead, it is an object of civic pride to the little town of Havre de Grace, Maryland, whose baseball field it adjoins.

Engineers can design bridges which achieve excellence in all three categories: performance, cost, and appearance. The key is to put all three issues on the table at the same time and work on improving them all at the same time, to not sacrifice one for the other.

FIGURE 1-16 *Salginatobel Bridge, Switzerland. Robert Maillart's masterwork of structural art.*

The goal is to bring forth elegance from utility. The product should be structural art.[3]

## Aesthetic Ability is a Skill Which can be Acquired and Developed by Engineers as Well as Anyone Else

Many engineers are not well prepared by their education or experience for the visual aspect of their responsibilities. However, aesthetic ability is not some mysterious quality bestowed by fate on a fortunate few. Engineers can learn what makes bridges attractive, and engineers can develop their abilities to make their own bridges attractive.

The outstanding bridges of John Roebling, Gustave Eiffel, and Robert Maillart show that engineers can produce beautiful bridges. In our generation we have the examples of Christian Menn, Jean Muller, and many others. But, producing beautiful bridges requires the commitment to do so and the willingness to learn how.

There are many tools available to help engineers improve their abilities in the visual aspects of engineering. This book presents a series of guidelines and the principles that underlie them. They are a useful base from which to consider the appearance of structures. However, they are only a beginning. Engineers should form their own opinions about what looks good, and work to develop their own aesthetic abilities. Chapter Two tells how.

## STRUCTURAL PERFORMANCE AND AESTHETICS

Structural safety cannot be compromised for the sake of appearance. That goes without saying.

With that criterion as a base, it is possible to go on to discuss the relationship of performance and appearance.

Many of the significant advances in bridge appearance have been made by engineers pioneering new structural materials, new construction techniques, and new methods of analysis in order to improve bridge performance. The bridges of John Roebling, Gustave Eiffel, and, in our century, Robert Maillart, Christian Menn, and Jean Muller are all examples. The fact that they improved appearance at the same time shows that these two qualities have factors in common and that improvements in one can and should improve the other. Finding improvements which do both is the engineer's challenge.

Robert Maillart's development of the three-hinged arch is a classic example of how this process can work.[4] Maillart began his career of concrete bridge design with the Stauffacher Bridge over the Sihl River in Zurich (Figure 1-17). Designed in the tradition of historic stone bridges, it gives no indication that the stone is merely a facing, and the loads are carried by a hidden concrete barrel arch.

His next assignment, in the rural community of Zuoz, was far from the urban sophistication of Zurich. Maillart was faced with a request to design a bridge that the tiny community could afford. He decided to strip away the stone covering and develop a shape that would make the most efficient use of the concrete that remained. The result was a three-hinged arch using a box-shaped arch, the first application of the box shape to concrete construction (Figure 1-18). The structure not only fit the town's budget, but it was an instant success with the community, and quickly became a significant landmark.

**FIGURE 1-17** *Stauffacher Bridge over the Sihl River in Zurich. Maillart's starting point for his three-hinged arches.*

FIGURE 1-18 *Zuoz Bridge, the first step.*

FIGURE 1-19 *Tavanasa Bridge. The prototype for Maillart's three-hinged arches.*

Unfortunately, after two years, the bridge developed vertical cracks in the spandrel walls, and Maillart was called back to investigate. He determined that the cracks were caused by differential shrinkage between the arch rib and deck, on the one hand, and the spandrel walls, on the other. He also knew that the stresses in the walls due to loading were very small, and concluded that the cracks posed no danger.

When he was next asked to design a bridge he wanted to use the same design which had been successful at Zuoz but he was faced with a decision about what to do about the cracks. Many engineers would have added material and reinforcing to prevent the cracks. Maillart had determined that the stresses in the walls were very small, and that the bridge could be redesigned without the walls. Therefore, he took the walls out. With no walls, there would be no cracks! The result is the bridge over the Rhine River at Tavanasa, which became the prototype for all of his later three-hinged arch structures (Figure 1-19). From here he went on to continuously refine the shape of this bridge type, looking for improvements in both the performance and aesthetic aspects of the form.

The structural success of the form can be understood by comparing it against the moment diagram for a three-hinged arch (Figure 1-20). The three-hinged arch creates maximum moments at its quarter points, exactly the point at which Maillart has placed most of his material. In other words, the bridge is thick where it has to be, and thin everywhere else. It shows how it works structurally. People respond on the aesthetic level to that demonstration, which is why Maillart's bridges are judged a success on aesthetic grounds as well as on performance and cost grounds.

The most familiar of Maillart's three-hinged arches is the Salginatobel Bridge (*see* Figure 1-16, page 12). In it he further developed his ideas, clearly differentiating the side spans and curving the arch. The bridge was selected by the Museum of Modern Art in 1949 as an outstanding example of structural art, has appeared in many books on modern art and architecture,

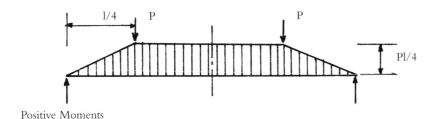

Positive Moments

**FIGURE 1-20** *Bending moment of three-hinged arch with concentrated loads at the quarter points.*

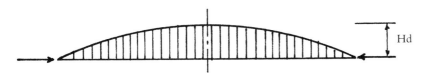

Negative Moments

Combined Moments (drawn on arch axis)

and in 1993 was named an engineering landmark by the American Society of Civil Engineers.

But even with the Salginatobel Bridge he was not satisfied. He decided, on aesthetic grounds, that the curve of the arch soffit was not satisfactory. He felt that there should be a noticeable break in the line of the underside of the arch to mark the presence of the center hinge. So, on his last bridges, he made the undersides of the arch segments almost straight, as shown in the bridge over the Arve at Vessy (Figure 1-21). He also continued to refine the form of the sidespans. His goal always was for improved structural performance, appearance, and economy, all at the same time.

As Billington puts it, "Maillart began with aesthetics, and then, with that basic consideration in mind, looked for the best structure where 'best' meant minimum materials, minimum cost, and minimum applied decoration."[5]

Of course, engineers always try to improve performance with no increase in cost, and often succeed. Maillart's difference was to also always try to improve appearance with no increase in cost, and he often succeeded.

Performance is sometimes used as a reason to rule out features which would improve appearance even though the feature will create no reduction in the performance of the bridge as a whole.

Engineers do not ask for an infinite factor of safety on any structure. It would cost too much. Nothing would be built. For any given structure and for any given technology, engineers arrive at an acceptable factor of safety based on the predictability of the loads and the consequences of failure. Once this factor of safety is decided upon, the engineer tries to apply it uniformly across the structure as a matter of economic efficiency. There is no point on

**FIGURE 1-21** *Vessy Bridge. Maillart's end point in developing the three-hinged arch.*

spending additional money on a feature if it won't make the structure, as a whole, safer.

The degree of redundancy is a characteristic that is an important contributor to safety. It is also subject to the same kind of question: How much is enough and how much is additional redundancy worth?

These questions must be settled first. Once they are settled, once the appropriate factor of safety and degree of redundancy are decided upon, the best possible appearance should be sought within these criteria.

Conversely, safety requirements beyond the established criteria should not be used as reasons to rule out features which would improve appearance. Mediocre appearance imposes its own disfunctions in community ugliness and dissatisfaction. Why incur those burdens to achieve something that is not necessary? By definition, enough is enough!

## COST AND AESTHETICS

Many engineers point to cost or issues related to cost, such as lack of design time or lack of political support, as excuses for not paying attention to appearance. Their attitude stems from a common belief that an improvement in appearance will automatically add cost. This is not necessarily true.

## The Potential Attractiveness of Structural Efficiency

As was explained previously in Five Fundamental Ideas, good appearance is often associated with bridges which efficiently respond to the flow of forces in the structure. They are thick where the stresses are highest, and thin where the stresses are lowest. Because such efficiency translates into a minimum amount of material, these structures are usually economical in cost. Thus, it is often true that a good-looking bridge is also a low-cost solution.

Indeed, some of the most attractive bridges of modern times were built because they were the most economical solution to the problem. The Swiss have a tradition of selecting bridge designs through competitions where cost and appearance are both criteria. All of the bridges Robert Maillart built as he developed his ideas for three-hinged arch bridges (Figures 1-16, 1-18, 1-19, and 1-21) were among the least expensive solutions proposed for their sites.

The design for Virginia's Maury River Bridge (Figure 5-44, page 164) reduces the spans of the main girders by almost half. The result is not only a

**FIGURE 1-22** *At Waterloo Bridge, London, long spans were required to provide space for a civic promenade, book market, and other uses.*

significant reduction in cost, but a striking appearance, as well. The bridge strides across its wooded valley with the grace of a steel greyhound.

Thus, it is not necessary to spend more money to achieve a good-looking bridge. Indeed a tight budget can and should act as a spur to creativity, encouraging a search for new approaches with both cost and aesthetic advantages. Improvement in appearance should be looked at like improvement in any other area of concern: safety, durability, or maintainability. Improvements in appearance, in the same way as improvements in materials, can be made which don't add cost and may even save money. The challenge always is to find ways of making improvements without spending more money.

If the improvement does cost more money then, just like for any other quality, the question becomes: Is the improvement worth the increased cost, keeping in mind that the bridge may be a feature of the landscape for a century or more? That question is discussed in The Costs of Responding to Larger Public Objectives next.

While it is not necessary to spend more money to achieve a good-looking bridge, the principle, unfortunately, does not work in reverse. Not every low-cost structure will be beautiful. One has only to travel the average American freeway to confirm that economy does not guarantee beauty.

Engineering problems permit many solutions. No matter how objective an engineer may be, he or she must still make some decisions where there is a degree of uncertainty, and must still make choices when alternative designs perform equally well or cost the same. It is in these decisions that the differences between beautiful and ordinary will be found.

## The Costs of Responding to Larger Public Objectives

Bridges are prominent features of many landscapes. They are justifiably called on to meet objectives beyond their transportation function. Engineers must ask themselves whether their cost analysis is really addressing all of the dimensions of the problem, including objectives that may not express themselves in the form of number of lanes, minimum clearances, and other physical criteria.

One frequent requirement is to recognize larger patterns of activity in the area around the bridge. A bridge near a civic center, for example, may benefit from longer spans than would normally result from the transportation needs alone. The longer spans may open up views to an important civic monument, or permit the easier passage of crowds for parades and civic celebrations. Bridges must frequently respond to the public's aspirations to achieve a specific visual quality for an area or a desire to create a symbol for their community: a "signature" bridge.

Once articulated by whatever public authority is in charge of the project, such requirements become legitimate public goals and therefore legitimate uses of public funds. Once such goals are established, only alternatives that meet the goals should be included in the cost analysis.

Citizens often request a specific historical look for their area. Usually they go on to unfavorably compare plain contemporary bridges to a historic bridge in their area—a historic bridge with the detail and ornament of an earlier era. They feel that the contemporary model can't carry the level of interest and the degree of symbolism of the older bridge, and so they ask for a bridge that looks like the older one.

Modern architecture has gone through a similar cycle. The early modern architects sought aesthetic appeal in the clear display of well-proportioned and carefully detailed structure. However, they also recognized people's interest in visual richness by providing thoughtful detail, appealing color, and interesting materials. In his icon of modern architecture, the Barcellona Pavilion (Figure 1-23), Mies van de Rohe designed an exposed structural system that had the elegance of a fine watch. But he also included walls of polished onyx and furniture of fine leather. His imitators compromised on the structural details and left out the onyx and the leather, and then wondered why people were quickly bored with their buildings. Architecture now faces its own demands for buildings which evoke the interest of historic structures.

FIGURE 1-23 *Interior of Barcelona Pavilion. Modern architecture which allowed for elegance and interest.*

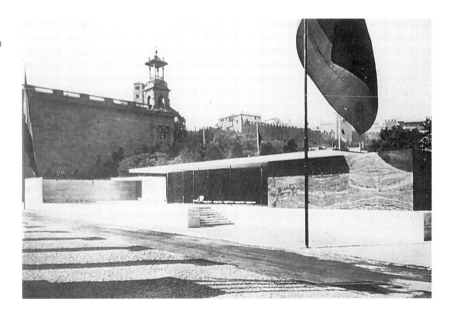

Before concluding that a request for a more attractive bridge requires an increase in budget, the engineer should provide the public with images of the great contemporary structures to see if shape and structure alone satisfy the public interest. Most members of the general public have no familiarity with the work of Maillart (Figure 2-32, page 53), Menn, Muller (Figure 1-2, page 2), and others, and find the work sufficiently breathtaking.

The wide circulation of images of the new Sunshine Skyway (Figure 1-2, page 2) showed how effective this approach can be. Soon every community with a bridge to build wanted its own cable-stayed bridge, regardless of the appropriateness of the site.

Shape and structure alone may not be sufficient in every situation, particularly for bridges with high pedestrian exposure. The first distant view and the view of the overall structure are the most important, but the view from close up and at oblique angles also attract and interest people and give them an additional level of perception to explore. If their speed or location permit, people enjoy detail and materials that can be appreciated close at hand as well as shapes that can be appreciated at a distance.

An analogy can be made with ice cream. Vanilla ice cream comes in both good and bad versions, and good vanilla can be very good indeed—but it can gain an added dimension with the right topping.

Many times, with creativity by the designer, the public's desire for additional detail and interest can be met without a significant increase in cost, and the engineer should endeavor to do so. However, at some point these criteria may require—and at the same time legitimize—additional cost, over and above what a the transportation function alone would indicate. Some agencies codify an additional budget for such situations. Caltrans for example, allows an additional 5 percent for significant bridges, and an additional 15 percent for "major" bridges.[5] The Federal Highway Administration has indicated a willingness to approve cost increases of as much as 15 percent for significant bridges.

At that point the test becomes: What does the public get for the additional money?

Lack of money is often given as an excuse to build an ugly bridge (which it is not). Unfortunately, having plenty of money is not a guarantee of building a beautiful bridge. It is possible to build a cable-stayed bridge in the wrong location and end up with a structure that towers over its neighbors and is quickly labeled an eyesore. It is possible to cover an ordinary bridge with decorative materials and have people wonder ten years later why it was ever attempted. To go back to the ice cream analogy, one can add an orgy of toppings to fine vanilla ice cream and produce a result that few find appetizing.

Having money doesn't mean that the discipline of economy and the criteria described in this book can be ignored. It means that they must be carefully applied so that the engineer can get the best possible improvement in aesthetic quality for the additional dollars.

FIGURE 1-24 *U.S. Naval Academy Bridge by Thomas P. Jenkins achieves aesthetic quality with longer spans and carefully shaped structural members.*

The section in Chapter Three on Determinants of Appearance will give some sense of priority for where the money would have the most positive effect. Often it will come not in surface add-ons but in the design of the structural members themselves, with longer spans, higher clearances, more graceful shapes, or by introducing to an area a structural type not previously seen there.

The new bridge recently completed over the Severn River in Annapolis, Maryland, adjoining the U.S. Naval Academy, shows the results of that approach. The design was selected as the winner of a competition in which both price and appearance were criteria, but some allowance for additional cost for aesthetic improvements was expected. The designer chose a haunched steel-box girder with flared columns. There are only two box girders, so that the slab overhangs and center span are substantial, requiring a 15-inch slab depth at some points. The bracing of the box girders is accomplished by boxed-steel diaphragms at the piers only. Special lighting of both roadway and bridge is included.

The result is a striking bridge with substantial shadow lines and an interesting underside. The impact is developed primarily by the shape of the structural members themselves, because that is where the designer chose to put the additional money.

Unusual detail, colors, and materials have their place, particularly in pedestrian areas, but the rule should be to use them in ways that enhance the overall structure and in ways consistent with the nature of the material itself. For example, a pattern incised in the concrete might be used to accentuate the point at which forces are transferred from one member to another, or a projection might create a shadow line that accentuates the overall shape of a structural member. See Chapter Five for examples.

A town's desire for a signature bridge is not an invitation to extravagance. Signature bridges hold engineers to the highest standards of efficiency, economy, and elegance, and at the same time create opportunities for fresh thinking and new concepts.

## Cost Estimating That Misleads

Improvements in appearance are often rejected because of misleading cost estimating.

Sometimes people say a change costs more because it is an aesthetic improvement when, in fact, it costs more because it is a change from the established practice. They mistake the cost of innovation for the cost of aesthetic improvement.

Any change, undertaken for any purpose, may well cost more the first time it is tried. Contractors working for a given transportation agency have accumulated habits, tools, and equipment suitable for current standard designs and details. Thus, the old standards will often be bid for less, regardless of the intrinsic cost savings of a new proposal. However, should a new proposal with an intrinsic cost advantage be instituted, within a short time the contracting industry will have adapted to it, and the cost advantages will be realized.

As an example, 50 years ago all plate girders were riveted. Asking for a welded plate girder was asking for a cost premium, whether the request was made for weight or aesthetic reasons. But enough engineers asked for welded plate girders that the industry became familiar with the technique and tooled up for it. Its inherent advantages prevailed, and riveting passed out of use. Now, asking for a riveted plate girder means asking for a cost premium.[6]

Improvements made for aesthetic reasons need to be given enough time to prove themselves. Special efforts must be made to ensure that builders fully understand the improvement, the reason for it, and how to build it. Contractors also like to see an improved product they can take pride in. Once they understand the reason for the improvement they will have positive suggestions on how to do it better. This enthusiasm will contribute to both economy and quality.

Standard designs and standard details can be both aesthetic problems and aesthetic opportunities. Many large bridge-building agencies build so many structures that, for efficiency's sake, they have developed libraries of standard designs and details. These are often pointed to as a reason not to undertake an aesthetic improvement, on the grounds that the nonstandard improvement would automatically add cost. However, the benefits of standardization are as equally available for attractive bridges as for ordinary bridges.

The California Department of Transportation (Caltrans) has built generations of attractive bridges based on standard elements. In the opinion of James E. Roberts, their chief bridge engineer, these are the least expensive bridges they can build.[7] All of the benefits of standardization apply. California contractors are familiar with the structures; they have accumulated stocks of standard forms and fittings. And the product is outstanding structures.

It's easy to understand the need for standardization to meet production needs. The question is: Why not standardize beauty instead of mediocrity? Why not grind out quality?

There are procedural traps which can mislead engineers trying to estimate the costs of improvements made for aesthetic reasons (and other reasons, too). Here are some frequent cases.

- *Suboptimization Trap.* All of the pluses and minuses of a change have to be added before a true picture is realized. For example, reducing girder depth may increase the cost of the girders in themselves, but the reduction in required vertical grades may save more in approach roadway and right-of-way costs.

- *Unit Cost Trap.* Often costs are compared on the basis of unit costs of material; so many dollars per cubic yard of concrete or pound of steel. This tends to give a misleading picture if there are significant differences in the alternatives beyond the quantities of material involved. For example, a decision to use a two-column pier in place of a three-column pier might involve more concrete in the pier. But, it may also produce offsetting savings in forms, footings, and placement of reinforcement because of the fewer columns.

- *Precision Trap.* Construction estimating is an imperfect art. It is a rare day when the engineer's estimate comes within five percent of the contractor's bid. The prices contractors bid for items changes from day to day depending on the size of their work load, the costs of materials, the availability of labor or equipment, and their degree of knowledge. Any feature or combination of features which costs less than five percent of the total cost of the bridge is essentially outside the range of precision of cost estimating. It might as well be treated as cost-neutral, given the inability of the designer to predict its eventual effect on the total price of the bridge.

## Design Time or Cost

The perceived need for additional design time is often given as a cost-related excuse to build ordinary bridges. Is true that the first time designers try to apply aesthetic ideas or techniques, there will be some additional time spent. As in any other situation, there is a cost for innovation. There is a learning curve to be faced; new Computer-Aided Design (CAD) techniques, training, and some experimentation must be expected.

However, once a design staff is skilled in questions of appearance, is equipped with the necessary design tools (3-D CAD, etc.), and has access to attractive standard details, it can turn out a good-looking bridge as quickly as an ugly one. The staff may, in fact, save time by avoiding the delay that occurs when objections are raised to an ordinary design. Why not do it right the first time?

## THE BRIDGE ENGINEER'S ROLE

Because the appearance of bridges is dominated by the shapes and sizes of the structural members themselves, appearance cannot be an afterthought or an add-on to bridge design. Concern for appearance must be an integral part of engineering. It is a difficult challenge.

As Billington interprets Maillart's view of it,

*The bridge art is, therefore, vision disciplined by technique; and more specifical-ly, a vision of the public landscape formed by economic constraints on public structures. It is a difficult art, with the artist continually struggling to control his elements in the face of public opinion, codes, budgets, and politics.[8]*

Many engineers see themselves as a type of applied scientist, analyzing structural forms established by others.[9] In the case of most everyday bridges the selection of form is based largely on precedents and standards established by the bridge-building agency. For example, the form of a highway overpass may be predetermined by the client agency to be a welded plate girder bridge because that is the agency's preference or because there are particularly cost-effective local steel fabricators or even because the steel industry is a domi-nant political force in that state, without any serious consideration of whether that is in fact the best form for that particular site. In other cases the form may be established by an architect or urban designer for reasons outside the structural requirements of the site.

Seeing oneself as an applied scientist is an unfortunate state of mind for a design engineer. It eliminates the imaginative half of the design process and forfeits the opportunity for the integration of form and structural require-ments that can result in structural art. Design must start with the selection of the structural form. All of the potential for creative structural art begins with

**FIGURE 1-25** *Maryland route 18 over U.S. 50, one approach to a two-span bridge.*

that decision. It is a decision that can be made well only by the engineer because it must be based on a knowledge of the forces involved and the forms best suited to handle them. Creative engineering design consists not in applying free visual imagination alone nor in applying rigorous scientific analysis alone, but of applying both together, at the same time. In the words of the Spanish engineer, Eduardo Torroja,

> *The imagination alone can not reach such [elegant] designs unaided by reason,*
> *nor can a process of deduction, advancing by successive cycles of refinement, be*
> *so logical and determinant as to lead inevitably to them. . . .*[10]

The art starts with a vision of what might be. The development of that vision is the key. Many engineers call the development of the vision conceptual engineering. It is the most important part of design. It is the stage at which all plausible possibilities and some not-so-plausible possibilities are examined in sketch form. The examination must include at a rough level of precision the whole range of considerations: performance, cost, and appearance. All that follows, including the aesthetic impression the bridge makes, will depend on the quality of the form selected. That is the stage often ignored or foreclosed, based on preconceived ideas or prior experience that may or may not apply.

The reasons often given for short-changing this stage include "Everybody knows that _____ is the most economical structure for this location," or "We always build _____ in this state," or "Let's use the same design as we did for _____ last year." When these thoughts are the starting point it is unlikely that the most promising ideas will ever appear. No design will occur. Instead, there will be a premature assumption of the bridge form, and the engineer will move immediately into the analysis of the assumed type.

That is why so many engineers mistake analysis for design, when design is more correctly the selection of the form in the first place, and is by far the more important of the two activities. Before there is any analysis, there must be a form to analyze.

Engineers also focus on analysis in the belief that the form (shape and dimensions) will be determined by the forces as calculated in the analysis. But, in fact, there are a large number of forms that can be shown by the analysis to work equally well. It is the engineer's option to choose among them, and in so doing he or she will determine the forces by means of the form, not the other way around.

Take the simple example of a two-span girder bridge (Figure 1-25), using an existing bridge, MD 18 over U.S. 50. Here the engineer has a wide range of possibilities (Figure 1-26). He or she can give the girder parallel flanges, or give it a haunch of a wide range of proportions. The moments will depend on the stiffness at each point, which in turn will depend on the presence or absence of a haunch and its shape. The engineer's choice of shape and dimensions will determine the moments at each point along the girder. The forces will follow the choice of form. Within limits, the engineer can direct the forces as he or she desires.

Now, let's examine which form the engineer should choose. All of them can support the required load. Depending on the specifics of the local contracting industry, many of them will be essentially equal in cost. All of them would perform equally well and all of them are comparable in cost, leaving the engineer a decision which can only be made on aesthetic grounds. Why not pick the one that he or she feels looks best? (See Figure 2-42 (page 58), for an equally valid version of MD 18.)

That, in a nutshell, is the process that all of the great engineers have followed. Quoting Billington, again in regard to Maillart:

> *The engineer cannot choose form as freely as a sculptor, but he is not restricted to the discovery of preexisting forms as the scientist is. The engineer invents form, and Maillart's career shows that such invention has both a visual and a rational basis. When either is denied, then engineering design ceases. For Maillart, the dimensions were not to be determined by the calculations, and even the calcula-*

**FIGURE 1-26** *Moments determined by the choice of form.[11]*

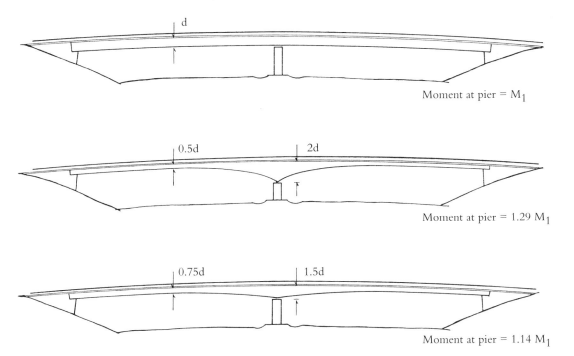

Moment at pier $= M_1$

Moment at pier $= 1.29\ M_1$

Moment at pier $= 1.14\ M_1$

FIGURE 1-27 *Engineering elegance in Seville, the Puente de la Barqueta by Juan Jose Arenas and Marcos J. Panteleon.*

*tion results could be changed [by adjusting the form] because a designer rather than an analyst is at work. Analysis and calculation are the servants of design.*[12]

At this point some will protest that other considerations (costs, the preferences of the local contracting industry, etc.) will indeed differentiate and determine the form. Too often that belief is based on unexamined assumptions, such as "The local contracting industry will not adjust to a different form," or "Cost differentials from (a past project) still apply," or "The client will never consider a different idea." Or that belief is based on a misleading analysis of costs as described in the previous section. Or that belief may be simply habit—either the engineer's or the client's—often expressed in the phrase "We've always done it that way." Accepting these assumptions and beliefs places an unfortunate and unnecessary limitation on the quality of the resulting bridge for, by definition, improvements must come from the realm of ideas not tried before.

As Captain James B. Eads put it in the preliminary report on his great bridge over the Mississippi River at St. Louis;

*Must we admit that because a thing has never been done, it never can be, when our knowledge and judgment assure us that it is entirely practicable?*[13]

At its base, the role of the engineer is to question those assumptions and beliefs, including his or her own, for each structure attempted. From that questioning will come the open mind that is necessary to develop a vision of what each structure can be at its best.

The engineering challenge is not just to find the least costly solution. The engineering challenge is to bring forth elegance from utility. We should not be content with bridges that only move vehicles and people. They should move our spirits as well.

## Using This Book

This book aims to help engineers improve the engineering of their bridges. Appearance will be a major concern, but not the only concern. Judgments about appearance must always be made in the context of judgments about performance and cost, and this book will concentrate on those relationships.

Chapter Two develops basic principles of aesthetics and perception in the transportation environment. The chapter ends with a statement of the visual priority of ten features of the bridge (superstructure, piers, parapets, etc.) according to their importance in creating the bridge's aesthetic impact. These elements are labeled the Determinants of Appearance.

Chapter Three suggests procedures to apply these basic ideas to bridge design.

Chapters Four and Five look at each Determinant of Appearance. The chapters present specific guidelines for each Determinant. The guidelines are presented not as absolute rules but as indications of what has worked well in previous structures. They are presented in the form of comparative sketches so that the engineer can decide for himself or herself how well they apply to the bridge at hand. The sketches are characterized as either "ordinary," representing problem designs or "better," representing markedly improved designs. The examples are accompanied by analyses of the underlying visual principles.

The guidelines incorporate a consensus opinion about how good appearance can be achieved. The consensus has been derived by analyzing the visually successful bridges of the modern era. It emphasizes simplicity, apparent slenderness, horizontal continuity, and the inherent attractiveness of efficient structural forms. The consensus has developed from several generations of experience with modern structures.

Chapter Six shows examples which incorporate the guidelines to a greater or lesser degree using actual bridges from typical locations. Again, bridges are characterized as "ordinary" or "better."

However, "better" is not "best." The better bridges are shown as targets to surpass, not models to copy. Every bridge is unique, and only its designer can recognize which of these ideas may apply, which must be adjusted, and when new ideas must be developed. "Best" is that unique design that precisely fits the situation at hand, using the best creative thinking of the designer to simultaneously solve the problems of performance, cost, and appearance.

Engineers should use these chapters as thought provokers, not thought inhibitors. They should be used as tools in observing bridges, and in making personal judgments about what works well and what does not.

Chapter Seven looks at the aesthetic responsibilities of bridge building organizations, the role of citizens and elected officials, and the responsibility of engineering organizations in improving the aesthetics of bridges.

1   Built by Caius Julius Lancer, one of the few Roman engineers of whom we have a record. He is buried at near one end of the bridge. His epitaph: "I leave a bridge forever to the generations of the world."

2   By legend the engineer was a shepherd who was guided by a divine vision. He was canonized as St. Benezet, and was buried in the chapel on the bridge.

3   David Billington, *Seminars with the Colorado Department of Transportation*, June 1994.

4   Billington, David P., 1979. *Robert Maillart's Bridges: The Art of Engineering*. Princeton, NJ: Princeton University Press.

5   Gloyd, Stewart, 1994. "California: A Quantified Bridge Aesthetics Case Study." Concrete International, Farmington Hills, MI: American Concrete Institute, February.

6   Billington, David P., 1989. *Robert Maillart and the Art of Reinforced Concrete*. Cambridge, MA: The MIT Press.

7   Roberts, J.E., 1990. *Esthetics in Concrete Bridge Design*. Watson, S.C. and Hurd, M.K., ed. Detroit: American Concrete Institute.

8   Billington, David P., 1983. *The Tower and the Bridge: The New Art of Structural Engineering*. New York, NY: Basic Books, Inc.

9   Billington, David P., 1982. *Thin Shell Concrete Structures*. New York, NY: McGraw-Hill Publishing Co., First edition, 1965.

10  Torroja, Eduardo, 1958. *The Structures of Eduardo Torroja*. New York, NY.

11  Calculated based on a typical non-composite two lane highway overpass with four girders and two equal 110-foot spans.

12  Billington, David P., 1989. *Robert Maillart and the Art of Reinforced Concrete*. Cambridge, MA: The MIT Press.

13  Petroski, Henry, 1995. *Engineers of Dreams*. New York, NY: Alfred A. Knopf.

chapter *two*

# UNDERSTANDING THE BASICS

*"There is a kind of human authority which needs no uniforms or symbols to make itself evident, but which makes a man stand out in a crowd simply because his movements and posture portray a powerful, controlled, and self-assured personality."*

—SINCLAIR GAULDIE, BRITISH ARCHITECT[1]

## STRUCTURAL ART

### The Keys to Success

In the example given in Chapter One, the better-looking bridges have the following characteristics in common:

- They are simpler.

- They are relatively thinner.

- The lines of the structure are continuous.

- The shapes of the structural members reflect the forces on them.

You will notice that I have named characteristics: simplicity, thinness, continuity. I have not named specific features, like Y-shaped piers or haunched girders. That's because most bridges differ from each other in important ways: The site requirements are different, the available technologies are different, the cost environment is different. If a new bridge seeks to achieve beauty by simply imitating the features of previous, successful bridges it will usually mis-

**FIGURE 2-1** *Eiffel Tower with diagram of wind-induced moments.*

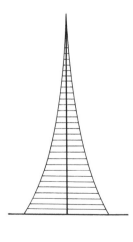

use those features. It will apply them in ways that are not appropriate to the bridge at hand. Characteristics, on the other hand, apply to any bridge.

Would other bridges with these same qualities also be considered attractive? Yes. A review of the work of outstanding bridge engineers will answer that question. Look at the work of Robert Maillart (Figure 1-16, page 12), Christian Menn (Figure 2-32, page 53), the California Department of Transportation (Figure 2-4, page 33), and the Tennessee Department of Transportation (Figures 1-14, page 11; 2-2, page 33; and others), and you will see that these qualities are apparent.

The most-admired modern structures create their visual impression with the forms of the structural members themselves. To take an example from history, think of the Eiffel Tower (Figure 2-1). The shape of the tower is a direct translation of the moments created by the wind forces acting on the tower. The tower's open framework of laced iron struts is a clear example of how to minimize the effect of the wind on a high tower. The tower was condemned by the art and architecture establishment of its time. Yet it survived to become the symbol of a city and a nation. It was designed by an engineer who had made his reputation designing bridges, bridges which exhibit the same talent for subtly shaping structure to respond to the forces at work.

Figures 2-2, 2-3, 2-4, and 2-5 illustrate more recent examples. All these bridges owe their qualities to the aesthetic impact of the structural shapes themselves. It is the structural elements that create the image.

We talked in Chapter One about the public's desire that their bridges take advantage of modern technology, make wise use of resources, achieve economic efficiency, and be responsible to the environment. To the extent that these attributes are evident in the appearance of the bridge, the public will find the bridge attractive.

We also said that people want their cities and towns to be attractive places to live. They want their bridges to be a positive part of these places. That means that the bridges should reflect some awareness of the things around them.

FIGURE 2-2 *Simplicity and carefully shaped "standard" elements result in slenderness and transparency in Tennessee.*

FIGURE 2-3 *Rigid-frame, Idaho. This rigid frame is thick at the joints, where the moments are the highest, and thin everywhere else.*

FIGURE 2-4 *California Interchange: One way to achieve unity is to design all elements with the same family of shapes, with the same standard details.*

FIGURE 2-5 *Maryland route 7 over the Gunpowder River. The arch rests lightly in this wooded park valley.*

These ideas can be generalized into the following principles which should be the aesthetic goals for any engineer designing a bridge:

- *Simplicity:* There should be a minimum number of different elements; elements doing similar jobs should be similarly shaped.
- *Apparent Thinness and Transparency:* Elements should appear slender; views through the structure should be preserved.
- *Structural Clarity:* Elements should be shaped to respond to the structural job they do; what each element does structurally and how it does it should be visible.
- *Variety within Unity:* There should be enough variety to hold people's interest, but all elements should contribute to a single whole.

FIGURE 2-6 *Delaunay painting of Eiffel Tower— painting responding to structural art.*

- *Appropriateness:* The bridge as a whole should have a clear and logical relationship to the things around it.

Judgments about appearance can be just as definitive as judgments about structural members, safety, or cost. As we shall see, judgments about appearance are based partly on facts (in this case, facts about how people see things) and partly on opinions (in this case, opinions about what people like about what they see).

With regard to appearance, the basis of fact is relatively narrower, and the basis of opinion relatively wider than in other areas of engineering. Therefore, these statements cannot be as prescriptive as those in the other areas. They should be used as guidelines, always with the understanding that there may be valid exceptions arising out of the needs of a particular site.

It is also important to remember that new materials, new ideas, and new techniques will call for new approaches to aesthetics which may violate the old rules. Gustave Eiffel is a classic example. His reaction to the new possibilities of a new material (iron) changed not only ideas about bridge aesthetics but ideas about painting, sculpture, and architecture as well. The art world was never the same after it saw the Eiffel Tower.

## Philosophical Underpinning

At this point a question naturally arises: Why do we agree that these particular characteristics make bridges more attractive? We do not *know*, in a factual sense—and therefore discussions of aesthetics necessarily become more speculative. However, in the centuries since the Greeks first codified their ideas on aesthetics, many theories about preferences in the realms of art and architecture have been developed. The theories can be organized into four categories: geometric, rationalist, sculptural, and structural.

### Geometric Theory

These theories are based on the idea is that we find certain things or experiences beautiful because they resonate with patterns built into our cog-

FIGURE 2-7 *Pont Neuf, Paris (1797), designed in the tradition of classical proportions.*

nitive systems. It is a common experience from music that certain combinations of sounds (chords) are generally judged to be beautiful, while others are considered dissonant, even uncomfortable, such as the sound of fingernails on a blackboard. Perhaps the fingernail sound causes our cells to vibrate in ways that disturb their functioning.

Many of the classical theories of proportion trace back to this idea. Rectangles proportioned according to the "Golden Mean" (1:1.618) were considered automatically superior because they supposedly appealed to some inherent inner sense of visual proportion. Classical Greek architecture was the first many of wonderful architectural styles based on mathematically determined proportions.

Recent scientific studies have created some support for this idea in the area of color. Exposure to certain colors is now known to have specific physical and psychological effects. In the bridge world, William Zuk has used statistical samples to determine a commonality of public preference for certain colors.[2]

### Rationalist Theories

This set of ideas states that we like objects whose shape clearly reflects its function. For example, a teapot with a comfortable handle and efficient spout will be more attractive than a teapot shaped without regard to these functional necessities. Shaker furniture has maintained its appeal despite the demise of the Shakers because of how clearly it is shaped to respond to its function.

FIGURE 2-8 *Shaker boxes use "swallowtail" joints to avoid wood fatigue from expansion and contraction. A model for ending cover plates?*

FIGURE 2-9 *Sculptured shapes with the goal of structural efficiency: The concrete shape acts compositely with the steel box to handle the high compressive forces in the negative moment area. Arenal Bridge, Cordoba.*

This theory applies more easily to objects with a single obvious function. Bridges fall clearly into this category. Buildings accommodating multiple functions are not as easily approached this way.

### Sculptural Theories

The goal of sculpture is to produce three-dimensional objects which have the sole purpose of evoking emotions or reflecting ideas. These theories state that we like certain objects because their shapes evoke emotions or reflect ideas which accord with our needs or value systems.

That does not mean that objects with other primary purposes, buildings and bridges for example, may not also evoke emotion or reflect ideas through their shapes. The Pont Neuf was intended to reflect the dignity and power of Paris as the capital of France.

There is a point where the sculptor's desire to create shape simply for the sake of its emotional impact conflicts with the economy required of the bridge engineer. A sculpture costing even $100,000 is a far different thing, in terms of the commitment of public resources, than a bridge costing $30,000,000. That is why the best bridge engineers have always embraced the discipline of economy in their work.

In our times, the equality of democratic governance, the efficacy of technology, and the need for economic efficiency are strongly held values. Objects that reflect these ideas will be appreciated.

The engineer's goals of economy and performance coincide well with these goals, as long as the engineer finds some way to reflect his or her efficiency in the appearance of the structure. The great engineers have found

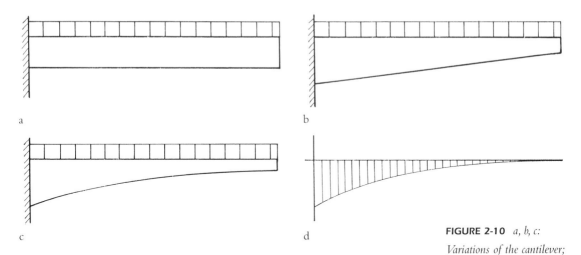

a

b

c

d

FIGURE 2-10 *a, b, c: Variations of the cantilever; d: Moments on a cantilever.*

ways to do that, which is one reason why their works have been judged beautiful by our culture.

### Structural Theories

These theories state that we like certain objects because they clearly reflect their structural behavior. The theory assumes that we all possess an inherent understanding of structure based on each person's struggle with gravity from the day we begin to walk.

The cantilever is an example of this idea which applies to bridges. To most people a cantilever is more attractive if it is thicker at its support and tapers toward its free end. People find it attractive because it reflects the cantilevers they are already familiar with: the shape of their own arms and legs or the branch of a tree. From this familiarity people develop an intuitive understanding of what the engineer knows from calculation: that the stresses in a cantilever are largest at the support, and therefore that's where most of the material should be. People will look at a cantilever of contestant depth and feel that there is something wasteful about it.

Study of these theories is indispensable for anyone who is serious about improving his or her aesthetic abilities. All of these ideas have something to contribute to bridge design. In this area there is much room for debate. Nevertheless, the results of the "exercise" given on page 6 of Chapter One, and the acclaim which bridges like the Salginatobel (Figure 1-16, page 12) have retained through the years can best be explained by the Structural Theory. Billington has placed these bridges in the category of Structural Art, an art of the same level as architecture, sculpture, and painting, but having its own characteristics.

**FIGURE 2-11** *Structural art in a simple pedestrian bridge, Maillart's Toss River Bridge..*

Structural Art is based on three disciplines:

- Efficiency: minimum materials controlled by safety.

- Economy: minimum costs controlled by serviceability and maintenance.

- Elegance: maximum personal expression of the designer controlled by the disciplines of efficiency and economy.[3]

This book is largely based on the Structural Theory and its goal is the creation of Structural Art. The ideas herein are guidelines for approaching that result.

## ANALYZING THE APPEARANCE OF BRIDGES

We perceive bridges primarily through the eyes. That means that success in bridge aesthetics depends first on recognizing the effects of light, shade, and shadow, color, and visual illusion. It also means that it is necessary to determine the positions and characteristics of likely viewers of the bridge. Viewers in cars are a special case, because they have a more predictable and limited range of views which tends to focus their attention on bridges. Our appreciation of a bridge is influenced to some degree by what is in view around it. The openness, motion, and horizontality of the typical highway environment will affect how bridges appear.

Finally, accurate analysis of the appearance of bridges can only be done through media which attempt to represent the three-dimensional reality of the structure: perspective drawings, models, and photographs.

# The Perception of Bridges

Let's start with the fact that our perception of a bridge is primarily through the eyes. Usually, we are too far away for any other sense to come into play. Often we are in a vehicle and perceive the bridge through the windows of that vehicle. Exceptions exist where persons on foot can approach some part of the bridge, such as the columns of a viaduct over a city street. In these cases, the sense of touch, the feeling of safety, or the noise of vehicles passing overhead might be involved. These exceptions will be discussed elsewhere in the guidelines. The discussions which follow are of visual perceptions.

Light, the medium through which visual perception takes place, is the heart of the matter.

Daylight is the universal light source for bridges and, in most cases, the only relevant one. The quality of daylight changes with the time of day and time of year, the degree of haze or cloud cover, the structure's geographic location and orientation, the orientation of the viewer, the season of the year, and the overall background colors of the environment.

Early morning and late afternoon daylight produces long shadows and rich-but-less-bright colors (Figures 5-40 and 5-41, page 163). Midmorning and midafternoon light produce average shadows and the true, bright colors. Noontime colors tend to be washed out by the bright light, and shadows are at a minimum. In the winter in the Northern Hemisphere the light fades, colors are generally not as bright, and the shadows are longer. At any time of year haze will dull colors and shadows, so there is less difference between the brightness of surfaces in or out of shadows. Finally, cloud cover eliminates shadows and dulls colors, giving them a gray undertone.

At any given location almost all combinations of clear sunlight, evening and morning light, haze, and fog will occur during the course of a year. But it is also true that certain combinations are more likely in some locations compared to others, and some are unique to their location. The brilliant light of the summer daytime Florida sun with its deep blue sky has no equivalent in Minnesota. Likewise, the thin, clear light of a Minnesota winter with its pale blue sky has no equivalent in Florida.

Characteristics such as these are dominant effects in their locales. They represent the type of light in which bridges are most often be observed. Engineers need to be aware of the characteristic light and sky color of their area.

The following are some observations about light in different parts of the United States. They need to be confirmed by personal observations on the spot.

FIGURE 2-12 *The effect of shadow: the horizontal shadow divides the girder into two horizontal strips, making it seem thinner, while the vertical shadows at the stiffners make them seem larger.*

FIGURE 2-13 *The effect of a visual illusion created by the lines of the abutment appear to "stretch" the girder, making it seem longer and therefore also thinner.*

In the Northeast and Midwest, summer brings clear sunshine and blue skies with sharp shadows; winter brings many cloudy days with indistinct shadows. Mid-Atlantic and Southeastern summer days tend to be hazy. Though there is plenty of light, the sky tends to be colorless, and the shadows are fuzzy. Winters bring clearer skies, but the sunlight is weaker. Florida has the strong light and blue sky described above. The Southwest has almost constant strong sunshine with deep blue skies. The West has similar light, though weaker in winter depending on latitude. The Northwest's light is affected by the frequent cloud cover; it is diffuse and relatively colorless because of the gray skies (Figures 5-36 and 5-37, page 157).

Because daylight is the medium of visual perception, the orientation of a bridge is a major influence on how it will be perceived. Surfaces that face south will be consistently the brightest; their shadows will change relatively little during the day, but change significantly from season to season; their colors will tend to fade quickest. Surfaces facing east or west will be in shade half the day and with strong, rapidly changing shadows the other half. Surfaces facing north will be in shade at all times; their colors will stay bright the longest. Figures 2-12 and 2-13 illustrate several of these effects.

The background against which a bridge is seen also influences the impact the bridge will make. East Coast and Midwestern background colors tend to be multiple shades of green in spring and summer; yellows, oranges, and browns in the autumn; and brown and grays in winter. California backgrounds are bright green in the early spring and brown the rest of the year.

Designers can't control daylight and background, and can rarely control orientation, but shadow and shade are susceptible to control. Overhangs, pro-

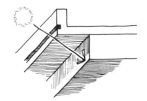

FIGURE 2-14 *Orienting surfaces to create areas of shade and shadow.*

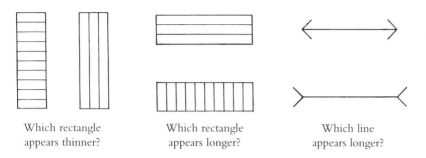

Which rectangle appears thinner?

Which rectangle appears longer?

Which line appears longer?

FIGURE 2-15 *Visual illusions applicable to bridge design. The bridge in Figure 2-13 embodies the concept on the right.*

jections, grooves, and recesses create areas and patterns of shade and shadow which help create the aesthetic impression (Figure 2-14). The brightness of surfaces can be changed by changing their orientation to the sky. Surfaces slanted toward the sky will be brighter than vertical surfaces or surfaces slanted toward the ground. The designer can also change the reflectance of surfaces, for example, by using white concrete, to accentuate the effect of light and shadow.

Nighttime illumination with headlights, or as incidental illumination resulting from roadway lighting luminaires, is rarely sufficient to do more than pick out major shapes. Given these limitations, plus the fact that most people's nighttime highway experience is largely occupied with the difficulties of the driving task, it is probably not worthwhile to be overly concerned with the appearance of most everyday bridges at night. The major exceptions would be those circumstances where the bridge itself deserves lighting because of its place in the environment, its symbolic importance, or where the use of the bridge requires lighting the space on or below it. Such situations are discussed in Chapter Five.

Since the viewer's aesthetic reactions to the bridge will be almost completely created by his or her visual perceptions, we must be aware that what people *perceive* is not always what is *there*. The visual sense is susceptible to manipulation and illusion. Illusion can work both to the design's advantage or to its detriment. It is the engineer's job to recognize where the potential for illusion exists, and put it to good use. The sketches above give examples of common visual illusions which have their applications to bridges (Figure 2-15).

## Viewpoints, Fixed and Moving

When an individual forms an aesthetic impression of a bridge, where the bridge is viewed *from* will strongly affect his or her impression. If the engineer wants to control that impression, it is important to know the likely posi-

FIGURE 2-16 *The traveler's viewpoint; also a good example of the strong shadows that can be created on a clear day by overhangs and projections.*

tion of viewers of the bridge. For a bridge over a park valley, these would be park users on the trails below (Figure 2-5, page 33); for a viaduct over a city street, these would be pedestrians and drivers on the street. For most bridges, there are many such viewpoints. For prominent bridges, the area of viewing may cover several square miles and incorporate whole communities within sight of the bridge.

The bridge itself creates new viewpoints overlooking the environment. For a bridge over a major barrier or at an entrance to a town, the act of crossing the bridge may have great symbolic importance. In the past, this was recognized by the placement of statuary, plaques, elaborate lighting fixtures, or viewing platforms on the bridge. While some of these devices may not be appropriate on a modern bridge, recognition of their symbolic purpose is still necessary.

In all cases the view by the user of the bridge itself must be recognized. Curving approaches often create dramatic views of the oncoming structure, and there are always overhead features and the insides of parapets to be considered.

Usually, not all viewpoints can be accommodated to the same degree; it is often necessary to assign priorities among them, perhaps giving more weight to the most numerous observers, or more weight to the view from the town square than to the view from the town industrial park.

Once the viewpoints are established, the engineer should evaluate the abilities of the observers at the various positions. For stationary or pedestrian viewers, the most important variables are distance and relative elevation. For bridges viewed primarily from a half-mile away, the major concern must be for overall shapes and the colors of large areas. Details will not matter. For bridges to be viewed close at hand, details and surface texture can become a major concern.

Most bridges are seen primarily from highways passing beneath them (Figure 2-16). It is a very controlled situation. The viewers are moving along a prescribed line (their highway lane) at a constant eye height and a constant rate of speed. The point at which the bridge first comes into view, the length of time that it is within view, and the size of the bridge within the visual frame at each point can all be predicted and are the same for each observer. The visual experience is analogous to that of a movie, where the windshield is the screen, and the designer controls what is presented on each "frame."

For viewers in cars, the most important variable is speed, and the second is distance to the bridge. As we travel faster and faster, two things happen to our visual perception: our field of view narrows (less and less is noticed on the periphery) (Figure 2-17) and our point of focus projects farther and farther ahead.[4]

Partially, this is a result of the physics of the situation: as speed increases, the periphery of the visual field moves across the field faster than the center, until it is moving too fast for the eye/brain to process, and becomes blurred. The only thing that stays in focus is the center of attention, the highway itself. Also, we have a subconscious sense of stopping distance: how far ahead of us are the events that we must react to *right now.* At highway speeds, those events are 300 to 500 feet or more in front of us, depending on how fast we're going, and that's where we focus.

All this means is that at 55 MPH our last and best view of a highway overcrossing is from about 300 feet away. By the time we get to the bridge, we are looking 300 feet beyond. The bridge itself, at that point, is a blur in our peripheral vision. The parts of the bridge that we see best are those that

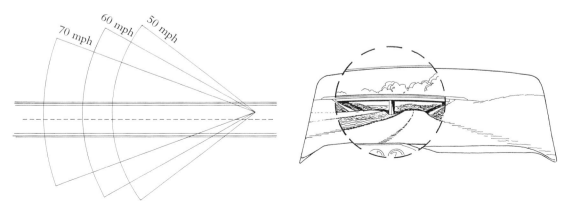

**FIGURE 2-17** *The cone of vision at highway speeds.*     **FIGURE 2-18** *The driver's area of focus at highway speeds.*

FIGURE 2-19 *Stone guardrails on the Baltimore-Washington Parkway establish a pleasingly curved, complementary line which adds to the traveler's enjoyment.*

are visible in front elevation. The undersides, the sides of the abutments, and piers are simply part of the peripheral blur. (We can, of course, make the effort to turn our head and look at an abutment wall, but even then the view will flash by so fast that few details will be recognized.)

These basics of perception also mean that at highway speeds the field of view in focus has narrowed to the point that the highway itself and its features occupy 80 percent of it, which means that the bridges are always on stage, front and center (Figure 2-18).

What are the implications of these facts? One is that any feature of the bridge that is meant to have a visual impact must be large enough to be seen at 300 feet. A second implication is that continuous horizontal lines, parallel to the line of movement, stay in focus and are easily understood and appreciated. If pleasingly shaped, they can be major sources of enjoyment (Figure 2-19); conversely, flaws in the horizontal alignment will be jarringly evident. That's why misalignment of a median barrier is so annoying.

Vertical lines, on the other hand, quickly move into the peripheral blur. A long, evenly spaced series of them will be perceived as an annoying flicker in the peripheral vision. Vertical elements that are large or close to the point of focus stand out in the peripheral blur and become prominent out of proportion to their physical position. This is why piers and abutments close to the edge of travel are seen as prominent and threatening, though they may be well outside the actual physical clearance envelope.

# The Effects of Surroundings

How a bridge is seen will depend, in important ways, on what else is seen around it at the same time. People will form a different perception of a bridge if it is seen against a backdrop of skyscrapers instead of a backdrop of mountains. Many bridges are seen in the specialized environment created by highway facilities themselves with their wide rights-of-ways and large interchanges.

## The Highway Environment

The essence of the highway environment is movement. Multiton metallic objects hurtle along curved paths at high speeds. Occasionally, groups of these objects merge and diverge in various patterns. At major interchanges, the patterns become quite complex and can involve vehicle paths crossing at multiple levels and locations. A concern for safety, if nothing else, would indicate large clear openings through structures, a minimum of barriers, and, when these are necessary, their orientation parallel, or at slight angles, to the lines of travel, with generous clearances.

These same features work to improve the driver's psychological comfort and aesthetic reaction. Large openings mean that the driver can see through to the other side and know what is coming next (Figure 2-20). Large openings also mean that potentially threatening vertical lines from piers and walls are out of the field of focus, leaving potentially pleasing horizontal lines and undistracted opportunity to create a positive impression.

Full realization of these potentials requires early and comprehensive communication between the road designers, bridge designers, traffic engineers, and landscape architects. Opportunities to coordinate all aspects of the highway at an early stage will result in improved safety, improved appearance,

**FIGURE 2-20** *404/410 Interchange, Toronto, showing large, clear openings.*

**FIGURE 2-21** *For most bridges the dominant dimension in the environment is horizontal.*

and probably less cost. Early attention to the appearance of the structures may result in slight alignment adjustments, which can often improve bridge appearance without compromising safety or cost. Early evaluation of sign design may identify safer locations for sign supports. Coordinated multidisciplinary attention can affect interchange layout as well. For example, moving a ramp gore from underneath a bridge moves it from the shadows into the light, which makes a significant difference in its visibility and safety.

Modern highway environments have been expanded to accommodate safety grading and large ramp radii. This means most highway bridges occur within a gently sloped landscaped area; the bridge itself is only a small part of the visual scene. The scene itself is predominantly spread out and horizontal. This is, of course, a matter of degree, which varies depending on the complexity of the highway and the shape of the natural surroundings. The basic point remains that the bridge itself is a relatively small object in a much larger landscape, where the dominant dimensions, compared to the bridge, are horizontal. This fact, combined with the horizontal nature of the vehicular movement which the structure carries, indicates that it is the horizontal elements of bridges which should be emphasized in most cases.

There are exceptions. Within a major multilevel interchange, a single, multilevel structure or a series of closely spaced and overlapping structures will be dominant enough to establish its own environment. The visual impact of this assembly needs to be studied to determine the structural/aesthetic approach that is appropriate. Figure 2-38 (page 55) shows an example from Tennessee where all of the bridges were designed as the same basic type of structure, steel-box girders. This structural type accommodates varying span and clearance requirements within a single structural form. The result is visual coherence, as well as a degree of openness with steel box structures similar to the result obtained by Ontario in Figure 2-20 with concrete, voided slab structures.

### The Natural Environment

The range of possible natural environments is immense. First, there is the question of shape, ranging from the absolute flatness of a tidal inlet between coastal barrier islands to the confining cliffs of a Rocky Mountain canyon. Then there is color, which changes from place to place and from season to season. Finally there are the differences in texture created by the presence or absence of vegetation, the varying types of vegetation, and the differences in rock and soil.

It is not possible or desirable to reflect all of these differences with specific features of the bridge. However, we must be aware of the effect these features will have on the public's perception of the bridge. In some cases, the selection of structural type and shape can be done in ways which reinforce the characteristics of the environment. An arch between granite canyon walls is an obvious example, which takes advantage of the natural efficiency of the arch in that situation. The Salginatobel Bridge (Figure 1-16, page 12) is a classic example.

### The Urban Environment

Urban environments are usually more confined. Urban structures often require retaining walls and are sometimes overshadowed by buildings. Here, every visual surface is man-made and often hard-edged, and the vertical dimensions are of the same order of magnitude as the horizontal dimensions. More emphasis on the vertical may be in order. However, the continuity of the driver's line of vision is still paramount—horizontal lines should follow the highway geometry as much as possible, with as much "visual space" as possible evident to the driver.

The viewpoints of pedestrians and slow-speed drivers become much more important in an urban environment. Sidewalks become more than just routes for passage. Opportunities to stop and enjoy a view should be considered, and hidden corners and exposure to high-speed traffic should be avoided. Small-scale textures, details, and special materials may not be noticed on a freeway, but they can be valued components of an urban structure.

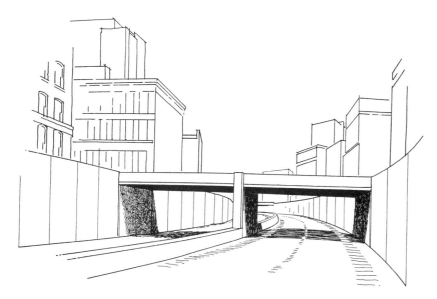

FIGURE 2-22 *An example of an urban freeway where the surroundings create a vertical emphasis.*

## Tools of Analysis

To accurately analyze the appearance of a bridge, techniques must be used which illustrate what people will actually see at the viewpoints they will see it from. The standard engineering tools are two-dimensional drawings: plan, section, and elevation. However useful these drawings might be as instructions to contractors, they are very deceptive in presenting what the bridge will actually look like. The typical two-dimensional elevation drawing is particularly misleading, since only the first columns of the piers appear in the drawing. In reality, all of the columns will be visible from almost every viewpoint.

The tools which must be used are those that portray the three-dimensional reality of the structure: models, perspective views, and photographs with the bridge inserted, but even these tools can deceive unless they are taken from an appropriate viewpoint. The typical aerial oblique rendering of a bridge is essentially irrelevant for this purpose. That view will only be available to occasional low-flying helicopter pilot (Figure 2-25). Drawings must be taken from the viewpoints of the most likely observers.

Views of bridges over highways should be taken at driver's eye height, from positions in the travelled lanes of the underpassing roadway, at distances of 300 to 500 feet. Views of bridges over water should be taken from the most important points along the nearby shore (Figure 2-26). Each bridge will have its own set of relevant viewpoints. Not all viewpoints can be covered by drawings. The designer may have to extrapolate from one drawing to other locations.

**FIGURE 2-23** *This bridge looks very simple in an elevation drawing.*

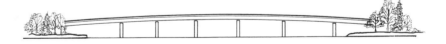

**FIGURE 2-24** *The actual view of the real-life bridge, however, is more complex.*

FIGURE 2-25 *The Sassafrass River Bridge, Maryland. The helicopter pilot's view, an attractive but irrelevant viewpoint.*

FIGURE 2-26 *The Sassafrass River Bridge, Maryland. Most people's view—the relevant viewpoint.*

Quick, three-dimensional sketches are the best way of trying out multiple ideas at the early stages of design development. The sketches in Figure 2-27 were done by Art Elliot when he was chief bridge engineer for the California Department of Transportation. They helped to resolve a dispute with nearby residents over the piers for the San Mateo Bridge (Figure 2-28).

*However, at the final decision making stage, perspective drawings must be absolutely accurate.* Small differences in girder depth or pier width can make enormous differences in the final appearance of the structure. All visible elements, such as signing, lighting, and guardrail, should be included. Conversely, all elements which will be below ground or hidden should *not* be shown. If visible, they will distort the analysis.

Structures designed on modern Computer-Aided Design systems (CAD) offer the possibility of easily generating three-dimensional views of alternate designs from the important viewpoints. Having access to such three-dimensional representations during the early design stage is so valuable that the CAD operator should be made an integral part of the design team from the very beginning. The designer can try out different designs and proportions at the sketch stage and quickly make adjustments, before too much time has been spent on details and calculations. This is too valuable a tool to be left unused until the formal presentation at the end of the process.

The CAD drawings shown in Figure 2-29 (page 51) were developed during the early stages of design for the new American River Bridge in Folsom, California. They resulted in a decision to use two columns instead of a wall at the piers. The three-dimensional view at this early stage avoided the wasted design effort that would have occurred had the change come later.

FIGURE 2-27 *Art Elliot's sketches of possible pier designs for the San Mateo Bridge.*

FIGURE 2-28 *The San Mateo Bridge as built.*

Perspective drawings from CAD systems can be superimposed on photographs taken from the relevant viewpoints. A series of such rendered CAD drawings over photographs is the most accurate method of presenting alternative bridge designs. Because of the sense of familiarity created by the photographic backgrounds, these drawings are particularly valuable at public meetings—the background is complete and easily recognized. Because of the accuracy of CAD, the bridge can be made to match the photograph. Viewers can get a good idea of the relative size of the bridge by comparing the drawing to familiar features of the existing scene.

Creating such drawings has its own technical requirements. Each CAD drawing must be done from the same viewpoint and eye height as the camera that produced the base photograph. The photographer should avoid wide-angle or telephoto lenses, as these will introduce distortions into the photo-

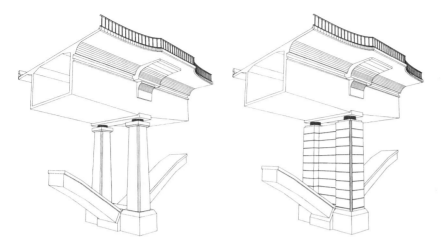

**FIGURE 2-29** *Perspective study, American River Bridge, Folsom, California.*

graph. The rendering of the CAD drawing to create photo realism requires a CAD operator with an artist's sensibility for shadows and reflections. Figure 2-30 (page 52), made for the type study for the new bridge over the St. Croix River between Minnesota and Wiusconsin, illustrates the degree of photo realism that can be achieved by a skilled operator.

Such drawings have two major limitations. For accuracy's sake they are limited to a field of view no wider than 60 degrees, which is the human eye's range for recognizing detail and judging distance. Second, the photo cannot show the effect of peripheral vision, or of the wider field of view we unconsciously take in by small horizontal eye movements. The result seems like an unreasonably limited slice of the actual structure. The temptation is to use wide-angle lenses for the photo and computer simulation in order to show more of the structure. Unfortunately this distorts the result by making the structure seem farther away from the observer than it really is. This limitation can be better addressed by incorporating the background itself into the computer model. Then animations can be prepared which allow the "camera" to pan over a long structure, as an actual observer would turn his or her head to take it all in.

A related problem with photos is showing the effect of movement around a structure. Multiple views can be created in the sequence of what a moving observer would see along a given path, essentially creating an animated movie. This requires using a series of carefully spaced photographs.

Unfortunately, at the current state of the animation art, entering and manipulating realistic and detailed topographic information requires unreasonable computational power and time. To compensate, the backgrounds are simplified, giving the product a cartoonlike quality. However, such presenta-

**FIGURE 2-30** *Computer-drawn views of the new St. Croix River Bridge, near Stillwater, Minnesota.*

tions can still be useful for judging size and shape, in relation to surroundings, and in analyzing proportions. Again, the emphasis should be on real eye heights and likely paths for actual observers. The computer can put the "camera" anywhere, from underground to swooping overhead. Designers can be seduced by this capability into concentrating on images that few real people will ever see.

Another promising technique is to record a series of views along a given path or to pan across a bridge site using a video camera. By carefully coordinating the positioning of the CAD model with the position of the video camera at each point, the rendering of the bridge can be inserted in each frame of the videotape. Unfortunately, this also is a difficult and expensive task requiring large computer resources, and is, at this point in the development of the technology, only applicable to the most sensitive projects.

Models can also be used. They have the advantage of allowing the viewer to move around the structure and select any viewpoint he or she chooses. Unfortunately, they have several major disadvantages. It is difficult for an observer to put himself or herself at a scale eye height. Failing that, the observer is in the same position as Gulliver in Lilliput. The view he or she is getting is the helicopter view, which few people will share after the structure is built. Models are also unwieldy to present to large numbers of people and are thus difficult to use in a public meeting context. Finally, if there are multiple alternatives, separate models or inserts must be constructed for each alternative.

## THE TEN DETERMINANTS OF APPEARANCE

How people react to a bridge depends on what they see first, and in what order. First impressions are rarely overridden by later information. People see the shapes of the big elements first, the structural elements. The color of the big elements is next, then, if time and distance permit, the details and their colors. It follows, then, that the ten most important determinants of a bridge's appearance are, in their order of importance:

1. **The vertical and horizontal geometry:** how high the structure is, whether it is curved in one or two planes, how is it positioned relative to prominent surrounding features.

   Before there is a bridge concept the geometry itself sets a line in space which can in itself be attractive or unattractive. The geometry establishes the basic lines of the structure, to which all else must react. A graceful geometry will go a long way to guarantee a successful bridge, while an awkward and kinked geometry will be very difficult to overcome with later decisions.

   Bridge engineers are often handed the geometry as a predetermined element. They should reserve the right to evaluate it and request changes if necessary to improve the appearance of the structure.

2. **Superstructure type:** whether the structure is an arch, girder, rigid frame, truss, or cable-supported.

   By establishing the overall shape of the structural members this decision establishes the most memorable aspect of the structure.

FIGURE 2-31 *Geometry, the starting point and base for all that follows.*

FIGURE 2-32 *At a glance, the shape of the Gantor Bridge superstructure establishes the viewer's impression (Switzerland).*

**FIGURE 2-33** *Pier placement establishes the relationship of the bridge to the West Virginia topography.*

**FIGURE 2-34** *These abutments frame a continuation of the Maryland countryside.*

**FIGURE 2-35** *The appeal of this haunched girder bridge in Idaho owes much to the shape of the superstructure and its blending with the piers.*

**FIGURE 2-36** *These memorable piers are shaped to reflect their function.*

3. **Pier placement:** which establishes not only the points at which the structure contacts the topography but also the shape of the openings framed by piers and superstructure.

   The success of the visual relationship between the structure and its surrounding topography will depend heavily on the apparent logic of the pier placement. For example, a pier near a water edge will appear more logical if placed on the shore side of the boundary, because people understand that it is easier to build a pier on land than in the water, and crossing the water is why the bridge is there in the first place.

   The openings between the piers have a shape which will influence the impression a bridge makes. Placing the piers to create well-proportioned openings will improve the appearance of the structure.

4. **Abutment placement and height:** which determines how the bridge starts and ends and, for shorter bridges, how the structure is framed.

   The abutment placement also establishes the shape of the end span opening, which can have a significant influence on what can be seen beyond the structure, and how well the structure relates to adjoining uses.

5. **Superstructure shape (and parapet and railing details):** the form of the structural members (and how the other elements of the superstructure are integrated with them).

   This is the point at which the structure can be shaped to respond to the forces on it. The intrinsic interest of the structure will be determined by this characteristic.

6. **Pier shape:** the form and details of the piers.

   From many viewpoints, particularly at oblique angles to the structure, the shapes of the piers will be a major influence on the impression created.

7. **Abutment shape:** the form and details of the abutments.

   For shorter structures, and from viewpoints near the ends of longer structures, the shape and detail of the abutment will be important. For structures involving pedestrians the provisions made for pedestrians at the ends of the bridge can be among the most memorable aspects of the structure.

8. **Colors:** the colors of the uncoated structural materials as well as the coated elements and the details.

**FIGURE 2-37** *The abutments of the bridge shown in Figure 5-37 (page 157) not only help frame the Rocky Mountain view, they give an indication of their role in supporting the girders.*

**FIGURE 2-38** *The bright yellow color of the steel box girders make this interchange a memorable milepost for travellers using I-440 in Nashville. This outstanding design for a complex interchange is made possible by the torsional stiffness of box girders.*

FIGURE 2-39 *Structural details, such as this combination of horizontal and vertical stiffeners, can serve a traditional ornamental role by emphasizing points of force transfer.*

FIGURE 2-40 *Signing, lighting, and landscaping can be integrated into an attractive whole.*

Color, or lack thereof, will influence the effect of all the decisions that have gone before. It provides an economical opportunity to add an additional level of interest.

9. **Surface textures and ornamentation:** elements which can add interest and emphasis.

Structural elements, such as stiffeners and bearings, can serve this function. Indeed, traditional systems of architectural ornament started from a desire to visually emphasize points where force is transferred, such as from beam to column through an ornamental capital. Patterns of grooves or insets, traditional materials, such as brick or stone, and details added strictly for their appearance are other possibilities.

10. **Signing, lighting, and landscaping:** not actually part of the structure but which can have great influence on the aesthetic impression a structure makes.

Decisions about the first five determinants are usually thought of as strictly "engineering" decisions. However, they are inescapably aesthetic decisions, as well. Decisions on determinants six through nine are the ones most often thought about when speaking of "bridge aesthetics," but it is almost impossible for decisions made about these elements to completely compensate for poor decisions made about the first five. A poorly shaped girder cannot be corrected by painting it an attractive color. A better idea is to make the best possible decision about the first five elements, and then use elements six through nine to accentuate and improve the positive qualities that have been created.

FIGURE 2-41 *All ten Determinants of Appearance make a positive contribution to this structure.*

The tenth determinant lists elements that are often added to the structure or placed next to it. Depending on their size, placement, and detailing, they can be irrelevant, positive, or very negative contributors to the appearance of the bridge.

## IMPROVING AESTHETIC SKILLS

The best way of improving aesthetic skills is by careful observations of the bridges seen every day.

Look at existing bridges. Go back to the same bridge at different times of day and at different seasons. See what the changing sun angle and changing light intensity does to what you see. Take a camera and photograph the bridges. Take a sketch pad, soft pencil, and/or Magic Marker and draw the bridges. Don't worry if the drawings are not very good. You don't have show them to anybody else. The important thing is to look at a bridge with a fresh eye, to see what it actually looks like, not what you think it *should* look like. The act of photographing or drawing will help you do that.

Compare your observations. Do you like the appearance of one bridge more than the next? Why? What feature appeals to you? Why does it have that positive effect? Does it add a shadow line, change the texture of the wall, make the girder look thinner? Keep notes on your photos and/or drawings, and organize them to use in your own designs.

FIGURE 2-42 *Comparative computer-drawn variation of Maryland route 18 over U.S. 50, Kent Island.*

Color is a subject that can best be learned with personal observation. Since bridges in general have such a limited range of color, it is necessary to look elsewhere to experience a wider range of the possibilities. Our appreciation of color is influenced by size and exposure, so that buildings furnish the nearest approximation of the effect of various colors. Look at the colors of buildings, and make judgements about what you see.

Bridges are usually seen against a largely natural background, so the effect of background colors must also be absorbed as well. Comparative observations and color photography are indispensable tools in this process.

This process can be formalized in case studies. The case study is a familiar feature of law and business schools. It summarizes the important facts about a given bridge in a few pages. These facts include a description of the major physical characteristics of the bridge, its structural capacity and safety features, construction and maintenance costs, and appearance. The study should also include an analysis of the success of the bridge and the presentation of alternative features which would improve future bridges of the same type. Figure 2-42 shows the results of such an analysis for the structure pictured in Figure 1-25, page 25. The key is an *integrated* study of each bridge, equally considering performance, cost, and appearance. Considering appearance without considering cost is just as irresponsible as considering performance without considering appearance.

This drawing above is the result of a case study developed for the Maryland Highway Administration.

Training yourself to think in three dimensions is an important skill. It encourages you to visualize, from the beginning, what the bridge will look like in real life. (It helps in understanding the performance aspects of bridge design as well.) As you design, try drawing elements in three dimensions even from the roughest beginning sketches. Your field observation sketches will give you practice. The better CAD programs have relatively easy-to-use 3-D modules. The designer can develop the concept in three dimensions first, and only reduce it to two dimensions when it is necessary to begin the construction drawings.

Many successful bridge designers have put on paper their ideas about bridge appearance. Some of these publications include specific and practical guidelines. Fritz Leonhardt's *Brucken*[5] is an example of such a book which includes many specific guidelines distilled from the author's experience. The Transportation Research Board has published *Bridge Aesthetics Around the World* [6] which is an international anthology of articles by 21 authors from 16 countries. It includes a comprehensive bibliography of everything written in English on the subject in the last 80 years. The American Concrete Institute recently published *Esthetics of Concrete Structures,*[7] another outstanding anthology containing many practical applications. David P. Billington's *The Tower and the Bridge* and his books on Robert Maillart[8] are also outstanding.

Books like these are useful sources of guidance and inspiration, and should be part of the library of any practicing bridge designer. Details and further suggestions can be found in the footnotes following each chapter.

1   Gauldie, Sinclair, 1969. *The Appreciation of the Arts 1, Architecture.* London: Oxford University Press.

2   Zuk, William, 1974. "Public Response to Bridge Colors," *Transportation Research Record.* Washington, DC: Transportation Research Board, vol. 507.

3   Billington, David P., 1983. *The Tower and the Bridge: The New Art of Structural Engineering.* New York, NY: Basic Books, Inc.

4   Tunnard, Christopher and Pushkarev, Boris, 1963. *Man-Made America, Chaos or Control?* New Haven: Yale University Press.

5   Leonhardt, Fritz, 1982. *Brucken.* Cambridge: The MIT Press.

6   Transportation Research Board, 1991. *Bridge Aesthetics Around the World.* Washington, D.C.

7   Watson, Stewart C. and Hurd, M.K. ed., 1990. *Aesthetics in Concrete Bridge Design.* Detroit: American Concrete Institute.

8   See Preface, page xii, and Chapter 1, page 30, for more books by Billington.

chapter *three*

# DESIGNING A BRIDGE: PRACTICAL PROCEDURES

*"Beauty will not unconsciously arise out of a search for economy. Rather, there are personal choices for the engineer to make, and he is to be judged on them."*

—DAVID P. BILLINGTON,
AMERICAN ENGINEER AND EDUCATOR

So now we have gone through all of these basic ideas and concepts. The moment of truth is at hand. The engineer is asked to design a bridge. A blank piece of paper is on the drawing board. How to start?

## DEVELOPING A DESIGN INTENTION

Before a designer can start on the bridge itself he or she must have an idea of all of the criteria that the structure must meet and all of the concerns that will act on the structure. He or she must then integrate these matters into a statement of intent.

Bridges being public works, this is inevitably a collaborative process. At the very least, the owner (or the owner's representatives) will be involved in setting minimum physical criteria and budgets. Financing and review agen-

FIGURE 3-1 *The engineer's starting point.*

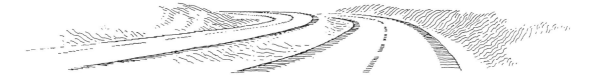

cies may also be involved in a major way. It is not uncommon, for example, for environmental agencies, the Coast Guard, or the Army Corps of Engineers to have a major say in span arrangements and bridge length. If the bridge is prominent in a community, or has historical or symbolic associations, community groups and historical societies will want a major role. This is the point at which to include members of the public and elected officials. By doing so the designer can have some confidence that the final result will address the most strongly held desires of the community.

All of these parties must be identified and invited into the collaboration process at this beginning stage, before any direction has been set. They should all be considered part of the project team, jointly charged with developing the best possible bridge for the site. This will ensure that every participant starts off with the same understanding of the project, and that all will feel like valued contributors. Also, the insights of nonengineering members of the team concerning the nontechnical issues will be particularly valuable at this stage. Finally, bringing everyone in at the beginning avoids the risk of having to redo work already done when a group consulted late in the process decides the result is not acceptable.

The next section will discuss techniques to make the collaborative process as productive as possible. This section will concentrate on the elements that must be considered in developing a design intention.

## Understand the Physical Requirements

The first thing to do is fully understand the requirements and the site. There will be the usual engineering requirements: horizontal and vertical alignment, required clearances, stream flows, foundation conditions, traffic, and loads. These will set the range of structural types that are reasonable.

## Understand the Visual Environment

The second thing to do is fully understand the visual environment. Here a camera is indispensable. Visit the site. Walk around it. Find the places the bridge will be visible from. Identify and prioritize the major viewpoints. Take pictures—in color. Lots of them. Get the important ones enlarged.

If the bridge is part of a larger project where the bridge's environment has not yet been built, then more imagination will be necessary. The highway drawings should be used to generate three-dimensional views from the likely viewpoints. These in turn can be placed on photos of the larger background to get a sense of what the site will be like.

FIGURE 3-2 *The underside of this German bridge provides an attractive and visually interesting ceiling, shelters the light rail stop, reflects daylight into the underbridge area, and supports the transit wire.*

It is also important, at this point, to get a sense of whether the night view will be important and in what way. Finally, the differences that will be imposed by the change of seasons need to be understood.

## Understand Nearby and Associated Uses of the Surroundings

The use of the surroundings needs to be understood. Will the bridge adjoin the town's Little League field? Do people picnic or boat or bicycle near the bridge? Under it? Will any of these uses change as a result of new development or new zoning? Is the town trying to improve its attractiveness to industry or tourism and should that affect the bridge? The presence of these activities will, of course, affect the selection of viewpoints, and the priority among them. It will also affect the criteria that might be established—for example, for the underside of the structure.

In any situation where there will be pedestrian usage under the bridge or for high bridges where the underside can be seen from many viewpoints the designer should consider the appearance of the underside. Such situations often occur over urban streets and in parks. In these cases the designer is creating an outdoor room in which the underside of the bridge is the ceiling (Figure 3-2).

Environmental requirements should be determined at this point. For example, the presence of rare marine life may restrict the options for pier placement, or restrictions on construction seasons caused by the presence of rare birds may influence the choice of structural type.

## Identify Symbolic Functions

Does the bridge have a symbolic function? What are the desires and aspirations of the people who will see or use the bridge? A prominent structure, such as a bridge near the center of a town will become a landmark which will come to symbolize the town. The people of the town will have strong feelings about what this bridge should look like, and those feelings need to be understood. Even less prominent bridges will have neighbors and users who will want to see a bridge which enhances their neighborhood and their daily travel. It is important to understand what it is about their neighborhood or their trip which they consider important.

## Determine the Boundaries of the Design

The boundaries of the design should be based on all the elements that will be seen together at the same time from the major viewpoints. All elements connected visually need to be visualized and developed together: bridge, retaining walls, noise walls, guardrails, signing, lighting, traffic signals, and landscaping. If the first person to see everything together is the contractor, then we should be surprised if it looks good.

## The Design Intention

The designer must then decide which of the factors he has learned will influence the design, and in what priority. All of the preceding information

FIGURE 3-3 *Flaming Geyser Bridge by Kevin Dusenberry, Washington. Restricted underclearance and its function as the entrance to a county park led to a design which answers both functional and symbolic requirements.*

should be organized and evaluated for its effect on the structure. Viewpoints with the highest priority should be identified. Environmental and land use information should be evaluated and criteria that could affect the structure should be listed. Critical aspects and features from the surroundings should be identified. The product should be a list of potential criteria for the structure. The list of factors, both "hard" and "soft," need to be considered, put in order, and integrated into a statement of all of the goals that the bridge is intended to address.

To go back to an earlier example, the presence of a nearby civic center may indicate benefits to be gained, in terms of views and space for crowd passage, from longer than normal spans, while the presence of crowds under the structure may add a desire to have an attractive underside. In other locations the color or form of nearby rock outcropping or buildings may be established as an important consideration. The preservation of significant existing views may be placed as a constraint on pier location or type.

In the project in Figure 2-30 (page 52) a new bridge over the St. Croix (a National Scenic River) near Stillwater, Minnesota, a type study and public involvement process developed a design intention with the following list of goals. The structure was expected to:

- maintain views up and down the valley;

- avoid calling attention to itself;

- complement the vegetation and topographical features of the area;

- limit piers in the water to eight, with the first river piers at least 300 feet off shore to avoid local mussel beds.

## COLLABORATION WITH OTHERS

Developing a design intention often can best be done by involving others—affected citizens, elected officials, or professionals from related disciplines. To be most productive the collaboration should carry over to the design stage.

### Citizen Participation

Bridges have long attracted detailed citizen interest beyond the usual not-in-my-back-yard reaction. For example, the Rainbow Bridge (Figure 3-4) over the American River has long been considered the defining landmark of Folsom, California. Images of the bridge appear in the masthead of the local newspaper and in the logos of several shops on the main street. When the

FIGURE 3-4 *Rainbow Bridge, Folsom, California.*

need arose to add an additional crossing nearby, the community was adamant about being intimately involved with the design of the new structure. The community wanted to be sure that the new structure would be of equal visual quality, and that its appearance would complement the old bridge.

Until recently, it has been difficult for engineers to respond to such concerns.

Appearance is in itself a difficult subject to deal with in the public sector. Facts don't apply to appearance to the same degree as other aspects of public works. The arena is largely in the area of opinions. Since everyone is a taxpayer, everyone believes their opinion is as good as anyone else's, to be heard equally.

A complicating fact is that most people, including engineers, have difficulty accurately imagining the appearance of the final structure based on engineering drawings. That makes agreement almost impossible. After all, how can we agree on or even discuss appearance when we each have a different image of the object in our minds?

In the past such problems could not be easily solved because of the difficulty and cost in presenting alternatives in ways which could be understood by the general public. Perspective drawings were expensive to prepare, were subject to artistic license which reduced their credibility, and were limited to fixed viewpoints. Models are also expensive and give a false impression of size. Now, with the advent of Computer-Aided Design (CAD) as discussed in Chapter Two, it is possible to economically prepare realistic depictions from multiple viewpoints. Citizen groups can easily understand what the bridge will look like, and become constructively engaged in judgments about the alternatives.

### The Foundation of Positive Citizen Participation

The first rule of citizen participation is to *listen*. That thought can't be overemphasized. The whole purpose of the citizen participation effort is to understand what citizens think about their design problem. There is only one way to do that: to listen to what they have to say.

It is not the easiest thing to do.

Most citizens start a citizen participation process by wanting to let off steam. They have some real or imagined dissatisfaction with the project or the agency, and they have to "get it off their chest." Either that or they have some pet idea about the project, which they also have to get off their chest. These statements can become quite emotional.

The natural tendency is for an agency representative or consultant to take the emotion personally and become defensive. The representative tries to explain or defend previous decisions or to explain why some pet idea won't work. These reactions are a mistake.

No useful exchange will take place until the attending citizens get their concerns off their chests. Until that happens, they aren't prepared emotionally to *hear* anything that the consultants or agency representatives might say. Indeed, an attempt to respond at this point will only confirm a frequent suspicion that the whole process is a sham, and that the agency is not really interested in hearing what the citizens have to say.

The only way to get over these hurdles is to listen.

Once the citizens see that the consultants and agency representatives are indeed interested in what they have to say, and understand what they say, then the emotion will dissipate, and they will be prepared to begin a useful dialogue.

The second rule of successful citizen participation is to avoid expert overload. As the project proceeds there is a risk that citizens will become intimidated by the professional knowledge of consultants and agency representatives and not volunteer anything of substance. Of course, this result makes the citizen participation process useless.

For example, citizens often say things or make suggestions that have obvious technical flaws. There is a tendency on the part of the professionals to immediately step in and correct the technical part of the statement. This reaction is a mistake. It only reinforces the perception of a knowledge gap between the citizen and the professionals. The better reaction is simply to let the matter pass and continue to listen to the rest of the message, which will often indicate areas of citizen concern or perception about their project of which the technical person is unaware.

If the technical flaw becomes substantive as the discussion proceeds, the professional can find a way to correct it at a later time, without seeming to contradict or "show up" the citizen's lack of technical knowledge.

Again, the best approach is to listen.

The use of technical jargon is related danger. Everything an engineer has to say can be said in plain language. One of the enjoyable challenges of citizen participation is rediscovering the plain language equivalents for all of the things we deal with. If the process continues successfully, the professional will find the citizens beginning to understand the technical concepts, even with the jargon.

Indeed, the best definition of a citizen participation process is that it is a mutual educational process between the engineers and the citizens. The engineers are educating the citizens about reasonable bridge types, costs, and other implications for the site in question. And the citizens are educating the engineers about community concerns, perceptions, and values for the site in question. Like any educational process, it must begin with a willingness on the part of *educatees* to listen to and understand the *educators*. The best way for both groups to get to this point is through face-to-face familiarity and dialogue.

Once the substantive dialogue begins, the agency and the citizens will have different but overlapping goals. The agency's goal will be to make citizens more aware of the real possibilities, constraints, and costs governing the engineering decisions, so they will be able to understand and accept a reasonable, cost-effective solution. The citizens' goal is to get the engineers to understand the community's concerns and aspirations, so that the engineers will be able to develop a feasible solution which responds to these concerns and produce a structure which meet the community's needs.

In the best of circumstances, the citizen participation acts as a spur to the engineers, unleashing their creativity and producing a proposal which is improved beyond what would arise out of a conventional engineering process.

### Useful Techniques

There are seven guidelines for a successful participation process:

1. **Tailor the Process to the Project.** The possibilities here range from an appointed citizen review committee to an open-to-everybody

FIGURE 3-5 *Folsom Citizens' Review Committee on field visit to the new bridge site.*

process. The best answer depends on the nature and number of the groups involved, the size and scope of the project itself, and the nature of the political body or bodies that are the final decision makers. The prime criterion should be to set up the process so that it meets the needs of these decision makers.

For the Folsom project the mayor appointed a Citizens' Review Committee with members representing all the interested groups and agencies, including several who opposed the bridge.

2. **Create Opportunities for Mutual Education by the Citizens and the Engineers.** The two groups need to have opportunities to develop a face-to-face relationship and discuss general topics of mutual interest before being faced with the stress of decision making on the project itself. A very valuable technique is a joint field visit to the site of the project. The citizens will be on familiar ground. Indeed, they will know more about some aspects of the site than the engineers do. This puts them on a more equal footing with the engineers, and makes them more receptive to comments from the engineers about the structural possibilities at the site.

3. **Encourage Citizen Participation in Developing the Bridge Alternates to be Studied.** Citizens will come to the process with a general idea or vision as to what they think the bridge should look like. It is very important for the engineers to understand what these visions are and to address them at an early stage. They may in fact be

**FIGURE 3-6** *One citizen's vision for the new American River Bridge.*

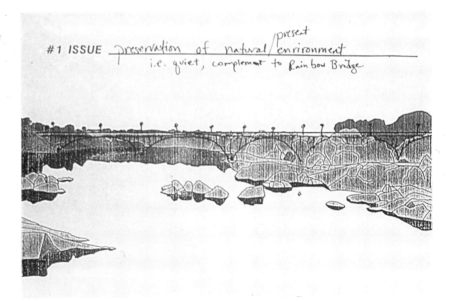

impractical. However, such ideas can be addressed in general terms in the first round of alternative evaluation. The impracticality, whether it be cost or structure, can be addressed at that time before too much time or money has been spent. If all of the citizen visions are not addressed at the beginning, their sponsors will not be able to let go of them. They will continue to raise their ideas, to the point that the whole process may be disrupted or delayed. If their ideas are addressed at an early stage, the sponsors will be able to move onto more practical possibilities.

By including the citizens in the development of alternatives from the very beginning, their "ownership" of the result is more likely, and it becomes less likely that a stop and restart will be necessary.

Of course, it is always possible that the citizens will come up with something that the engineers had not thought of. This possibility has to be recognized and encouraged.

At Folsom a line drawing of the site was abstracted from a photograph (Figure 3-6), with the profile of the new structure added. The members of the Citizens' Review Committee were asked to sketch on the drawing their visions of the structure. A clear predominance of the drawings were for arch bridges, but other possibilities also appeared.

4. **Present All Alternatives in Three-dimensional Form Showing the Bridge in its Actual Setting.** Even engineers have difficulty visualizing what a bridge will actually look like using engineering

drawings alone. It is almost impossible for nonprofessionals to do so. If the attempt is made the results will be, at best, misleading impressions, and, at worst, endless arguments over differences in impressions, none of which are accurate.

The alternatives that are available to resolve this problem, such as three-dimensional CAD-based drawings over photographs, were discussed in the Tools of Analysis section of Chapter Two.

5. **Full Disclosure of All Technical and Nontechnical Information, Including Cost.** If the citizens are to be full participants in the decision-making process they need to have access to all the information. Citizens are taxpayers. The major engineering constraints need to be explained. The cost implications need to be explained. Faced with realistic and credible information about cost they will, in most cases, draw the logical conclusion. Engineers should remember that citizens may consider it logical, in view of the importance that they attach to the bridge, to spend some of their money on features added simply for their contribution to the appearance of the structure.

6. **Provide Multiple Iterations of Review and Narrowing of Alternatives.** The alternatives selection process should start with a wide range of alternatives, at least four, to give citizens a full range of the possibilities, and to provide for further education of the citizens and the engineers as to their mutual areas of concern. Some ideas or concerns may not be aroused until a proposal is placed on the table. The process needs to allow for incorporation of these ideas, with revision, extension, and reevaluation of the possibilities in a second or even third round of review.

Even the initial round of alternatives should include rough costs. The initial round is also the place to review any citizen alternatives that have support, but are not particularly reasonable. Once they see the cost and other technical information citizens will more than likely move on to more reasonable alternatives.

Multiple rounds of review also allow for the deferral of details to the later rounds of review. There is no need for the basic decisions about structural type to get hung up at the beginning because of debates about railing details.

In the Folsom example four alternatives were developed, responding to the committee's sketches (Figure 3-7). The presentation included rough costs. Based on this information, the committee narrowed their focus to two: the three-span deck arch and the haunched girder.

**FIGURE 3-7** *Preliminary alternatives for the Folsom structure.*

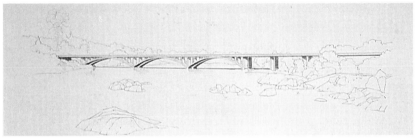

Three span deck arch

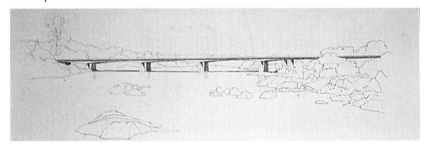

Three span haunched girder

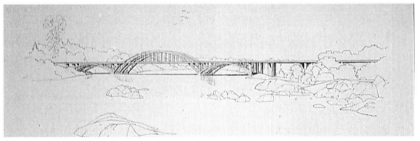

Three span through arch

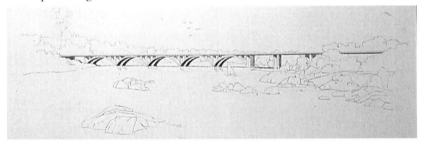

Five span deck arch

7. **Presentation to Elected or Appointed Body and/or the Larger Public for Ratification and Approval.** Even with the best citizen participation process there may remain a disgruntled minority who feel that their views have not been appropriately heard or reflected in the final decision. In order to forestall the later derailment of the process by

this group, the selected alternative should be a given a formal review process in which the formal commitment of the appropriate decision-making or elected officials is received. This will make it more difficult and less likely for those individuals to change their minds at a later date should objections surface.

At Folsom, once the committee had made up its mind, their findings were referred to the City Council for ratification. When the project was later petitioned to referendum (based on objections to the location, not the design) the members of the Citizens' Review Committee became the nucleus of a group which successfully supported their adopted proposal.

The Folsom project then moved into final design, based on the committee's preference for a three-span arch. However, the comparative cost of providing earthquake resistance for an arch versus a haunched girder proved to be overwhelming. The City Council finally decided on a three-span haunched girder, detailed to complement the Rainbow Bridge, with arch ribs added to the main spans entirely for appearance.

A community participation process conducted along these lines makes possible reasoned debate based on a common vision of what the new bridge should look like. While time-consuming in terms of man-hours, the process may well save calendar time by resolving issues in an orderly and timely manner, rather than though an endless series of contentious hearings and redesigns. The process will result in a clear and specific mandate for the appearance of the new bridge.

FIGURE 3-8 *Final design for the new American River Bridge at Folsom, California.*

Through application of previous processes, projects can be developed of which both engineers and citizens will be proud.

## Collaboration with Other Visual Professionals

Visual professionals who are willing to take the time to understand the special nature of bridges can offer a positive contribution to engineers. Architects can advise on the visual aspects of span arrangements, proportions, and the shapes of major elements. They can be particularly helpful at offering suggestions on railings, walkways, and materials encountered at the street and pedestrian scale.

Urban designers and landscape architects have a different contribution to make. They are skilled at articulating the visual and physical relationships between buildings and open spaces. Their ideas can often be valuable in suggesting parameters and design features that will improve the fit between the bridge and the community. Examples might include providing a berm to screen the noise and view of traffic from a nearby residential area, or providing a median opening for a structure carrying dual roadways to allow light penetration and a wider range of uses to an area under a structure. Sculptors can advise on the shapes of major elements and assist with issues of ornamentation.

Color can become a complex issue requiring refined sensibility. Color consulting has developed as a specialty on its own. Even trained visual professionals get assistance in this area; engineers can, too.

The engineer must be sure that his or her collaborators understand the basic issues involved in bridges. They must be aware of the difference in size between bridges and the objects they are used to dealing with. Even the average everyday bridge is much larger than the average building and *very* much larger than the average work of art. Size relates as well to dollars, placing more importance on the discipline of economy. As we have seen in Chapter One, size also affects perception, as does movement. The visual professionals must take the time to understand all of these issues. Otherwise, the engineer and the visual professionals will be constantly at odds with each other, and the design will suffer.

**FIGURE 3-9** *This pedestrian bridge owes its form to a productive collaboration between an urban designer and its engineer, Jorg Schlaich.*

The best mechanism for collaboration is an interdisciplinary team working together from the beginning of the project under the leadership of the engineer. The team should function in a collegial fashion with respect all around for the skills and knowledge of each professional and the special contributions each can make. All should be encouraged to comment on, and contribute to, all decisions, even the early "engineering" decisions covering, for example, geometry, on which so much else depends. Each professional must take the responsibility to explain the reasons for each of their comments in plain language the others can understand. Each has the responsibility to listen carefully to those explanations.

The engineer should not be shy about asserting his or her own aesthetic views. If the engineer has developed his or her own aesthetic abilities, he or she will have an understanding of the emotive power of a well-designed bridge, and the positive contribution that such a form can have to a larger scene—an appreciation that the visual professionals may lack unless they have taken the time to make their own study of bridges.

In the end it must be clear that the decisions are being primarily driven by the engineering balance of performance, cost, and appearance. If something can be made visually better, in a way that improves or at least does not reduce structural efficiency, then it should be considered by the engineer.

## FREQUENT CONSIDERATIONS IN DEVELOPING A DESIGN INTENTION

### Corridor and Urban Design Themes

Major highways incorporate a number of bridges which are often seen in close succession or even at the same time. Concern for the quality of the sequential experience requires that the appearance of all of the bridges be considered together. Concept themes should be considered on all new and reconstructed routes during the earliest stage of design. This is particularly important when some of the bridges are to be done by different designers or different agencies.

A design theme can be developed by selecting a common vocabulary of bridge elements, and applying them more or less consistently to all of the bridges on a given route or in a given area. For example, a standardized parapet profile can be developed and used consistently throughout a series of bridges. Standardized colors, certain surface materials, or a standardized texturing for retaining walls and abutment walls are other obvious devices to develop a theme.

**FIGURE 3-10** *The difficulty of finding a compatible theme to meet many different situations.*

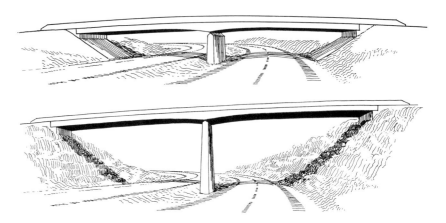

A concept/theme does not require that all structures be identical. Variations along a route can be used to influence the user's frame of mind, such as gradually reducing spans as the highway moves into an urban area. The theme becomes one of change or difference. But the change or difference must be controlled and compatible over the entire route.

The major challenge is to reconcile the common features of the theme with the need for each bridge to address its particular structural requirements. If all of the bridges are essentially similar in their structural aspects, the problem is obviously simplified. However, where a wide variety of structural situations exist, it becomes a more difficult challenge to find a theme which allows each structure to develop its own efficiency, economy, and elegance while still being a contributing part of a larger ensemble. In such cases, reliance on a structural element (say, a standardized pier design), may produce disappointing results when the element gets stretched to meet all of the different situations (see Figure 3-10). Better in those cases to rely on nonstructural elements (parapet profile, color, surface texture) to carry the theme.

Structures in interchanges must be given special consideration since several of them are usually visible at one time, and they may even be physically interlinked. This means not only application of the common elements resulting from a design theme, but also close coordination by the designers of each structure.

Themes may not be appropriate for all corridors or all structures within a corridor. The exception to the rule makes its own statement. However, the designer should remember that the absence of a theme is in *itself* is a theme, with its own set of perceptions and reactions.

On occasion a bridge will be required to respond to an urban design theme established to encourage a certain design flavor in a larger area of

**FIGURE 3-11** *Appropriate use of traditional materials on walls and piers, U.S. 50 over U.S. 301, Queenstown, Maryland.*

**FIGURE 3-12** *Problematical use of traditional materials to face a bridge girder.*

which the bridge is a part. The legitimacy and success of such efforts, with regard to the bridge, depends on the nature and specificity of the urban design requirements. If the requirements set general requirements for the use of certain materials, colors, or details, they can usually be accommodated within the engineer's disciplines of efficiency, economy, and elegance. However, if they establish specific requirements which compromise engineering criteria, they should be strongly resisted.

For example, one frequent requirement is the use of a traditional material, such as brick. Such materials can easily and sensibly be accommodated when used in their traditional fashion as walls and piers (Figure 3-11). However, if the requirement extends to mandating the use of brick to face the bridge girder, then substantial cost and durability problems will have been inflicted on the bridge. These problems will have been incurred without producing an offsetting improvement in aesthetic quality. Most people will find the sight of brick suspended in midair over distances of 150 feet unsettling, not attractive.

## Bridges in Historic Areas and Towns

In a historic area, people will often feel that the bridge should blend in or be consistent with the architecture of the town. This is a difficult idea to implement.

Historic towns are built with the technologies and materials available in their times: brick, stone, cast iron, and/or wood. The architectural details are suitable for those materials and reflect the aesthetic and social values of those times.

**FIGURE 3-13** *Capital Center Structures, I-35E, St. Paul, Minnesota.*

We, on the other hand, have available to us high-strength steel and posttensioned concrete. It is not unusual for us to build multispan structures as long as a city block with spans of more than 200 feet. It is impossible to make a highway bridge, as long as a whole block of colonial buildings, look like Georgian architecture. The attempt will result in something which is neither a good bridge nor good architecture and is very expensive as well.

If traditional materials are used, it is best to use them in traditional ways. Brick facing, for example, can be used for piers and abutment walls, reflecting its traditional function as a load-bearing material.

Figure 3-13 shows a set of structures that was built in the monumental center of St. Paul, near the Minnesota capital building. Rather than placing the ashlar stone of the capital building on the bridge superstructure, the designer imitated the stone with precast concrete, and then used it at locations in piers and retaining walls consistent with the historic use of stone.

The best idea is to build a modern bridge which is as true and as high-quality a reflection of our era as the historic buildings are of theirs. The Naval Academy Bridge shown in Figure 1-24 (page 21) was built as a result of an international competition. The bridge is in Annapolis, Maryland, a colonial town which still serves as the state capital. During the judging the jury, which included representatives of the nearby neighborhoods and the local historical society, decided that the best bridge was one that embodied all the modern virtues of simplicity and transparency. Their reasoning was that, since the existing scene was of such high quality, the new bridge should preserve the focus on the existing elements, and not become itself the centerpiece.

## Replacement and Duplication

Placing a new bridge next to, or near, an old one or replacing an old bridge with a new one are situations where hard-and-fast guidelines cannot be given, and which depends very heavily on the situation as it exists in the field.

As existing freeways are rebuilt and expanded, there will be more and more situations where it is necessary to duplicate or expand an existing bridge.

A thorough field review and documentation, including multiple color photographs of the old structure, should be undertaken in order to assist in developing the new. The review should use the guidelines outlined in this book as criteria. Often, this kind of careful study and analysis will produce its own ideas.

It is usually not possible or desirable to reproduce the existing structure exactly. New structural techniques, new materials, and new functional requirements will make that an unreasonable solution. However, it is possible to construct the new bridge alongside the old so that the ensemble is visually consistent and attractive. Effort should be directed at looking for common features which can be reinterpreted in modern technologies. For example, a beloved 80-year old concrete arch is nearby. Perhaps a precast concrete arch could be built, with longer spans suitable to the modern material, but with the same general shape. Or, perhaps, there are details of railings or lighting on the old bridge which can be incorporated in a new structure while the major structural members themselves are shaped to take advantage of new materials. The bridge shown in Figure 6-29 (page 209) is an example of this approach.

If the old bridge is not attractive, or if an old bridge stands alone rather than being part of a group of similar structures, then it may be better to make the new bridge completely independent. However, if the old bridge has good qualities, then these qualities should be carried over to the new bridge (and preserved on the old bridge).

The desirable features can be made the basis of common details, common proportions, and common structural systems which are used in both new and old structures. The new features need not be literal reproductions of the old. For example, it may not be necessary to construct new fieldstone abutments to match old abutments. Recent advances using form liners and individually stained "stones" make it possible to reproduce the look of fieldstone in cast concrete (see the discussion of Surface Patterns in Chapter Five). However, it must be well done or the sham will be quickly apparent and will make both new and old look tawdry. The new abutments could also be made of plain concrete similar in size, shape, color, and/or proportion, and achieve the desired consistency.

In the Folsom Bridge example discussed in Citizen Participation, above, column shapes, capitals, and deck brackets from the existing Rainbow Bridge were emulated in the new structure. The goal was to establish a correspondence with the old structure (Figure 2-29, page 51), but use details shaped and sized for the new.

FIGURE 3-14 *At the proposed new Peace Bridge over the Niagara at Buffalo, NY, the spans and structure type emulate the existing bridge, but the arch ribs are tapered and the bracing simplified to reflect modern methods.*

Color offers a quick and obvious way of establishing correspondence between old and new. If a new steel bridge is to be built next to an old one, it is a simple matter to paint them the same color or a related color. Concrete may offer similar possibilities. For example, if the older pier cap is to be given an epoxy finish for maintenance purposes, the same finish can be applied to a similarly shaped new pier cap adjacent.

The introduction of a new crossing on an existing route, such as a beltway, creates a real challenge to establish a positive relationship with what exists. This requires a thorough evaluation of the location: noting existing structures near the new, their pier placement and shapes, color, and details. This does not mean that the new must match the existing. A choice needs to be made: Should the new structure attempt to compliment the existing structures, or should it make its own statement?

When all of the existing structures are similar and very close together (300 feet or less) it is probably better to closely complement the nearby structures. The approach is to tie the new to the old with common features, details, or color. For example, a two-span continuous crossing in an area with four-span bridges could be tied to the older bridges through a similar pier design or parapet profile.

Paradoxically, when all of a series of closely spaced structures are different, it is probably better to select the best one and attempt to complement it, rather than insert a new variant into the visual cacophony.

However, when existing bridges are more widely spaced more flexibility exists, and engineers can look to criteria outside the freeway itself, such as the desire to emphasize the presence of a nearby town, as reasons to complement or not complement existing bridges.

## Reconstruction and Rehabilitation

It is also possible to reconstruct old bridges to incorporate new requirements and materials while still respecting their original design intent. When older bridges are rebuilt or rehabilitated the question becomes how much, if any, of the old detail should be restored? This question can be answered by determining the answers to two others, of what visual quality is the detail and how important is it to the historical record and/or the community's image of the bridge?

If the answers are that the old detail is of very high quality and/or it is very important to the community then every effort should be made to restore it to its original quality, or to incorporate this detail in new forms with the new materials used in reconstructing the bridge.

If not, the reconstruction should seek to simplify the appearance of the bridge in ways which bring out whatever positive qualities exist in its structural members and form.

## CONCEPTUAL ENGINEERING

## Exploring the Possibilities

Once the design intention has been established conceptual engineering can begin. Conceptual engineering is the stage when all plausible options and some not-so-plausible options are examined in sketch form.

It begins with the quick generation of a wide range of possibilities, going beyond the usual and accepted options with a quick development of at least the first five Determinants of Appearance. For each option the possibilities of geometry should be investigated first, then structural type, pier locations, shapes of the major members, etc., through pier and abutment shape. Color, railings, and surface treatment—the more detailed determinants of appearance—can be left for later.

Starting with a wide range of seemingly unusual options is critical. By definition, improvements will come from new ideas, ideas beyond the cur-

**FIGURE 3-15** *Portage Viaduct over the Genesee River, New York, an extreme example of the transparency possible with thin structural members.*

rently understood range of possibilities. By starting with a wide range of options the designer is less likely to miss that key idea that will lead to an improved structure and, perhaps, to a great bridge.

Promising structural concepts should be sketched in three dimensions to get a sense of how they will appear in finished form. Rough calculations, sufficient to set major member sizes and get preliminary costs, should be done. The next step is an equally quick evaluation. The less-promising alternatives should be discarded and the more promising should be refined.

Then the review and evaluation process should occur again, always looking at structural effectiveness, cost, and appearance at the same time. At each successive stage, the drawings should be more accurate and more carefully rendered.

It is very helpful to keep the public involved during this part of the process. In this way designers will have some confidence that their interpretation of the public's ideas is correct, improving the chances that the final result will get a positive reception. Often, seeing the drawings will call to the public's mind concerns not voiced earlier. Better to get these on the table at this early stage than to have to come back and deal with them during final design.

There will be dead ends and blind alleys. Sometimes the process will have to be recycled if, for example, a decision to change structural type indicates that a change in vertical alignment is warranted. Through the generation and review of multiple alternatives, the process will narrow down to a basic concept that meets all three criteria: efficiency, economy, and elegance.

One can imagine how this process might go for a project crossing a valley. Part of the design intention may be a desire to keep open views up and down the valley. In response to this concern the designer might start off with a set of alternatives that relies on large spans to keep the views open. Figure 3-16 shows a solution of this type. The side effect of long spans, of course, is that the structural members themselves become quite large, creating in themselves an impediment to the views.

The designer might try a different approach: alternatives with very short spans supported by a multitude of very thin members (Figure 3-15). The

**FIGURE 3-16** *This arched structure from California shows a good way to bridge a highway cut; the sides of the cut contain the thrust of the arch both structurally and visually. Figure 4-16 (page 100) shows that a rigid frame is a clearly different but equally valid design concept for a similar problem.*

views are still available, only now they are seen through a transparent lacework of thin structural members.

The aesthetic impression of the second set of alternatives is obviously quite different, as are the structural and cost implications. (With the shorter spans, this approach actually presents some possible economies.) The point is not that one approach is better than the other, but that there are many possible solutions to a given problem, and the more that are considered the better the chance that the unique solution will be found which best fits the design intention.

Once the most promising concept has been selected, the formal Type, Size, and Location presentation can be prepared. Engineers often consider this the point at which 30 percent of the design is complete.

## After Type, Size, and Location

It is only after the basic concept has been selected that detailed calculations and engineering drawings should be started. This is also the point at which secondary elements such as railings, colors, and signing and lighting, elements lower on the list of Determinants of Appearance, can be developed consistent with the selected structural concept.

Such details are critical to the final aesthetic success of the structure. As the great German architect Ludwig Mies van de Rohe put it, "God is in the details." The development and selection of details must remain true to the intentions of the original concept. Throughout the final design process details should be drawn in three dimensions to ensure that they contribute to the design concept. Significant changes should be reviewed to ensure that the design intention has not been compromised.

This part of the design process holds particular hazards if there is a change in personnel between the preliminary, conceptual engineering, and the final design stages. Large bridge-building organizations sometimes organize their staff into preliminary and final design groups, or perform the preliminary design in-house and leave the final design to a consultant. There is great danger that something significant will be lost in the transition from one group to the next. There must be a continuing review function for the first group throughout the final design process to ensure that all changes are positive.

## Selection and Standardization of Details

Standard details have an important place in bridge design. They are especially important when they represent the distillation of hard-won functional experience, as in a crash-tested railing. Indeed, many agencies attempt to design their bridges by agglomerating standard details. When some surface detail has proven to be attractive on one bridge, it is particularly tempting to apply it to all subsequent bridges.

Any success experienced through these approaches will be sheer coincidence. Bridges are too unique. Each deserves a fresh look. The functional aspects of standards will always apply. The visual aspects need to be reconsidered for each bridge. Some will apply completely, some will apply partially and have to be modified, and some will not apply at all, and new details will have to be developed to fit the specific situation. California addresses this problem by having a range of standard details covering the majority of bridge situations. The California bridge illustrated in Figure 2-4 (page 33) demonstrates a good use of standard details.

An important part of the role of the engineer is to carefully review the standard details that will apply to his or her bridge, and suggest an alternative wherever the existing standard would compromise his or her design intention.

chapter *four*

# A Design Language: Guidelines for the First Five Determinants of Appearance

*"Perfection is finally achieved not when there is no longer anything left to add, but when there is no longer anything to take away. It is as if that line which the human eye will follow with effortless delight were a line that had not been invented, but simply discovered; had, in the beginning, been hidden by nature and, in the end, been discovered by the engineer."*

—Antoine de Saint Exupéry,
French Aviator and Author

Chapters Four and Five take bridges apart and look at the appearance of each element: superstructure, piers, abutments, parapets and railings, surface colors, and textures and ornamentation. The guidelines address problems which appear over and over again in bridge design.

This is not meant to imply that bridges can be designed in pieces. Each element must be considered in relation to the whole. Instead, the guidelines should be seen as a type of language. Just as in a written language, the guidelines can be combined in numberless ways to arrive at a statement that is uniquely suited to each structure.[1] In Chapter Six we will analyze example structures by showing how the guidelines have been applied, or not applied, in more or less successful combinations.

The guidelines in Chapters Four and Five are organized around each Determinant of Appearance. They are numbered according to the Determinants of Appearance for reference in later discussions. Chapter Four looks at the Determinants of Appearance that are usually thought of as purely engineering decisions, even though they have the most important impact on the appearance of the bridge. Chapter Five covers those Determinants of Appearance in which aesthetics is usually thought to have more of a role, even though they have less influence on appearance than the first five.

The guidelines describe solutions for each Determinant of Appearances which have worked well in existing bridges, as judged by the reaction of engineers, visual professionals, and the public to these bridges. However, they should be seen as hypotheses—subject, as in science, to continual review and potential change as technologies, social needs, and aesthetic ideas change.

Each guideline is coupled, whenever possible, with a principle of perception or other factor which underlies it. This gives the engineer the opportunity to judge the guideline for himself or herself and to modify it without losing the principle upon which it is based. The guidelines are stated in a general and abstract way, so that the engineer can adapt them as appropriate to individual preferences and local conditions.

## GEOMETRY

This is the first and most important Determinant of Appearance. It includes the basic geometry of the highway or transit line as it relates to surrounding topography and other structures.

The bridge engineer is often presented with the geometry as a finished product with little opportunity to influence it. Since geometry is the most important determinant of appearance, this situation can present the bridge engineer with insurmountable aesthetic problems. He or she must seek to influence the geometry in ways that will improve the chances for aesthetic success. Often, small adjustments in the horizontal and vertical alignments can make enormous improvements in appearance with no appreciable effect on safety, cost, or by particular clearances or control points. The question should always be asked and the analysis made, just to make sure no opportunity is missed.

### *Look for the Shortest Apparent Distance Between Points*

This sounds too obvious to have to worry about. However, sometimes the bridge engineer's analysis of the site shows that the highway alignment creates a crossing which does not *look* like the shortest distance across the obstruction. In these cases it is sometimes possible to make small shifts which allow the bridge, for example, to spring from a topographic promontory, or to take advantage of a protrusion of the shoreline.

### Construct Horizontal and Vertical Alignments from Long, Continuous Curves

Vertical and horizontal alignments made up of long, continuous curves and tangents will look better than alignments made up of short, discrete segments. Because of the extreme perspective foreshortening that takes place in the highway environment, short curves will look like kinks in the alignment. Since we expect to find gradual changes in direction in the highway environment, especially when traveling at high speed, an alignment which seems to require a sudden change of direction will look disturbing and out of place.

Closely spaced curves in the same direction should be connected as compound curves, without an intervening tangent. Reverse curves should have only enough tangent to provide for a graceful superelevation reversal. The best way to reverse curves is with spiral transition curves or compound curves that approximate spirals.

### Relate Curve Length to Structure Length

How long a curve needs to be is a question that can only be answered in the context of the specific bridge. To start with, a curve which looks good is almost always substantially longer than the minimums set by the American Association of State Highway Transportation Officials (AAHTO). Second, the curve length should bear some relation to the length of the bridge. For bridges less than 2,500 feet long, with one horizontal or vertical curve, the

**FIGURE 4-1** *A too-short curve will look like a kink from many viewpoints.*

**FIGURE 4-2** *This generous curve in California is consistent with people's visual expectations on a high-speed highway.*

FIGURE 4-3 *The appearance of this Maryland pedestrian bridge is improved by the crest vertical curve.*

curve should be no less than half the length of the bridge. The length is better if it approximates or exceeds the length of the bridge.

### *Analyze the Effect Superelevation Transitions have on Parapet Alignment*

An analysis needs to be made of the effect of superelevation transitions on the parapets. Because the top of the parapet is near driver's eye height, and because of the foreshortening effect of perspective, the horizontal and vertical alignment of the parapet is very visible. In bridges with shoulders and/or sidewalks, the effect of superelevation transitions can be exaggerated. Vertical curves can add more complication. On any bridge with multiple curves, the parapet profiles should be plotted at an exaggerated vertical scale and checked for kinks and awkward curvatures.

### *Where Possible, Use a Crest Vertical Curve on Overpasses*

Even a very slight crest vertical curve will give a bridge a slightly arched appearance which most people find appealing.

### *Adjust the Horizontal Alignment to Simplify Column Placement*

One of the most difficult aesthetic problems is dealing with multiple pier designs within the same structure, such as mixing multicolumn frames with hammerheads. Sometimes the need for multiple column types can be reduced or eliminated by changes to the horizontal geometry without affecting cost or safety.

# SUPERSTRUCTURE TYPE

Superstructure type is the second most important determinant of appearance. Superstructure type is usually heavily influenced by the conditions of the site and the required spans. Given the proportion of the bridge cost associated with the superstructure, its type will usually be determined by combined economic and structural considerations. However, there are situations where two or more different superstructure types are comparable on economics and performance, and appearance can come into play. Or, situations can arise where a different superstructure type will provide a major improvement in aesthetic quality at a small increase in cost. Finally, there are many variations of layout and arrangement within a given structural type where improvements in appearance can be achieved at little or no increase in cost.

This book concentrates on the 60- to 500-foot span range where girders are the most usual type of superstructure. However, rigid-frame bridges and arches are also possibilities in this span range for the right site. Trusses and cable supported bridges have also been used, though more rarely and generally under special conditions.

Since most superstructure types are built in both steel and concrete, the choice of material by itself does not determine structural type. However, considerations of material choice and structure type are intertwined. For example, certain types, such as box girders, are generally easier to build in concrete than in steel. Material choice is discussed in more detail below.

The discussion that follows concentrates on the aesthetic aspects of the decision. It assumes a prior understanding by the reader of the structural possibilities and the economics of the various options.

## Influences on the Choice of Superstructure Type

There are many factors which influence the choice of Superstructure type. All must be understood and weighed together in order to arrive at a the best solution.

- The geometry of the roadway to be carried exerts a major influence, particularly if it tapers or is curved in plan. Structural types which can be curved or tapered to match offer an overriding simplicity. (*See* Figure 4-5.)

- The span requirements and required vertical clearances will determine the proportions and size of the bridge, as well as set the boundaries on what is economical and even what is physically possible.

FIGURE 4-4 *Two bridges of substantially different depth.*

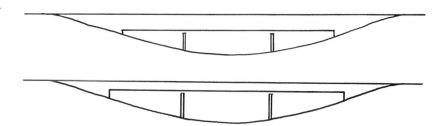

- The nature of the topography and foundation conditions at the site will be major influences. For example, arches and rigid frames look best in steep ravines, valleys, and deep cuts where the arch/frame can spring from the hillsides, or crossing rivers with steep banks or river walls. They also work better structurally because of the ability of such locations to resist the horizontal forces imposed by an arch/frame.

- The location of important viewpoints and nearby land uses should influence the structural type. For example, the underside of a structure over an urban street or park will be visible to many people. I-girder bridges are difficult to make attractive from the underside because of the visually complicated bracing details and because the fascia girders shadow all the other girders. The underside becomes a dark, complicated, and somewhat threatening place inhabited by pigeons and worse. The condition is worsened by weathering steel, whose dark matte surface soaks up whatever light may be available.

- If the structure is intended to carry a symbolic role, then that can most effectively be satisfied through the choice of structural type. For example, if it is desirable for the structure to frame an important view, then a structural type with a curved, arched soffit will be an effective choice (*see* Figure 5-37, page 157).

## Effects of Material Characteristics

Usually, material choice is heavily influenced by the cost of the material in the locality, the availability of experienced contractors and fabricators, ease of construction at the specific site, and environmental factors such as the presence of a corrosive environment. However, the choice can also dramatically affect the appearance of the structure, and these effects should be considered.

The choice of superstructure material can affect appearance in four ways: apparent thinness, shape, details, and color. The typical precast girder is significantly deeper than a steel welded-plate girder of equivalent span. This difference in depth has a major effect on the superstructure's overall appearance. However, by the use of appropriate posttensioning, poured-in-place and precast segmental concrete structures can be made almost as thin as steel structures.

Poured-in-place concrete girders can be built with a smooth surface of any shape, as long as the contractor can economically build the form work. Steel girders are sharp-edged and are limited in shape by the need to fabricate them from plates and rolled sections. Standard precast girders have characteristic shapes and are limited in the ways they can be economically connected.

Differences in details enforced by the material choice need to be considered. On steel bridges, bolts, stiffeners, bracing plates, and splice plates will be visible, and their appearance needs to be considered. With concrete box girders, all details and connections are typically internal and unseen.

Concrete and A588 weathering steel have strong characteristic colors. Superstructures may need to be coated to offset the effect of material color. For example, to achieve visual continuity in a long structure, it may be desirable to coat steel box girders with a light, warm gray so they look like adjacent concrete box girders. The lighter concrete or light-colored paint on steel is advantageous for bridges where pedestrian use of the underside is important because more light is reflected into the underbridge area.

If coating is not desirable, then the natural color of the material should be a consideration at the time of material selection. This can be particularly important when there will be significant pedestrian use of the underside of the bridge. For example, A588 weathering steel attains a dark brown-black color, which provides an unpleasant "ceiling" for a pedestrian space, and needs to be offset with additional lighting or other measures. However, if few pedestrians are likely to be present, then color, being lower on the scale of importance for determinants of appearance, is a less significant consideration for selecting the superstructure material. (See Chapter Five for more information on color.)

No one of these characteristics is good or bad by itself. All need to be considered in choosing the superstructure type in order to create a unified design for the overall structure.

The material decision begins with the design intention, which may dictate a material based upon the desired structural conditions or visual concerns. For example, steel was required for the river crossing shown in Figure 1-13 (page 8) in order to meet design intention requirements for maximum vertical clearance while still connecting to existing streets. The choice of steel also allowed the assembled girder to be rolled into place to replace an existing truss in a minimal amount of time.

If the design concept does not require a specific material, then the choice can be made on cost. The chosen material can then be detailed to meet the requirements of the design concept.

## General Considerations

Certain criteria should influence all bridges. We saw in the section on Geometry, above, that relative slenderness is an advantage. It is in the choice of structural type that this characteristic is most strongly established.

### Relative Slenderness Should be Sought When Picking Superstructure Type

Choosing continuous steel plate girders rather than simple spans will immediately improve the looks of the structure (*see* Figure 4-3, page 88). Precast concrete I beams will look (and be) heavy compared to continuous steel girders because of their greater depth for a given span. Post-tensioned concrete slab bridges can look very light because of their minimal depth.

### Maintain Continuity of Structural Form, Material, and/or Depth

The bridge should be a single unified concept. Changes in structural type or depth to accommodate differing span conditions should be made smoothly, and similar structural shapes, materials, and/or colors should be used to tie the structure together.

If the main span or spans require a change to a different type, such as an arch, truss, or rigid frame, the maintaining of an appearance of continuity

FIGURE 4-5 *Tapering the girders makes all of the spans look like one continuous girder.*

FIGURE 4-6 *The constant depth girder of Oregon's Alsea Bay Bridge is an element of continuity across different structural types.*[1]

becomes more difficult. Arches and frames often are combined with a series of girder-approach spans. Combining these two different forms in one structure can seem visually confusing. Either selected features of the main structure should be extended over the approach spans, or a major pier or other vertical feature should be used between the two types of structure to visually clarify where one type of structure starts and the other stops.

### Find Elements of Continuity Between Adjoining Types

As an example of extending selected features of the main structure over the approach spans, a deck stringer for an arch can be matched with a girder of the same depth on the approach spans. Deck overhangs can be kept constant from a girder span to a deck truss. The end span of the truss can be tapered to the same depth as the girder. The same color or material can be used on both types. The more consistent elements there are, the more continuous the structure will seem.

## Girder Bridges

For bridges with spans less than 500 feet, under most conditions and with today's technology, the most cost-effective structure is a girder bridge. Within the girder category, there are choices to be made between straight and curved girders, between I-girders and box girders, and between steel and concrete.

FIGURE 4-7 *This bridge with chorded girders demonstrates the variable slab spans and the visual confusion that results.*

### *Use Curved Girders for Curved Roadways*

Curved girders are better than straight girders on chords for all but the most-gentle curvatures.

Curved girders eliminate the variable deck overhangs (and scalloped shadows) of spans on chords. They also eliminate all of the structural tinkering necessary to fit straight girders to circular curves and still meet clearance requirements and fixed pier locations (*see* Figure 4-4, page 90). In more basic terms, curved girders are better because the structure itself therefore reflects the lines of motion which are the dominating features of the transportation environment, and which are, in fact, the structure's reason for existence.

If straight girders must be used, they should all be of a similar length so that the variations of deck overhang occur in a constant rhythm along the structure.

### *Consider Box Girders or Posttensioned Concrete-voided Slabs for Prominent Bridges, Bridges with Curvature, or Bridges Where the View of the Underside is Important*

Box girders, both steel and concrete, have been used in prominent locations because of their relative thinness, because of the clean, simple appearance of their undersides, and because their torsional stiffness often allows thinner piers and more flexible pier locations.

The design of steel box-girder bridges has been hampered by a tendency to use too many boxes. The bridges have been treated like plate-girder bridges with adjacent bottom flanges connected. This approach misses the opportunity to take full advantage of the torsional stiffness of box girders and adds unnecessary cost and visual complication. Designers should seek to use as few widely spaced box girders as reasonable.[2]

Box girders are an advantage because their flat underside reflects light into the underbridge area, and the bracing details are mostly hidden.

**FIGURE 4-8** *The torsional stiffness of box girders improves load distribution and allows wider spacing than for I-shaped girders.*

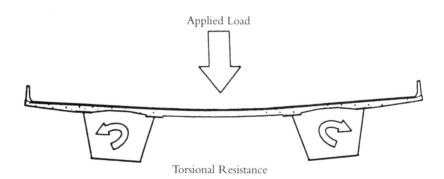

FIGURE 4-9 *This underside view of the new Naval Academy bridge at Annapolis shows the value of few widely spaced girders in its clean and bright appearance.*

FIGURE 4-10 *The curved lines of this integral girder bridge flow past the piers and are continuous from one end of the bridge to the other.*

### Consider Abutment-restrained Girders When Vertical Clearance is Minimal or When It is Desirable to Frame a View Through the Structure

Three-span girder bridges can be built with the end spans hidden within the abutments. The center span can be treated as a fixed-end girder, with maximum moments at the abutment. The resulting structure allows longer spans than a simply supported girder, and allows the midspan depth to be reduced. Figures 5-37 (page 157) and 6-3 (page 186) show how abutment-restrained girders can be thin at midspan; their curved bottom edges effectively frame the views beyond.

### Consider Integrally Framed Cross Girders

Integrally framed cross girders have also been used in high exposure locations because they minimize the size of the pier, provide for more flexible pier location, and emphasize the visual continuity of the superstructure (Figure 4-10).

Integrally framed cross girders can be particularly effective in improving the appearance of I-girder bridges, both steel and precast concrete. If carefully detailed, they can provide structural redundancy and need not add significant cost.

### When Adding Girders to Accommodate Splits and Widenings, Do So in a Clear, Systematic Manner

Splits and widenings to accommodate ramps can result in a hodgepodge of half-girders and odd spacings, particularly when working with steel or precast concrete I-girders.

**FIGURE 4-11** *This method of adding girders at a ramp junction presents an easily understood pattern.*

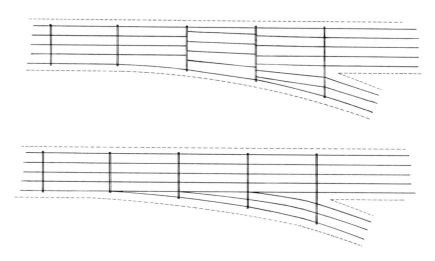

## Arches/Frames

Arch and rigid-frame bridges less than 300 feet in span are rarely economical in today's technology. However, they continue to have strong visual appeal because of their shape. They are definite possibilities for the right site.

### *Arch and Rigid-frame Bridges Look Best Where the Surroundings "Contain" the Visual Thrust of the Arch*

Even tied arches look best contained in river valleys with high bluffs (Figure 4-12). Thrust blocks can provide the same sense of "containment" on flat sites if they are large enough.

### *Rigid-frame Bridges Look Best with Legs That are One-quarter to One-half the Span Length*

Rigid frame bridges need height to allow for a graceful length of leg. Rigid frames with short legs tend to look stubby (Figure 4-13). These consideration is less of a problem where the legs are enclosed triangles (Figure 4-14). Then the bridge can fit into most sites. Rigid frames can be very slender at midspan. They will be visually more successful the more the elements are shaped to reflect the change in stresses across the structure. (*See also* Figures 2-3, page 33; 2-21, page 45; and 6-14, page 190.)

## Trusses

In recent decades, truss bridges have rarely been used at this span range because of cost, maintenance and appearance. However, there is now renewed

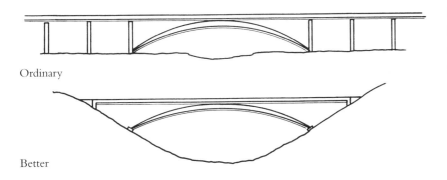

Ordinary

Better

FIGURE 4-12 *An arch bridge needs a site which contains the structural and visual thrust.*

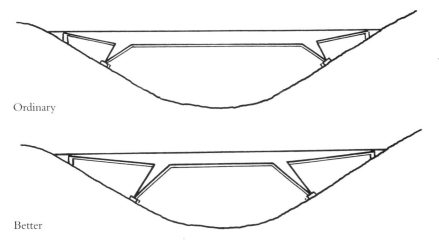

Ordinary

Better

FIGURE 4-13 *The importance of height to a rigid frame bridge.*

interest in truss bridges for local roads. Also, prefabricated truss bridges are often used as pedestrian bridges. Finally, several concepts for composite and prestressed trusses are in the experimental stage, and the availability of high-performance steel may lead to more economic trusses. It is likely that there will be more serious interest in trusses for shorter span bridges in the years ahead.

The keys to good appearance in truss design are:

- A graceful overall shape.

- Simplicity: a minimum number of members.

- Consistency: all the members should be at consistent angles. For example, a truss with all diagonals at a 60 degree angle will look better than a truss that mixes diagonals and vertical members.

- Small and attractive connection details.

**FIGURE 4-14** *This triangular frame looks good even in a site with a low clearance.*

## Cable-supported Structures

Pedestrian bridges offer some possibility for suspension and cable-stayed designs in this span range. These possibilities are discussed in Chapter Six in the section on Pedestrian Bridges.

Vehicular-suspension and stayed-girder bridges are generally economical only for spans in excess of 500 feet and are beyond the scope of this book. Books offering guidance for such bridges can be found in the Bibliography. However, some shorter-span cable-stayed bridges have been built economically to fit specific situations, as illustrated in Figure 3-3 (page 64).

## PIER PLACEMENT

Pier placement begins with providing for under roadway clearance requirements, hydraulic requirements, navigational channels, and foundation conditions. Added to these should be visual criteria. These are of two types: providing a pattern of piers which is visually logical both within the structure and relative to nearby topographic features, and providing for desirable lines of sight through the structure.

### With Few Exceptions, There Should be an Odd Number of Spans

With an even number of spans a duality is produced which most people find uncomfortable. Usually there is something to be crossed: a channel, river, roadway or ravine. People expect that to occupy or appear to occupy the center of the structure. A pier in midriver or midroadway is an obvious conflict.

However, there are important exceptions to this guideline. Wherever there is a strong symmetry in the area being spanned, with an obvious pier location at its center, then an even number of spans is preferable. Frequent examples are a typical freeway with dual roadways or a river with an island in the middle. Also, for very long bridges with more than seven or eight spans, the fact that there is an odd or even number of spans is not noticeable.

### Place Piers in Logical Relation to Topographic Features

Placement with regard to topography and shorelines can be critical.

1. *Piers should not be placed at the deepest part of a valley or man-made cut.* This position will produce the tallest possible pier. In addition to the cost problem observers will find this obvious lack of logic disturbing.

2. *Place piers on natural promontories.* This approach will produce shorter piers and will look more logical than a pier placed next to a promontory.

3. *Place a pier on land at or near the shoreline, more or less symmetrically placed with regard to both shorelines.* Common sense calls for a pier (or abutment) on land at or near the shoreline. Deviations from this guideline should have a visually obvious reason, such as a shoreline roadway, to explain them.

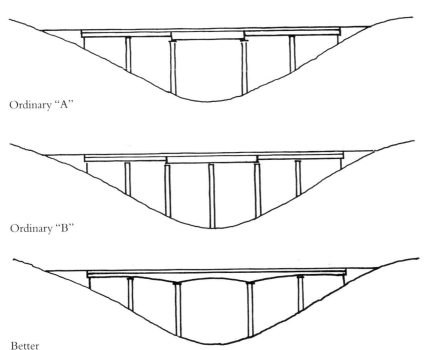

Ordinary "A"

Ordinary "B"

Better

**FIGURE 4-15** *Schematic A suffers from a discontinuous superstructure. Schematic B has several problems: an even number of spans and a pier at the deepest point of the valley as well as a discontinuous superstructure. Compare with the schematic at the bottom.*

*For Arch and Rigid-frame Bridges, Springing Point Placement is Critical*
Place the arch or rigid-frame springing points on topographic features which appear to resist the horizontal as well as the vertical reactions.

1. *For arches and frames over water the shoreside springing point of an arch or rigid frame should be on shore near the shoreline to give the structure a strong visual end point to the diagonal line of the arch or frame.* If the arch ends in the water a large foundation element should be created to provide a strong end for the arch and visually contain its horizontal thrust.

2. *For both arches and rigid frames in hilly topography, try to find natural locations on the valley walls (such as a rock outcrop) or cut side walls (as on a bench) to place the springing.*

*Consider Superstructure Costs and Foundation Costs Together When Developing Optimum Span Lengths*
Typically superstructure costs increase and foundation/pier costs decrease as spans get longer. These relationships can be plotted as curves showing the change in element cost at various spans. By adding the two curves together the true effect of various spans lengths can be determined. Figure 4-17 shows an example of a combined cost curve.

Often the combined curve does not show a clear minimum. When considering the difficulties of accurate cost estimation, the only logical conclusion is that the effect of longer spans is negligible over a significant range. In such cases span lengths should generally be set at the long end of the range. Fewer piers will mean fewer foundations, less surface disruption, and a more open view through the structure, particularly at oblique angles.

**FIGURE 4-16** *This rigid frame starts at a logical point, the benches of this man-made cut, which visually contain both the horizontal and vertical reactions.*

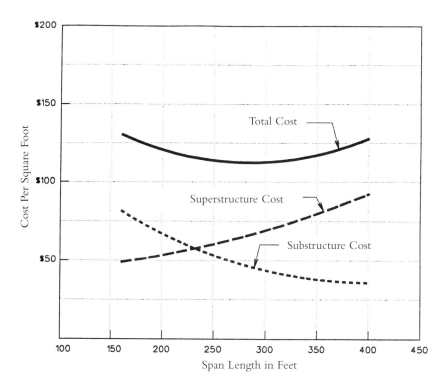

FIGURE 4-17 *A typical total cost curve; the curve changes with each project.*

### In General, Span Length Should Exceed Pier Height

Throughout the bridge, it is the *relative* sizes of the major elements that have the strongest effect on the visual impact.

For pier placement, the key proportion is span versus vertical clearance or, a better way to look at it, span versus the overall shape of the space beneath the bridge.

Generally, the bridge will look better the more the horizontal dimension of this space (the span) exceeds the vertical dimension. There is a visual span limit for low bridges, but economics will probably take effect before the visu-

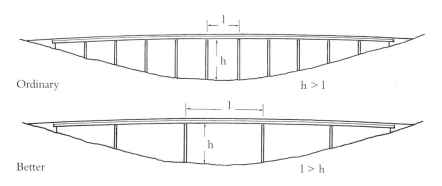

FIGURE 4-18 *Emphasizing horizontal proportions in pier placement.*

FIGURE 4-19 *Multispan bridges will look better with consistent proportions of span to height in all spans.*

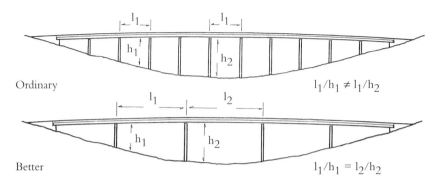

al limit is reached. Conversely, for very high bridges, economics may make it unfeasible to make the span significantly greater then the height.

Most bridges are in an environment where the horizontal dimensions of the bridge itself and its surroundings are much greater than the height of the bridge. The longer the spans are, relative to pier height, the more the bridge will seem to be complementary to its environment. Also, logic says that the reason for the bridge is to cross something, and additional piers only get in the way.

This idea can reach a point of diminishing returns when the pier and girder elements become so massive as to overwhelm the site.

### Ratio of Height to Span Length Should be Similar from Span to Span

Once the ratio of span to height ($l/h$) has been established for the main span, the secondary spans should vary in proportion to their individual heights in order to maintain the $l/h$ ratio approximately constant for all spans. The bridge will have much more unity if these *proportions* are consistent, regardless of span lengths.

### Open Up Spatial Corridors Through the Structure

The width and continuity of spatial corridors through the bridge should be made as generous as feasible. The intrusiveness of the bridge in the town or landscape will depend on the degree that this is accomplished. It is particularly important in interchanges, where the ability to see beyond the bridge is a matter of safety as well as appearance.

As was discussed in Chapter Two, actual sight lines need to be recognized. For example, a multicolumn bent will look simple when seen end-on (as in an elevation drawing), but the hidden columns will be very apparent in the more normal diagonal views. A group of such bents can become a "forest" when seen from the usual angles. Figure 6-28 (page 208) shows how a forest of columns can block sight lines through the bridge. Figure 6-25 (page 202) is an example of how the problem can be reduced.

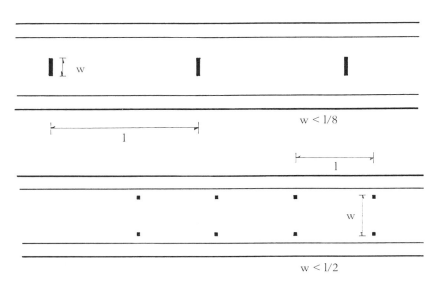

FIGURE 4-20  *Ratio of pier width at the base to span length for single-shaft piers.*[3]

w < 1/8

FIGURE 4-21  *Ratio of column spacing and span length for two or more columns.*[3]

w < 1/2

- *For single-shaft piers, span lengths and overhangs should be adjusted so the pier width does not exceed one-eighth of the span length.*

- *If multiple column piers are planned, the span should be set so that the total width of the column group does not exceed one-half of the span length. See also the section on Pier Shape in Chapter Five, page 33.*

## Skew Structures

The needs of highway and transit geometry often enforce crossings of other facilities at sharp angles, or skews. These situations pose visual as well as structural challenges. At skew angles down to about 60 degrees a standard girder bridge can be adapted without major effect on the appearance. However, at lower angles piers and abutment walls become substantially elongated. These elements become larger portions of the visual scene, to the detriment of the structure's overall appearance. Also, the nearer part of the superstructure becomes larger than the more distant part, and the distortion can be disturbing. These effects tend to be underestimated by engineers viewing the structure in elevation drawing, resulting in many unsightly skewed bridges. Preparing a three-dimensional driver's-eye-view will show the problems and suggest some solutions.

Addressing the problems of skew structures requires considering superstructure type and shape, pier placement, and abutment placement all at the same time, as a decision made on one will have major impacts on all the others.

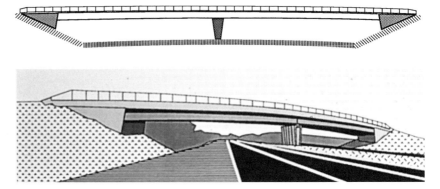

FIGURE 4-22 *Compare this elevation drawing of Maryland route 18 over U.S. 50 to what the observer actually sees in Figure 4-23.*

FIGURE 4-23 *Actual appearance of Maryland route 18 over U.S. 50; this is a computer abstraction of the photo in Figure 1-25 (page 25).*

### Select Superstructure Types That Allow Large Overhangs and Few Supports

Adopting a superstructure type that has larger overhangs narrows the piers and helps compensate for the skew elongation. The desirable goal is a super-structure that can be supported on a single round or elliptical pier. Not only does this minimize the visual presence of the pier but it presents much more flexibility in the placement of the pier in complex interchange situations.

Box girders and posttensioned concrete-voided slabs lend themselves to this situation because their torsional stiffness allows for larger overhangs and creates the possibility of handling the torsional reactions at the abutments only. Ontario has built many interchange structures that take advantage of this property (Figures 2-20, page 45; and 4-24). These structure types also provide for the possibility of integral pier caps whose soffits are flush with the soffits of the longitudinal girders. The pier caps can thus extend over the under-crossing roadway without causing a clearance problem.

### For Very Wide Structures Use Multiple Girders with a Single Column at Each Beam

This eliminates the visual distraction of an elongated pier cap (Figure 4-25). There is a danger in the extreme case that the appearance will become confining and tunnellike to the driver.

### For Sharp Skews Place a Beam at Each Edge of the Overpassing Roadway, Then Place Columns at the Edges of the Underpassing Roadway

This approach can result in a very open appearance. Recent concerns about the redundancy of two-girder systems have discouraged this type of structure. However, using box girders, which are internally redundant, or paired I-girders can address this concern.

FIGURE 4-24 *This Ontario structure's post tensioned voided slab has great torsional stiffness; torsional forces are carried to the abutments, allowing single intermediate columns which open up clear views through the structure.*

FIGURE 4-25 *Using a single freestanding column for each girder can avoid an unreasonably long pier cap for skewed structures.*

See also the discussions of skewed bridges concerning abutments in the following section, girder shape later in this chapter, and pier shape in Chapter Five.

## ABUTMENT AND WALL PLACEMENT

The placement of abutments and walls in the visual field will influence the size and appearance of both superstructure and piers, as well as creating elements which in themselves can be positive or negative features. The positive or negative nature of their contribution will depend significantly on where they are placed relative to other features and the topography.

### Abutments

The abutment's function is to get the bridge started at one end and bring it back down to the ground at the other end. Its visual job, as well as its structural job, is to mediate between earth and structure. The "right" decision for an abutment depends on the designer's design intention for the structure.

One-span bridges are the simplest structures. Abutment placement is *the* key element in determining the overall proportions of the bridge. For two-, three-, and four-span structures the abutments are a lesser part of the total structure, but are still major elements because both abutments are seen at once, and frame the structure. For these bridges and particularly for highway overcrossings the specific placement of the abutment is crucial to the appearance of the bridge.

The range of possibilities is demonstrated by the history of highway overcrossing design. The design of highway overcrossings starts with the required clearance envelope of the underroadway. In the early days of highway bridge building, that was the limit of the bridge, and bridges looked like Figure 4-26.

Designers soon realized that high walls create an uncomfortable degree of enclosure for motorists as well as cut off the view through the structure. They also are safety hazards. So they added piers at the shoulder edges and moved the abutment to the top of the slope, as shown in Figure 4-27.

While this was a big improvement, the added void areas on either side are relatively small and cut off from the major space by the piers, while the piers themselves are still safety hazards. More recent structures eliminate the side piers and move the abutments back down the slope to a point set by safety clearances and structural economy. Structures began to look like Figure 4-28.

The safety problems are now gone, and the view through the structure is much more extensive. This whole process is an excellent example of the incorporation of aesthetics in structure design. Each step was made for a functional reason as well as an aesthetic reason. At each step the superstructure costs more, but there were offsetting savings in the substructure. In some cases, these savings totally offset the additional cost; but even where they did not, the new designs were accepted because designers felt that the improved safety and improved appearance were worth the additional cost.

The determining visual variables for abutment placement are girder depth, abutment height (the height of the abutment wall at the bearings), the clearance under the structure, and the ratios between these variables.

The possibilities vary from massive retaining walls to minimal pedestal abutments perched on the edge of the embankment. The smaller the abutment height, the lighter and less prominent will the bridge appear; the greater the height, the more anchored and heavy will the bridge appear, and views through the bridge will tend to be framed or, at the extreme, enclosed.

### Relate Abutment Height to the Maximum Height of the First Span

The point at which the abutment starts to be a dominant element is when it is greater than one-third the maximum height of the first span. Heights greater than that should be avoided unless a visual dominant abutment is a desired feature (Figure 4-26).

### Make Minimum Abutment Height One-half Girder Depth

At heights less than this, the abutment will not look big enough for its job. It will also be quickly obscured by landscaping.

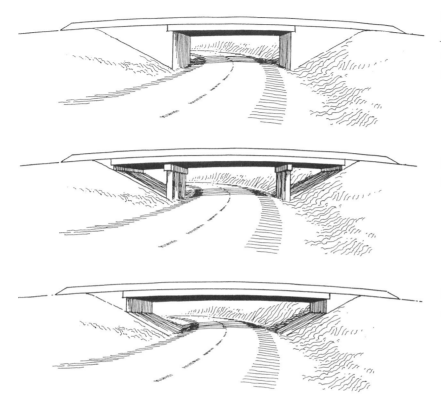

FIGURE 4-26 *Visual confinement and safety problems on a bridge with high abutments.*

FIGURE 4-27 *Opening up the view somewhat.*

FIGURE 4-28 *More view and more safety, too.*

### *Use Minimum Height Pedestal Abutments (h = 1/2d) with Three- or Four-span Bridges*

In order to achieve reasonable end spans with a three- or four-span bridge, the abutments are usually pushed to the top of the slopes. The applicable guideline here is to use a minimum height, so that the abutment doesn't disappear completely.

Figure 2-16 (page 42) shows how a minimal abutment extends the length of the structure and emphasizes its thinness and horizontally.

### *For Structures Where Both Abutments are Visible at the Same Time, Use the Same Height/Clearance Ratio for Both*

A common problem for abutment placement is a structure on a vertical grade, so that one side is higher than the other. Using either a common abutment height or a common distance from the first pier results in an unbalanced appearance (Figure 4-30).

Landscaping at abutments can become a major determinant of the visual impact of the bridge, particularly for small abutments (where the height is

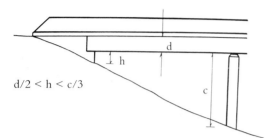

$d/2 < h < c/3$

**FIGURE 4-29** *The desirable range of abutment heights.*

less than one-half the girder depth). Abutments of this size can be obscured by landscaping after a few years' growth. Whether this is good or not depends on the designer's overall concept for the bridge. In one- or two-span bridges, hidden abutments will leave the viewer with doubt about how the bridge is supported. Bridges of three or more spans may give the impression that the end span is cantilevered, particularly if the end spans are also tapered and thus make the apparent lack of an abutment more plausible.

**FIGURE 4-30** *When a structure is on a vertical grade, so that one side is higher than the other, the abutment proportions should be kept similar.*

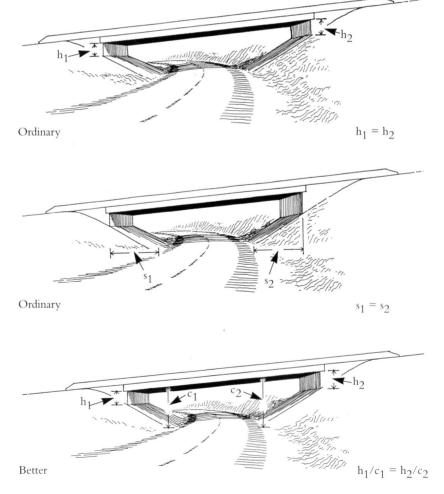

Ordinary $\quad h_1 = h_2$

Ordinary $\quad s_1 = s_2$

Better $\quad h_1/c_1 = h_2/c_2$

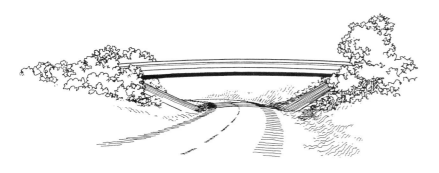

FIGURE 4-31 *The effect of abutments hidden by landscaping: The bridge has no visible means of support.*

### Use Abutment Wing Walls Which Parallel the Upper Roadway

The abutments will usually look best if the wing walls parallel the upper roadway because this visually "stretches" the structure, making it seem longer and thinner. The end of the wing walls also provides a place to terminate the approach roadway guardrail.

Wing walls which simply bisect the angle between upper and lower roadways should be avoided, because they create a major object unrelated to either roadway. They also create triangular areas of landscaping, top and bottom, which are hard to plant and maintain. Finally, they require an additional guardrail and a separate parapet end block to accommodate them.

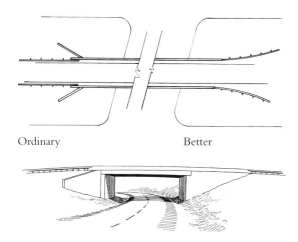

Ordinary                    Better

FIGURE 4-32 *Aligning wing walls with the upper roadway simplifies construction, maintenance, and guardrail placement, and improves appearance.*

FIGURE 4-33 *The wing wall would have been improved by aligning it with the upper roadway.*

**FIGURE 4-34** *This right-angled abutment keeps the roadway edge open and reduces the size of abutment walls. The brick on the abutment is a use of a traditional masonry material which is consistent with its historical role and structural capability.*

### With Skewed Structures, Consider Moving the Abutments to the Top of Embankments and Place at Right Angles to Overcrossing Roadway

Heavily skewed bridges create difficult abutment problems. If the abutment wall is kept parallel to the lower roadway it can get quite long and the slopes of the adjoining embankment can become large enough to become a major visual problem. All of this can be worsened by the large wing walls required to adapt a conventional girder bridge to a skewed condition.

Placing the abutment further up on the embankment and at right angles to the centerline of the overcrossing roadway (Figure 4-34) reduces the visual problem by reducing the amount of fill near the roadway. While it does require longer spans, there are compensating savings in the length and height of abutment walls, as well as significant simplifications in analysis and construction.

The designer must be careful in establishing the height of the abutment on skewed bridges. As the bridge is lengthened the depth of the structure is drastically affected, sometimes defeating the goal of creating a slender structure, so that structure depth becomes more of a problem than abutment height.

With wider bridges (greater than about 50 feet) and still lower angles, these ideas no longer suffice.

### For Extreme Skews, Align the Wall with the Lower Roadway, Then Flare with a Graceful Curve

Structures on extreme skews can generate wing walls which become quite long and costly. They can be designed to become a positive feature in the scene. When aligned in a smooth curve related to the lower roadway they help guide the driver through the underpass, reduce the tunnellike aspects, and provide a sense of transition to the high abutment wall.

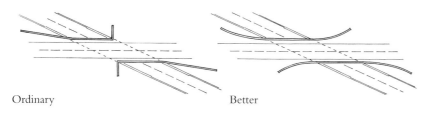

**FIGURE 4-35** *Smoothly curved walls help guide the driver through the underpass.*

Ordinary                    Better

Driver's view, curved walls

### *In Depressed Roadways with Parallel Retaining Walls Treat the Abutment Wall as an Extension of the Adjoining Retaining Walls*

See Figure 2-22 (page 47) for an example of a depressed roadway with continuous retaining walls where the abutment becomes an extension of the retaining walls.

### *For Bridges Longer Than Four Spans, Locate the Abutment in Relation to Nearby Features*

The above considerations are most important for bridges of four spans or less, where both abutments are visible from important viewpoints. For larger bridges, the abutments are a smaller proportion of the structure, and may not even be visible from many key viewpoints. Abutment placement and height will be a function of pier placement and span length throughout the structure rather than a function of the appearance of the abutments themselves. Abutment placement will have a lesser, though still important, impact on the appearance of the total structure. The more important consideration for longer bridges will be the effect of the abutment on its immediate environs. How well the abutment fits the topography, or matches up with an existing street pattern, will be an important consideration.

If there is an undercrossing roadway near the abutment then abutment position and height should be determined using the previous guidelines. If the abutment is on a natural hillside it should be placed to take advantage of a natural promontory or outcropping. In an urban area it may be appropriate to align the abutment with a building line or setback line. The goal is to find a location that will appear obvious or "natural" in the total setting.

## Retaining Walls

Retaining walls mediate between the existing topography and the roadway geometry. Both of these elements are fixed. As a result wall height and position are often seen as a mechanical connection of the two, resulting in walls with a haphazard, almost accidental shape. However, there are choices that can be made to improve wall appearance by conscious adjustments in wall position and height.

### For a Wall Between a Lower and an Upper Roadway, Locate the Wall Closest to the Upper Roadway

This approach creates space at the edge of the lower roadway, where it will be appreciated by drivers, and increases safety by moving the wall further from the travel way. The upper roadway will require a guardrail anyway, so nothing is lost there. This position will also allow the wall alignment to be independent of the geometry of the lower roadway, which will contribute to the next guideline.

### Align Walls in Continuous Horizontal Curves Related to Roadway Geometry and Topographic Features

Highway environments are made up of continuously curved surfaces. Anything composed of straight edges and angles will seem out of place and even threatening. Walls on curved alignment fit the highway environment; walls aligned in jogs and offsets look out of place.

FIGURE 4-36 *Moving a retaining wall back from lower roadway edge creates more space for travelers, increasing both apparent and actual safety.*

FIGURE 4-37 *This retaining wall seems abrupt and arbitrary.*

*Shape Wall Tops in Continuous Curves Reflecting
and Smoothing out the Topography*

The curvilinear rule applies to wall profiles for the same reason as for plan alignment. A smoothly curved top profile will look like it belongs in the scene. A profile of jumps and bumps won't.

It may seem like the above guidelines would not apply in urban areas. However, since the "topographic features" in urban areas are streets and buildings, applying the guidelines will, in fact, lead to more rectilinear walls that will seem in place in the urban scene, while still recognizing the visual needs of road users.

## Noise Walls

Noise walls can be very large elements in the visual field. Since it is not usually necessary to parallel the highway alignment, designers find themselves with flexibility to follow the vagaries of local drainage or property lines. However, this often results in a jagged alignment which seems to jerk into and away from the roadway and has an inconsistent relation to the topography. A stepped, jagged top profile can compound the problem.

Many of the rules of retaining walls apply here as well. Control of the horizontal alignment is particularly important.

*Align Noise Walls in Long Smooth Curves Related
to Major Topographical Features*

If the wall is a proprietary wall which depends on a zigzag alignment for its stability, then the overall alignment of the wall should be established in smooth curves.

Such curves can easily be accommodated by the precast concrete panel systems used for many noise walls. Radii as low as 250' require a deviation at each post (often spaced about 12' apart) of only a few degrees, which is well within the construction tolerances of the precast system.

*Profile the Top in Long Smooth Curves or Regular Small Steps
with a Minimum of Height Variation*

Because of its position within the visual field the top of a noise wall is often the most prominent highway element in the scene, particularly if the wall color contrasts with its background. Wall profiles are influenced both by topography and a required acoustical profile. The elements affecting the latter are usually not visible to the driver. Finally, walls are often built from systems of large rec-

FIGURE 4-38 *While this brick noise wall has an attractive surface, its zigzag alignment and jagged profile conflict with the smooth curves of the roadway and topography.*

FIGURE 4-39 *This noise wall follows the top of the slope with a series of smooth curves.*

tangular panels. The result is a wall which proceeds in irregular and apparently irrational vertical steps, with no visual relationship to anything else in the scene. The effect is as disquieting as seeing the jagged edges of torn paper.

The goal should be to shape the top of the wall in some obvious relationship to the topography visible to the driver. Changes in vertical elevation should be made with multiple, identical small steps, rather than a few large jumps.

*Visualize Both Retaining and Noise Walls with 3D Drawings*

Before finalizing wall designs, develop three-dimensional sketches from the driver's viewpoint showing topographic background as well as the wall The three-dimensional result of decisions for both retaining walls and noise walls cannot be adequately predicted from viewing plan and elevation drawings.

## SUPERSTRUCTURE SHAPE, INCLUDING PARAPETS AND DETAILS

At this point the superstructure type will have been selected and pier and abutment locations set. Now is the time to shape the superstructure to reflect the forces on it in ways that improve its appearance. At the same time choices made now can positively affect the appearance of the pier shapes and abutment shapes to be established later.

The major visual design goals are apparent slenderness, lightness, and continuity, with the structure shaped at each point to efficiently resist the forces upon it. In girder bridges the ideal will give the appearance of a slender, horizontal, perhaps subtly shaped ribbon running from abutment to abutment, and resting lightly on the intermediate piers.

Since the structure is in fact quite heavy and deep the challenge is to make it *seem* thin and light through a selection of girder depth, shape and details. For example, the haunches and small exposed bearings of the U.S. Naval Academy Bridge in Figure 1-24 (page 21) create the illusion that the main span is resting on four points, and therefore must be very light indeed.

The design of the cross section and, in particular, the edge profile, has a major impact on the overall appearance of the bridge because the parapet and fascia girder are often the most visually prominent parts of the bridge. This is especially true for highway overcrossings because parapets are such an important feature of the structure's elevation view.

## Superstructure Shape and Depth

The major elements to be settled are the superstructure depth, shape, and slab overhang, as they will have a powerful effect on appearance. The overhang, along with the parapet fascia, provide the strongest opportunity to make the bridge *seem* more slender than it really is. Two relevant guidelines are to minimize girder depth and to maximize the overhang, which are to some degree contradictory. A balance must be sought between them that will result in the best combination of performance, cost, and appearance.

### Seek Girder Arrangements Which Emphasize Apparent Thinness and Horizontality

In the typical highway environment the horizontal is the dominant dimension. As we saw in Chapter One, most people will find the structure that appears the thinnest and with the most horizontal emphasis as the most attractive. The techniques available are:

1. **Maximize the overhang; maximize girder spacing.**  Maximizing the overhang creates a strong shadow on the fascia girder which visually divides the girder horizontally (taking advantage of one of the visual illusions shown in Figure 2-15, page 41) or places the girder entirely in shadow. The shadow thus cast by the deck overhang can be effective in reducing the apparent depth of the fascia girder. This can be a particularly important feature in long single-span structures.

   Maximizing the overhang pays dividends in the substructure as well, particularly for skewed structures. The pier caps and abutment end walls can be shorter, and fewer pier columns may be required.

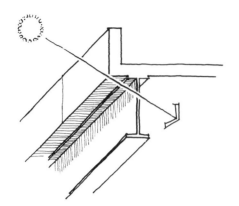
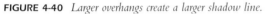

**FIGURE 4-40** *Larger overhangs create a larger shadow line.*

**FIGURE 4-41** *Box girders can more easily accommodate large overhangs.*

Large superstructure overhangs allow fewer and/or narrower columns per pier, which means that oblique views through the structure are less likely to look like a forest of columns. The amount of the overhang will also allow more light to enter the underbridge area, because the fascia girder is farther back from the structure's edge.

The need to have scupper outlets inside the fascia girder is often given as a reason to limit the size of overhangs. There are several solutions to this problem discussed on page 130.

Maximizing girder spacing allows a larger overhang without varying slab depths. With I-girders a limit will be reached for narrow ramps, since a minimum of three girders is required for redundancy. Box girders have more internal redundancy and torsional stiffness and can more easily accommodate large overhangs.

The drawback for this guideline is that it requires that more load be carried by each girder, which may require a deeper girder, thereby somewhat offsetting the effect of the deeper shadow line. Which combination of depth and overhang is best must be determined for each structure. The following is a useful target:

2. **The minimum overhang should equal the girder depth.** This proportion will place the girder or a significant part of it in shadow most of the time, thereby minimizing the apparent depth of the structure. Figure 2-16 (page 42) shows the effectiveness of this approach.

*Keep Structural Depth Constant or Smoothly Varied Over the Bridge*
Since people observe bridges by sweeping their eyes along the length of the structure, any abrupt changes in girder depth will be jarringly obvious.

Constant or smoothly varying depth will make the structure more unified. It will also make the structure *appear* longer, and therefore thinner. The eye judges relative thinness by comparing length to depth, so making the girder seem longer will make it seem more slender also. Structural continuity is a big help here, since it keeps everything visually continuous as well.

With girder bridges the spans will often vary in length over the bridge. It will be necessary to change girder depth, provide haunches, or do both in a single bridge. Transitions between girder depths should be made with girders which are tapered or have a curved lower flange (Figure 4-42).

### Consider Haunched Girders Where Feasible

Haunches are important because they visually demonstrate the concentration of forces in the bridge and make the bridge seem thinner by reducing the average depth while leaving the length the same. Haunches provide

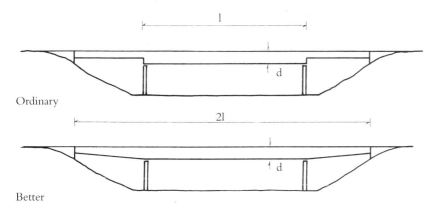

Ordinary

Better

**FIGURE 4-42** *Visual continuity makes the bridge seem thinner because the whole bridge is seen as one long unit, while the maximum girder depth stays the same.*

**FIGURE 4-43** *Poor pier placement and discontinuous spans add to the confusion of this urban viaduct.*

**FIGURE 4-44** *Structural continuity creates the possibility of orderly pier placement for this Colorado bridge even with the complex undercrossing roadways.*

FIGURE 4-45 *Visual (and structural) weight added by a "fishbelly" haunch.*

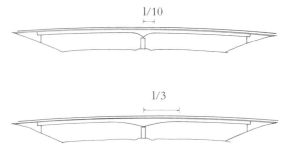

FIGURE 4-46 *The effect of short versus long haunches.*

an important point of visual interest as well. If haunches are not feasible, the structure will depend for its interest primarily on the proportions of the girder, particularly its relative thinness, as compared to the other features of the structure.

- *Make haunches long enough to be in proportion to the span length.* The moment diagram is a good guide (i.e., bring the haunch out to the point of inflection). In order to reduce fabrication costs of steel girders, the splice point can be set at the point the haunch begins, and the haunch depth can be set so that flange plate thickness changes only at the splice point, which eliminates the need to butt weld flange plates.

- *Use pointed haunches because they concentrate visual interest at the point of force transfer and better reflect the flow of forces.* "Fishbelly" haunches make the girder look heavier and waste material.

FIGURE 4-47 *Haunches demonstrate the flow of forces and make this Colorado bridge seem thinner.*

- *Haunches are usually better when formed by smooth curves.* Parabolic curves work well. Straight lines can make the haunch seem shorter if the break point between the haunch and the rest of the girder is too obvious. Then the girder appears to be divided at that point. If using straight lines, make the angle at the beginning of the haunch no greater than 5 degrees.

- *Haunches shouldn't get deeper than twice the midspan depth, or the midspan will look too fragile and the haunch will look too heavy.*

- *Conversely, the depth at the haunch should be not be too close to the midspan depth or the haunch will be imperceptible—1.3 times the midspan depth is a*

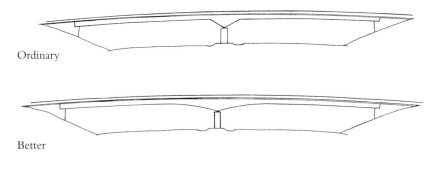

Ordinary

Better

**FIGURE 4-48** *Forming a haunch with straight lines and a sharp break makes the haunch seem short.*

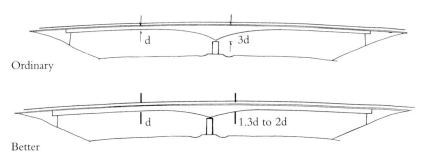

Ordinary

Better

**FIGURE 4-49** *Too much depth at the haunch makes the girder look heavy.*

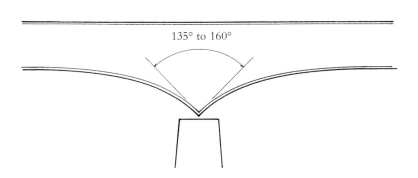

135° to 160°

**FIGURE 4-50** *The desirable angle at the bearing point.*

*reasonable minimum (see Figure 2-12, page 40 for an example of too small a difference).*

- *The angle at the point of the haunch should be between 135 and 160 degrees; otherwise the bearing point will seem too delicate.*

### Consider Use of a Haunch with Skewed Structures

Skew structures can create illusions about span length and depth. The nearer span will seem longer and deeper than the balance of the bridge, often resulting in a distorted appearance (*see* Fig. 4-23, page 104). A haunch may correct this problem.

Reshaping a skewed girder to add a haunch makes it appear thinner and compensates to some degree for the distortion caused by the skewed alignment. Compare Figure 1-25 (page 25) to Figure 2-42 (page 58).

### With Rigid Frames, Give the Legs Enough Slant to Maximize Their Lengths and to Give Full Play to the Visual Illusion of Additional Length

Frames are inherently interesting shapes to start with. Shaping the frame to respond to the areas of minimum moment enhances that interest. Shaping rigid frames and delta frames takes exploration. Much depends on the relative lengths, vertical clearance, and shape of the side slopes. Written guidelines can be misleading—better to make sketches of multiple shapes, as seen from the important viewpoints, than pick the one that seems most graceful.

The leg width at the joint with the girder should approximate the depth of the girder, and both girder and legs should taper to a minimum at the supports. Figures 2-3 (page 33) and Figure 6-24 (page 201) show nicely proportioned rigid frames.

### For Arches, Shape the Arch Rib to Reflect the Flow of Forces, with the Thinnest Section at the Hinges

Arches are also inherently interesting forms to begin with. Reducing the section in areas of reduced moment will make the structure even more attractive. Salginatobel owes its fame to Maillart's application of this simple idea (Figure 1-16, page 12).

### Keep Deck Supports (Spandrel Columns) Similar in Thickness over Bridge's Entire Length

With regard to the deck supports, a heavier support at the arch abutment is usually structurally unnecessary and visually interrupts the lines of the bridge. Figure 3-4 (page 66) shows the Rainbow Bridge in Folsom California, an arch with a heavy pier at the arch abutment. The main span would seem much more continuous with the approaches without these elements.

*For Frames and Arches, Keep Sway Bracing and Flooring System to Simply Arranged Minimum Number of Members and in a Clear, Consistent Relationship to the Main Members*

No matter how graceful a frame or arch looks in an elevation drawing, the three-dimensional real-life view can be significantly degraded by a confusion of secondary bracing members.

The bridge in Figure 6-24 (page 201) recognizes and controls this potential problem.

## Parapets

Parapets and railings serve functions for both people on the bridge and below the bridge. Since each side has its own requirements, the two have to be reconciled during the design process.

The first issue to be faced is whether any of the parapet can be open, or whether it will be entirely solid. The overall superiority of the Jersey barrier from a safety point of view has settled this issue in most cases in favor of a solid barrier parapet. However, this forecloses much of the driver's view from the bridge, and also restricts the options available in using the parapet to influence the appearance of the bridge elevation. Development of open bridge rails with equivalent safety characteristics has proceeded to the point where these can now be considered as long as the specific design has been crash tested. The discussion below starts with the solid part of the deck edge. Railings are discussed in subsequent sections.

The parapet is an important influence on the overall appearance of a bridge because it—and the girder—determine the visual depth/span ratio of the superstructure. This ratio is one of the strongest influences on appearance. The viewer's judgment of the visual span-depth ratio is subject to manipulation via one of the visual illusions discussed earlier.

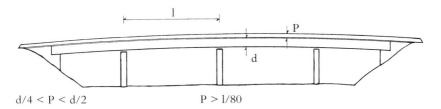

$d/4 < P < d/2$          $P > 1/80$

**FIGURE 4-51** *The visually desirable parapet height.*

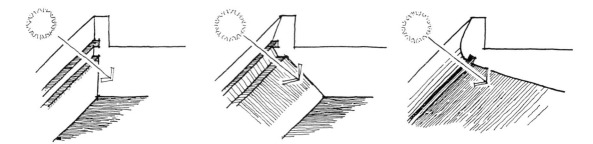

FIGURE 4-52 *The effects of cross section differences on appearance.*

One key dimension is the height of the parapet relative to the exposed depth of the girder. The German engineer Fritz Leonhardt[3] suggests the following guideline:

***Keep the Parapet Height Between 1/4 and 1/2 of the Exposed Girder Depth with a Minimum of 1/80th of Span Length***
For most medium-span bridges the standard Jersey barrier parapet will be higher than this ideal. Attention should then be turned to ways of making the barrier appear thinner. These are discussed below.

***Break up the Face of Parapet Horizontally Using Incisions, Recesses, or Sloped Planes***
The apparent depth of the parapet itself is subject to manipulation through visual illusion. The available techniques are:

- *Divide the parapet fascia into separate horizontal surfaces by shadow and/or physical breaks.* Elements which create apparent horizontal division in the combined girder-parapet will make the bridge seem longer and the combined girder-parapet seem thinner. The relative size of these divisions also makes a difference. Evenly spaced divisions do not seem as effective or attractive as uneven divisions, where one horizontal element is thicker than the next. (Figure 4-52, left).

- *Change the relative brightness of different fascia surfaces by changing their angle so that they catch more sun, or no sun at all (Figure 4-52, center).*

- *Remove the divisions between fasia surfaces by introducing curvature, which leaves the viewer fewer clues by which to judge thickness (Figure 4-52, right).*

***Any Parapet Pattern Should have Dominant Lines Which are Horizontal***
Horizontal details should be emphasized in the selection of patterns for the parapet. Vertical details will interrupt the dominant lines of the bridge and make the parapet look deeper.

FIGURE 4-53 *Keep the emphasis of parapet patterns horizontal.*

Spaces between vertical divisions in the parapet should be at least three times parapet depth. There is an exception for vertical patterns which are so closely spaced that they read as textures rather than distinct vertical lines. The pattern tends to hide drainage stains and construction irregularities. Form liners which create patterns of closely spaced vertical projections ("fins" or, if irregular, "fractured fins") have been used to create these textures, and can even be slipformed. (*See* Figure 2-40, page 56.)

### Recognize the Slab/Parapet Joint with a Significant Groove or Recess Incorporated in the Parapet Design

The choice of construction technique will have an important influence on parapet details. The best results can be obtained when the parapet covers the slab edge. This allows for any irregularities in the slab edge to be eliminated and produces the best control of alignment. It also eliminates staining the parapet face by roadway drainage seeping through cracks at the slab/parapet joint.

FIGURE 4-54 *Incorporating the slab parapet joint in the parapet design.*

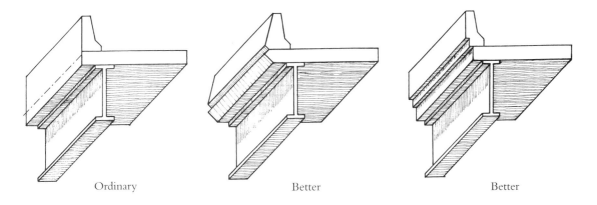

Ordinary                    Better                    Better

However, the relatively greater difficulty of forming the element covering the slab edge has led some agencies to leave the slab edge exposed. If it will be exposed, the slab/parapet construction joint must be recognized; it is impossible to effectively camouflage it. The construction joint should be incorporated into parapet patterns aimed at making the parapet look thinner. Slip forming technology is now able to produce reliable and well-aligned results. Slip forming requires that the parapet face be set back slightly from the slab edge in order to provide an offset to guide the form.

Precast parapets have been experimented with; however, they have proved to be difficult to align accurately in the field. Precast, stay-in-place forms for the parapet provide many options for shape, color, and finish, can be produced to higher tolerances and a denser surface than field-place concrete, and are easier to align. Precast panels attached to poured-in-place parapets are another attractive option.

### When Designing the Parapet Face Use Details Large Enough (4 Inches Minimum) to be Recognized at Highway Distances

Parapet details have a particularly strong impact on highway overcrossings, since the parapet and fascia girder are usually the most visible parts of the structure. Any parapet features must therefore be large enough to be seen and appreciated at highway distances and speeds.

### Use Shapes on the Parapet Which are Consistent with Either the Girder Cross Section or the Pier Shapes or Both

Precast 1-girders have characteristic faceted edges which should be emulated with faceted shapes on the parapet. Steel wide-flange or welded I-girders and box girders have thinner, sharp-edged shapes which can be emulated in the parapet details. Or, since the visual characteristics of steel girder cross sections are not particularly distinctive, the cue can be taken from a memorable pier shape.

### Check Parapet Profiles at Points of Superelevation Transition Using Profile Drawings with Exaggerated Vertical Scales

Because the top of the parapet is a nearly horizontal line parallel to the line of sight of a driver on the bridge, any flaws in the alignment, whether due to design or construction, will be magnified. At the design level problems most often crop up at transitions of superelevation, since the parapet profile is driven by pavement and shoulder cross-slopes.

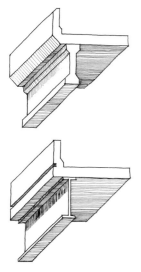

**FIGURE 4-55** *With precast girders the parapet shape should be from the same family of shapes as the girders.*

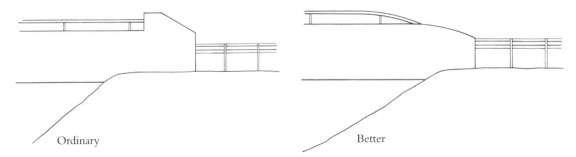

Ordinary                    Better

FIGURE 4-56 *Simplifying the parapet ending while accommodating guardrail and other features.*

### Prevent Railings and Fences from Creating Drainage Stains on the Parapet

Because of the prominence of the parapet, drainage stains have a significant affect on the bridge's appearance. These results primarily from dirt, de-icing salts and corrosion products from the fence or railing, and are worst at the railing posts. One or more of the following techniques should be applied:

- *Slope the parapet top slightly to drain toward the roadway side of the parapet.*

- *Provide incisions on the parapet face under railing posts to control drainage streaks.*

- *Use corrosion-proof fence and railing materials.*

- *Coat the parapet with a stain-resistant finish.*

- *Provide closely spaced vertical striations in the parapet to hide stains.*

### End Parapets, Railings, and Pedestrian Screens by Tapering Them Down or Flaring Them Away from the Traveled Way, or Doing Both; Do not Use Vertical End Blocks

At each end of the bridge the parapet has the visual job of gracefully ending or beginning the bridge, and the functional job of providing a place for the approach guardrail and right-of-way fence to tie in.

The goal is to make the transition as smooth and continuous as possible, with a minimum number of separate elements. Aligning the abutment wing wall with the upper roadway helps by allowing the parapet end block and wing wall to be combined.

### Incorporate Attachment Details for the Guardrail and Right-of-way Fence into the End of the Parapet

This approach fits the overall goal to emphasize the horizontally of the bridge and its continuity with the approach roadway. It also has safety benefits.

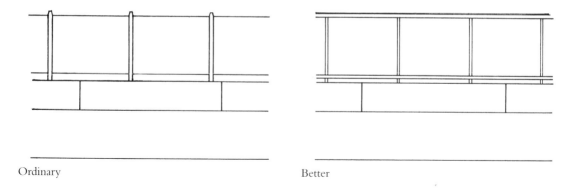

Ordinary                                                Better

**FIGURE 4-57** *The horizontal members of screen support and railing systems should dominate; the relationship of posts to parapet divisions should be consistent.*

# Railings, Pedestrian Screens, and Bridge Noise Walls

Railings, pedestrian screens, and noise walls will be seen together with the parapet and the structure itself. All these elements need to be considered together.

Railings can be positive features on a bridge, particularly if they substitute for all or part of a solid parapet. Open railings have been successfully crash-tested and are greatly appreciated by bridge users, particularly in scenic areas. A pedestrian screen or noise wall on a bridge complicates matters because it can make the parapet seem three times as high, with comparable negative effects on the proportions of the whole structure.

### Railing, Screen, and Noise Wall Design Should be Done Together and Coordinated with Parapet Design

In particular, the post spacing and vertical divisions of the parapet should be in a consistent relationship.

### Major Horizontal Railing and Screen Members Should be Significantly Larger Than Vertical Members and not be Interrupted at the Vertical Members

As with the parapet itself, the details of railings, pedestrian screens, and noise walls should maintain a horizontal emphasis.

### Curved or Slanted Posts Contribute to the Horizontal Emphasis by Eliminating All Vertical Lines

Figure 5-41 (page 163) shows how slanted or curved supports put the horizontal members in the dominant position.

*Use Materials, Details, and Colors for the Pedestrian Screen Which are as Transparent as Possible, and Which Make Clear That the Screen is Separate from the Parapet*

The goal is to keep the screen from increasing the apparent depth of the bridge. This can be done by making the screen a visually different element than the rest of the bridge. Color, pattern, and texture are all tools to achieve this visual difference. For example, the screen should have a clearly different color than the parapet it is mounted on. Pedestrian screens are often seen against the sky. Colors such as light blue gray or gray will tend to take on the sky color and seem to disappear. Pedestrian screens seen against wooded or rocky backgrounds can take their cue from those backgrounds.

*Clamps, Elbows, Junctions, and Other Fittings Should be Compact, Simple and Rust Proof, and Integrated with the Major Members Wherever Possible*

The goal here is to keep the appearance of the railing or screen as simple as possible and to prevent these functional but secondary elements from distracting from the appearance of the bridge or the railing/screen itself.

*Design Noise Barriers with a Pattern or Color to Visually Separate the Barrier from the Bridge*

Noise barriers must be solid. However, as with screens and railings, the goal is to keep the barrier from increasing the apparent depth of the bridge. The barrier can be made to seem separate from the structure by differences in color, pattern, and/or texture. Some noise barriers on structures have been successful using specific pictorial or abstract designs on the community side.

At each end of the bridge a graceful ending of the noise barrier is necessary. Since the overall goal is to emphasize the horizontality of the bridge and its continuity with the approach roadway, the barrier alignment should curve smoothly away from the bridge to meet the barrier alignment on the nearby roadway. The top profile should also be smoothly curved.

## Superstructure Details

The point at which the girder connects to the pier is crucial visually as well as structurally.

*Differentiate Bearings from Moment Connections*

The rule is simple: only material needed to resist forces should be present, leading to a different appearance at a bearing than at a moment connection.

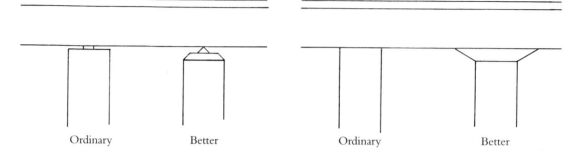

| Ordinary | Better | Ordinary | Better |

**FIGURE 4-58** *A bearing compared to a moment connection.*

- *Use high bearings, pedestals, or chamfers at pier tops to visually attenuate the bearing point.* This approach elongates the bearing or raises the bearing on a small pedestal so that it is silhouetted against the sky, visually separating the superstructure from the pier with what appears to be a tiny element. This makes the bridge seem light in weight, in the same way that a waiter, by carrying a heavy tray on his fingertips, makes the action seem effortless. This approach also avoids any visual interruption of the horizontal lines of the superstructure, which makes the structure seem longer and more slender. Figure 3-2 (page 63) shows one way this can be accomplished. The bridges in Figures 4-1 (page 87) and 4-9 (page 95) show another way. Compare Figure 4-1 with Figure 5-19 (page 143) to see the importance of this effect. In no case should pilasters be used to hide the bearing.

- *For moment connections thicken and round the joint area to accommodate the stress concentrations that occur.* Based on their familiarity with moment connections in their own experience (their own shoulder and hip, tree branches), people recognize the point of stress concentration, expect that there will be more material there, and are disappointed when the shape of the structure does not match that expectation. Figures 6-24 (page 201) and 5-20 (page 143) are good examples of an appropriate moment connections.

### Design the Pattern of Stiffeners on Steel Fascia Girders to Support the Design Intention

Steel, used as a bridge material, is typically not thought of as patterned. However, the spacing of stiffeners on a girder or the intersection of flanges at a truss connection create patterns which will be recognized. Because of the prominence of the fascia surfaces, the stiffeners on steel-plate fascia girders are especially significant visual features. They will create an impression, which should be controlled.

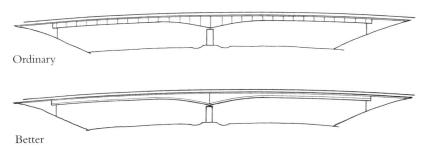

Ordinary

Better

**FIGURE 4-59** *Vertical stiffeners will make the girder seem heavier than a comparable girder with horizontal stiffeners.*

- *Continuous, evenly spaced vertical stiffeners should not be placed on the exterior of fascia girders.* Evenly spaced vertical stiffeners will divide the girder vertically and make it appear thicker. If vertical stiffeners are necessary on fascia girders, they should be placed on the interior face of the girder.

  There are three exceptions to this guideline. If the stiffener spacing exceeds the girder depth by at least a factor of 2, the resulting rectangles have a dominant horizontal dimension, and the visual problem is much reduced.

- *If the spacing of vertical stiffeners is allowed to vary continuously in direct proportion to the shear stress the resulting rhythmic pattern may be visually strong enough to override the thickening effect.* The bridge shown in Figure 6-51 (page 230) has some spacing variations, but does not carry the idea far enough to create a visually convincing result.

- *Vertical stiffeners are desireable at bearing points, where they confirm people's intuition that something important is happening at that point.*

- *Horizontal stiffeners on the outside of fascia girders have a positive visual effect: they subdivide the girder horizontally and make it appear thinner.* Engineers should be aware that current fatigue requirements inhibit horizontal stiffners in the tension area.

- *If the girder is haunched, a partial horizontal stiffener over the support curved to a pattern complementary to the lower flange will reinforce the visual effect of the haunch* (Figure 4-60).

### Take Advantage of Structural Needs (Stiffeners, Bearing Plates, etc.) to Develop Attractive Details Which Accentuate the Points of Stress Concentration and Transfer

Bracing details are often more visible than most engineers realize. Bracing will be visible wherever pedestrians are nearby. The higher the structure the more visible the bracing. It can have a much larger impact on the

FIGURE 4-60 *The combination of curved horizontal stiffener and vertical stiffener complement the curve of the haunch and concentrate attention on the point of weight transfer.*

final appearance of the structure than can be predicted from elevation or section drawings. The result can undermine the best efforts on the design of other elements of the structure. As one bridge neighbor was heard to say, "From most angles the bridge looks fine, but from below it looks like the underside of an old car."

The goal should be to reduce the amount of such features, simplify those that remain, and design them so that they generally follow the main lines of the structure.

### Consider "Compact" Steel Plate Girder Sections with Less Girder Depth, Wider Flanges, and Thicker Webs

This approach may well offer overall economy as well by requiring the fabrication and erection of fewer stiffeners and less bracing. This is an area where engineers are often deceived by basing their design on the minimum weight of steel, not realizing that the resulting thin sections require many additional secondary bracing members, and that the effort of handling and erecting these secondary members may offset any cost savings in the primary members.[4]

### Design Bracing to be Seen

Simplification is the key. Patterns with few members arranged in simple and consistent configurations should be used. Complex patterns distract the eye and interfere with any positive effect created by the main structural members.

- *Use patterns with all diagonal or all right-angled members.*
- *If diagonal bracing is used, keep all members at the same angle relative to the superstructure.*
- *Use a few large bracing members rather than many small members.*

## Scuppers, Drain Pipes, Conduits, and Utilities

These functional necessities are not usually thought of when the design intention for the bridge is initially conceived. However, they creep onto the structure in the final stages of design and sometimes overwhelm its best features.

FIGURE 4-61 *Simplified bracing patterns will improve the appearance of the underside.*

### Eliminate Drainage Inlets on Bridges Where Possible

The best answer is just to not have drainage inlets on the bridge. This can often be achieved on shorter bridges by adjustments to the vertical geometry to eliminate sumps on the bridge, changes to the shoulder cross slope to allow it to carry water farther, and other relatively minor changes. Placing inlets on the roadway at the ends of the bridge is one obvious strategy.

### If Scuppers are Absolutely Necessary, Avoid Piping Systems

Recent water quality restrictions have reduced the applicability of this approach, but it is still the best idea. Drainage pipes, in addition to their visual drawbacks, are notorious maintenance problems.

- *When placing scuppers look first for a location where water can be permitted to outlet just below the bottom of the girder.* For bridges over bodies of water, this can be almost anywhere in the bridge. For bridges over land, potential locations cannot be over paved areas and must fit into drainage patterns of the area below. A splash block below the outlet will usually be required.

- *Design scuppers so the outlet falls on the inside of the fascia girder and still accommodates the desired overhang.*

- *With scuppers which outlet through the parapet integrate the outlet design with the design of the parapet.* This will place restrictions on scupper locations because, as visible elements, their location must be coordinated with the overall concept of the bridge.

FIGURE 4-62 *Piping at this structure for Washington, D.C.'s Metro is designed to be seen, with parallel large radius curves and few fittings.*

### If Drain Pipes Must be Installed, Hide Them in Spaces Between Girders and Within Piers

Pipe systems embedded within piers should be avoided in cold climates because of freezing problems. An alternative is to place the drain in a groove in the pier where it seems to be part of the pier but is still accessible for maintenance.

### If Drainage Systems Must be Exposed, Frankly Acknowledge Them as Another Design Element

- *Pipe systems should be kept as simple as possible, using large-radius curves and as few fittings as possible.* For example, it is better to run a pipe in one simple run down the face of a column rather than install five elbows to get it around to the rear.

- *Wherever drain pipe are exposed, run them in lines which are either parallel or at right angles to the main lines of the structure.*

- *Paint drain pipes the same color as the structural element they are mounted against.*

Conduits and utilities impose similar problems as drainage systems, and should be approached using the same basic ideas. In addition:

These ideas won't eliminate visual problems with drainage, utilities, and other piping, but they will at least help make these elements a more positive part of the structure.

---

1  This notion was introduced by Christopher Alexander in the following books on architecture. Alexander, Christopher, 1979. *The Timeless Way of Building.* New York, NY: Oxford University Press, and Alexander, Christopher; Ishikawa, Sara; Silverstein, Murray; Jacobson, Max; Fiksdahl-King, Ingrid; and Angel, Shlomo, 1977. *A Pattern Language: Towns-Buildings-Construction.* New York, NY: Oxford University Press.

2  Price, Ken, 1993. "Economical Steel Box Girder Bridges." *Transportation Research Record 1393 Structures.* Washington, DC: Transportation Research Board.

3  Leonhardt, Fritz, 1982. *Brucken.* Cambridge, MA: The MIT Press.

4  Nickerson, Robert, 1996. "The Economical Use of Steel for Bridges." Videotape, Chicago, IL: American Institute of Steel Construction, November.

chapter *five*

# A DESIGN LANGUAGE: GUIDELINES FOR THE SECOND FIVE DETERMINANTS OF APPEARANCE

*"The next note must seem fresh but inevitable."*

—LEONARD BERNSTEIN,
AMERICAN COMPOSER AND CONDUCTOR

This chapter looks at the second five determinants of appearance: pier shape, abutment shape, color, surface texture and ornamentation, and signing, lighting, and landscaping. Once the first five determinants have been positively applied, decisions made about these elements can add to the interest and success of the bridge.

## PIER SHAPE

Piers can be a major element in forming people's impression of a bridge. This is particularly true of girder bridges, where the superstructure does not present as much opportunity to create a memorable image. There is no single correct type of pier; what is appropriate and good looking on a narrow ramp overpass will be different than what is appropriate and good looking on a wide dual structure. There should be a clear visual relationship between the substructure elements, meaning that potential abutment features need to be kept in mind when developing pier shapes.

The appearance of piers is heavily influenced by their proportion: how long they are relative to their height. As piers get taller, the engineering challenge may increase, but the aesthetic challenge decreases. In other words, it's

**FIGURE 5-1** *Short and tall piers defined.*

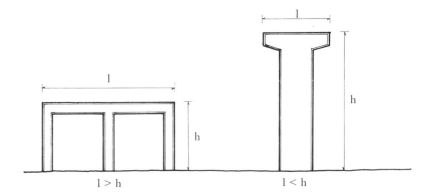

easier to make a tall pier look good than a short pier. In order to highlight the differences, these guidelines are divided into two categories of piers: short piers, those that are longer than they are high, and tall piers, those that are higher than they are wide. Obviously, drawing this line between the two categories is arbitrary, and there is a continuum of shape involved. However, there are enough definite differences in the aesthetic problems involved with the two types of piers to make it worthwhile to analyze them in this way.

Longer multispan structures present particular difficulties with pier shape. They may have piers of significantly different height and/or width, some of which fall in the short category and some in the tall category, and all of which have to be accommodated within the same family of shapes.

## Short Piers

Why are short piers so difficult? Because the pier cap is such a large portion of the total pier.

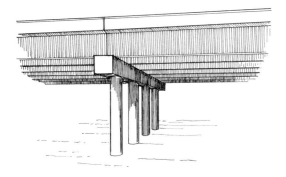

**FIGURE 5-2** *The prominence of the pier cap and especially its end surface. The pier cap end visually attaches to the superstructure and makes the bridge seem thicker.*

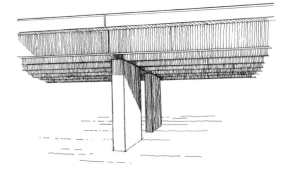

**FIGURE 5-3** *Integrating the pier cap into the superstructure removes it as a visual element.*

The pier cap introduces a third element into the visual scene. The overcrossing roadway/superstructure is one element; the columns with their vertical lines are another. The pier cap is clearly not part of the superstructure, but not clearly part of the columns either, especially if the columns are geometrically separate shapes. The mind and the eye have a hard time dealing with the complication introduced by this third element, and it becomes a distraction.

The end of the pier cap compounds the distraction. The end of the pier cap is at about the same plane as the parapet fascia and fascia girder. It is generally out from under the shadow of the overhang and is a relatively bright surface. Visually, the end of the pier cap "reads" as part of the superstructure, which interrupts the lines of the superstructure and makes the superstructure appear deeper.

### Use Piers Which Eliminate or Minimize the Pier Cap

The key to improving the appearance of a short pier is eliminating or minimizing the pier cap, or incorporating it in the superstructure.

- *Use pier types with no cap.* Enhanced diaphragm framing can be used to combine girder reactions over a narrow column, or the pier cap can be integrated as a cross girder into the superstructure (Figures 4-10, page 95 and 5-21, page 143).

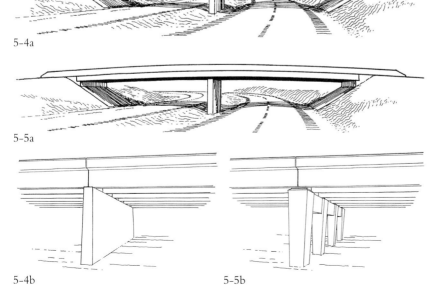

5-4a

5-5a

5-4b

5-5b

**FIGURE 5-4** *Simple wall pier means no pier cap or pier cap end.*

**FIGURE 5-5** *Pier cap recessed behind front column.*

**FIGURE 5-6** *A minimal pier cap end; dominant end dimension is horizontal.*

A solid shaft or wall can be used for support. Since the wall can be made relatively thin, this can result in an elegant structure. Indeed, care needs to be taken to be sure the wall does not look too thin for the size of the superstructure. The leading and trailing edges of the wall can be shaped to add interest. When the wall gets long because of overcrossing width or skew, the lack of visibility through it will be a problem.

- *Recess the pier cap behind the front column or otherwise unify the pier cap and columns so as to minimize the pier cap as a separate element.* One variation of this option is to make the cap thinner than the columns. Another is to unify the cap and columns by design into a single continuous form. These options eliminate the end cantilever. They may not be appropriate in situations involving a family of adjacent piers, some of which are hammerheads.

**FIGURE 5-7** *The circular inset here adds interest to the large pier cap face.*

- *Minimize the end elevation of the pier cap by keeping the vertical dimension significantly smaller than the horizontal by tapering the pier cap cantilever in one or two dimensions, sloping all or part of the end surface, sloping the pier cap sides so that the end elevation is a keystone shape, or by some combination of these techniques.* The effect of these shapes is to make the cap seem more a part of the girder.

- *On prominent, square pier cap ends, add a recess or other detail to differentiate the cap from the parapet.* If for some reason these abovementioned techniques cannot be applied and the pier cap must remain square and prominent, detail the end elevation so it is clearly differentiated from the superstructure.

- *For skewed structures use one column per girder or girder pair, which eliminates the pier cap as an element; do not use solid (wall) piers as side piers as they cut off the view completely.* Because of the

additional pier length on skewed bridges and because the far-side piers of skewed structures are more visible than the near-side piers of typical highway overcrossings, pier design becomes more important on skewed bridges and at the same time more difficult.

A variation which is particularly effective for skewed bridges is to use individual rectangular columns aligned with the girders, which creates a "venetian blind" effect on the undercrossing roadway.

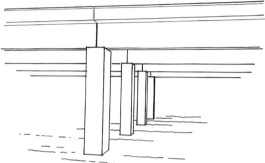

FIGURE 5-8 *With one column per girder, there's no need for a pier cap.*

### Limit Taper of V-shaped Piers

V-shaped piers eliminate the pier cap. However, when short, they create another visual problem because they are counterintuitive: they are thinnest where visual (and structural) logic says they should be thickest—at the bottom. The problem can be alleviated by a proper degree of the taper and the proportions of the total width to the width of taper.

Tapers which are too extreme produce piers which look top heavy and illogical. The viewer will ask, "Why not just carry the pier right down to the ground?" Or, a taper which looks reasonable on a short pier will produce a pier that is too wide at the top when applied to a taller pier. Finally, when the bottom width sets too thin compared to the total width, these piers will look unstable, as if they were about to topple over.

- *Keep taper to slopes of 1:4 or less for piers tapered lengthwise; 1:16 or less or piers tapered across their width. Use less for taller piers.*

- *Make the base width at least one-half of pier width.*

### Limit Taper of A-shaped Piers

Piers tapered in the other direction, narrow at the top and wide at the bottom, can suffer from similar problems in reverse. A taper which looks reasonable on a short pier will produce a pier that is too wide at the bottom

FIGURE 5-9 *V-shaped piers with too much taper will look top heavy.*

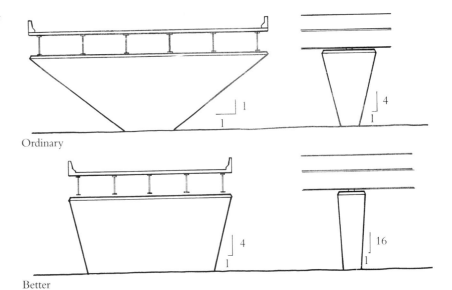

Ordinary

Better

when applied to a taller pier. The pier will start to look like a pyramid. Use the same slopes as specified above.

### Form Hammerhead Piers into Structurally Logical Shapes

Short hammerhead piers produce similar problems of proportion. While it is difficult to give specific rules, shapes that are structurally logical will also generally be visually logical. The key relationships are:

- Cantilever length compared to pier height. A cantilever which is longer than the distance between its underside and the ground will appear unnecessary and wasteful.

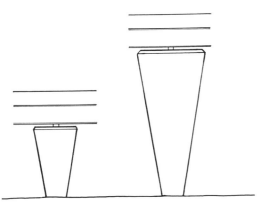

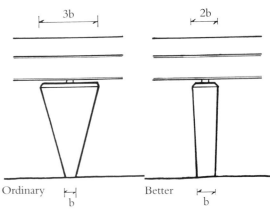

FIGURE 5-10 *The danger of using the same taper on piers of different heights.*

FIGURE 5-11 *V-shaped piers which are too narrow at the base will look unstable.*

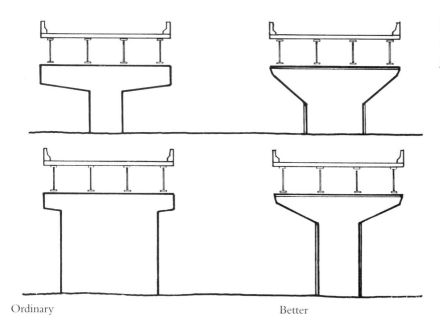

FIGURE 5-12 *Dos and don'ts of short hammerhead piers.*

Ordinary                    Better

- Base length compared to top length. If base width approaches top width the cantilevers will be so short the question will be: Why did the designer bother to add them?
- Cantilever depth at the shaft compared to shaft length. Thin arms on long shafts will look fragile.
- Cantilever depth at the shaft compared to depth at the tip. Cantilevers should be noticeably deeper at their support than at their tip. Based on their familiarity with cantilevers of their own experience (their own arms and legs, tree branches) people expect a cantilever to be thinner at the end, and are disappointed when the shape of the structure does not match that expectation. Of course, a tapered shape is also more effective structurally.

### Minimize Cantilever Ends Using the Same Techniques as for Pier Cap Ends (see Figures 5-6 and 5-7)

The cantilever ends will create the same visual problem as discussed above for pier cap ends.

### Make Pier Width Proportional to Superstructure Depth, Span Lengths, and Visible Pier Height

On short piers width should be considered for its visual effect. (On tall piers structural and economic issues tend to make this decision.) Piers notice-

FIGURE 5-13 *Pier widths should relate to superstructure; proportions should take safety mounds into account.*

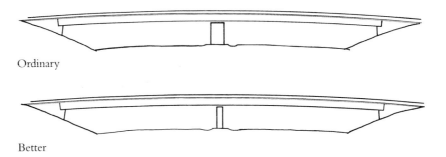

Ordinary

Better

ably thicker than the depth of the superstructure will look heavy and squat. Pier proportions should recognize that an open railing significantly changes the apparent thickness of the superstructure. Use of a mound for pier protection will shorten the apparent height, and may indicate that a thinner pier is necessary to avoid a squat appearance.

Designers are often tempted in the name of economy to keep column diameters the same over several different bridges of differing heights resulting in unattractive proportions in some of the structures. Some minimal cost savings may result, but the potential savings should be weighed against the loss of visual quality.

## Tall Piers

Tall piers are easier to design because both structure and aesthetics point in the same direction: consolidation of vertical members into one or two shafts. Engineer and laypersons alike can appreciate the economy of consolidating reactions into fewer members for the longer journey to the ground. Nature itself has offered a familiar model: the tree.

### Use No More Than Two Columns/Piers at Each Pier Line

If more columns are necessary for unusually wide structures, they should be paired. Because tall piers are so prominent a group of them can look like a forest of columns. Minimizing the number of columns reduces this effect. Pairing columns helps by creating a greater sense of visual organization. See Figure 6-25 (page 202) for a good example.

### Recognize and Accentuate the Verticality of Tall Piers

- *Use simple, vertical shapes. If both horizontal and vertical members are present, emphasize the vertical members by making them larger or more continuous than*

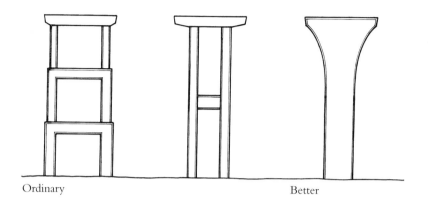

Ordinary

Better

FIGURE 5-14 *The targets for tall piers: simplification and vertical emphasis.*

*the horizontal members.* If the required length of pier at the top is narrow enough, a single vertical shaft will suffice. A single vertical shaft on a wide bridge will look—and be—too massive.

- *Taper or flare the vertical members to be wider at the bottom.* Because of wind, seismic, and other horizontal loads the stresses are largest at the bottom; the pier should be, too. Piers will look too squat if the taper is too great. Tapers of 1:24 to 1:80 work well in most situations, with the lesser tapers applicable to taller piers.

- *Integrate shaft and cap.* The pier operates as one element structurally, so it ought to look like one element. The tree analogy, specifically the trunk/branch joint, can provide clues about the shaping of the shaft/pier cap intersection. The cap/branch should be thicker at the joint and thinner at the end. There is no structural reason to be restricted to straight lines. Curves more accurately reflect the flow of stresses, and they add visual life to the structure.

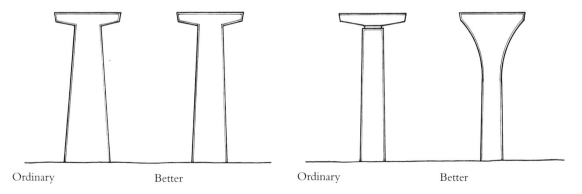

Ordinary            Better                     Ordinary            Better

FIGURE 5-15 *The effect of too much taper.*          FIGURE 5-16 *The necessity of integrating pier cap and shaft.*

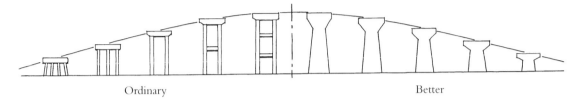

Ordinary                              Better

**FIGURE 5-17** *Families of piers varying by height.*

There is a temptation to get carried away with this shaping process, and venture into the realm of nonstructural design. The shapes indicated by structural needs are exciting enough.

## Families of Piers

### Design a Group of Piers of Varying Heights as Variations of the Same Basic Shape

It is not uncommon for multispan bridges to have piers of widely varying heights. Bridges over shipping channels or bridges over deep ravines are examples. One pier by itself may look fine, but many piers of differing heights seen at the same time may create visual cacophony. The designer is challenged with creating a family of pier designs which look good both individually and as a group, whether the individual pier be tall or short. Simply changing from one type to another, for example, multicolumn bents for the short piers and hammerheads for the tall piers, will always look like a camel of a compromise. Usually it is better to pick a single type, say a hammerhead or a two-column frame, and vary its proportions through the different piers in a logical and continuous way.

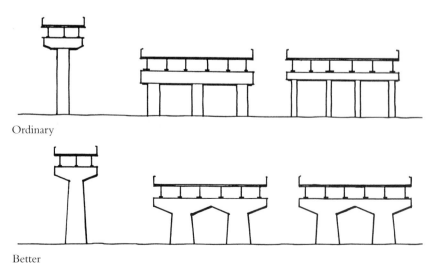

Ordinary

**FIGURE 5-18** *Families of piers varying by width.*

Better

FIGURE 5-19 *This group of piers has too many different shapes to be a family.*

FIGURE 5-20 *These piers accommodate multiple widths with consistent shapes and details.*

FIGURE 5-21 *Integral pier caps provide flexibility to match ground plane changes while keeping a consistent appearance of superstructure.*

FIGURE 5-22 *The piers of the Bong Bridge in Duluth, Minnesota, create interesting compositions from many angles.*

### Design a Group of Piers of Varying Widths as Assemblies of the Same Basic Shape

An even more difficult problem is introduced when a bridge varies in width over multiple spans or branches, as when a ramp leaves a main line.

With hammerhead piers, wider piers can be made by assembling a series of hammerheads placed tip-to-tip. As the bridge widens or branches, it is a fairly simple matter to add another hammerhead to carry the additional structure. The side-by-side hammerheads can be connected structurally to improve their efficiency without changing the basic concept or its visual impact. Since they then become rigid frames, their shape continues to be consistent with structural logic.

With a one-column-per-girder arrangement more girders can be handled by just adding more columns. This works well with widely spaced girders, especially box girders. With closely spaced girders, it can degenerate into a forest of columns.

FIGURE 5-23 *The haunch seems unsupported on this bridge from Europe.*

FIGURE 5-24 *The bearings allow a bit of sky to show through between the superstructure and substructure, emphasizing the continuity of the superstructure and making it seem light in weight.*

Integral pier caps have major visual advantages in this situation. The bridge becomes a structural ribbon riding above a few, simply shaped columns, with considerable flexibility in their placement on the ground.

### Keep the Slopes and Curves of Adjoining Piers Consistent

This approach will result in piers that create pleasing compositions when seen together from the major viewpoints. When designing a series of piers which will be seen at an oblique angle, so that they line up one behind the other, the shape of the visual voids between the piers should be considered as well as the shape of the piers themselves (Figure 5–22).

## Nuances of Pier Shape

### Keep Pier Designs Simple

Because most piers are usually seen in groups and by people traveling at high speeds who have little time to understand and appreciate complexity, keeping each pier simple is usually the best strategy.

- *Use a minimum number of elements in the pier design. One shaft is better than two columns, two columns are better than three, etc.* For structures which stay low to the water, single shafts or walls will be best of all.

- *Use simple patterns of large, easily seen elements.*

### Use a Wall, Column, or Fan-shaped Hammerhead Under a Haunched Girder

Haunched girders resting on cantilevered pier caps can seem insufficiently supported. The curves of the haunch direct the eye toward the ground in expectation of solid support continuing directly to the ground under the point of the haunch. If the support is not there, as in a cantilevered pier cap end (Figure 5-23), the viewer will feel that the girder is hanging in midair.

As discussed in the section on Superstructure Details in Chapter Four, the joint between pier and superstructure is crucial to the appearance of the bridge as well as its performance. The joint should be designed to make clear its structural function. That means that a joint with a bearing will look noticeably different than a moment connection.

### Attenuate Bearing Pads so That the Superstructure Stands Clear of the Substructure

Consider tapering the pier and/or chamfering the top (see Figure 4-58, page 128). There is no moment at a bearing, only axial compression and some shear, so the dimensions can be relatively small. If the superstructure appears to rest on a point it will appear lighter and thinner than it really is. This technique will also accentuate the horizontal sweep of the superstructure. The effect is the strongest when an observer can see right through the structure between the girder and the substructure.

The top of the pier cap can be chamfered to assist in this effect. A chamber also reflects the stress transition from the small base plate to the larger area of the pier.

A chamfer or taper also brings the pier to a clear visual termination, so it does not appear to be a short piece of a longer shape (cylinder, etc.), which happened to be sliced off by the superstructure.

### There Should be a Consistency in Shape Among the Pier, Girder, and Parapet

In order to achieve unity in the structure the shapes of the major elements should have some common characteristic.

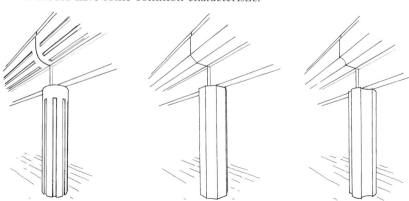

FIGURE 5-25 Sample techniques for making piers appear thinner; note consistency with parapet patterns.

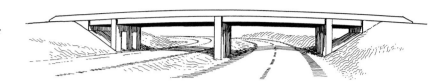

Use piers formed with planes and straight edges with precast concrete I-girders, and rectilinear box girders, which are formed of planes. Use piers withcurved surfaces with box girders having curved surfaces.

The I-shape of steel wide flange and welded plate girders is less dominant visually than other girder types. The choice of pier and parapet shape can be made based on other considerations. However, there should still be a commonality of shape between pier and parapet.

### Use Facets, Curves, Grooves, and/or Recessed Panels to Reduce Apparent Thickness of Piers

Where appropriate as part of the overall design, columns can be made to appear thinner by breaking them up into multiple surfaces with facets, curves, recessed panels, or vertical incisions.

The technique used should be consistent with the details used on of other parts of the structure.

### Avoid Pilasters at Pier Caps

Pilasters or closure walls are sometimes used on pier caps to hide the bearings. They have the effect of interrupting the horizontal sweep of the bridge, breaking it up into segments which thereby appear thicker than they otherwise would. Since the bearings are hidden, the viewer is left in doubt as to how the bridge is held up.

### Integrate Pier Protection into the Pier Itself

When a pier is in a median or next to a shoulder, protection for errant vehicles must be provided. The standard answer is a guardrail, which introduces still another element into the visual field while changing the appearance and proportion of the pier (as well as introducing hazards of its own). Better approaches should be found.

- *Use a tapered mound to deflect vehicles.*
  Figure 2-12 (page 40) shows how tapered mounds protective devices can be effective.

- *Integrate the pier design with a Jersey barrier.*

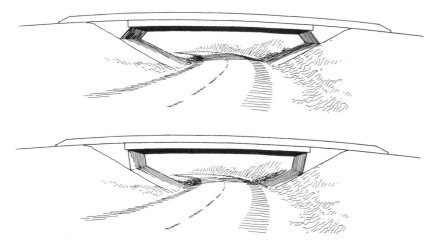

**FIGURE 5-27** *Sloping the abutments in will frame the opening and make the bridge seem more continuous.*

**FIGURE 5-28** *Sloping the abutment out makes the superstructure appear longer.*

The thickness of the pier should be reduced to reflect the shorter apparent height of the pier and the consequent change in proportions which will result.

## ABUTMENT AND RETAINING WALL SHAPE

Abutments and adjoining retaining walls can be major contributors to the appearance of a structure, especially for structures of four spans or less. The shapes and details should be chosen to enhance the design intention and the features of the rest of the structure. Independent retaining walls can also be major features in the highway scene. Their appearance deserves attention.

### Abutments

The apparent length of the bridge and the apparent height of the abutment can be influenced by sloping the face of the abutment.

*Use Slope of the Abutment Face to Influence the Structure's Appearance*
- *Consider sloping the face of the abutment inward to frame the opening and create a sense of transition between abutment and superstructure.*
- *Consider sloping the face of the abutment outward to emphasize the separation between abutment and girder and make the superstructure appear longer.*

*End Parapet and Railings in Ways Which Support the Design Intention*
The parapet, railing, and pedestrian screens come to their ends at the abutment. How these elements end will have a major impact on appearance.

**FIGURE 5-29** *Example of Type 1.*

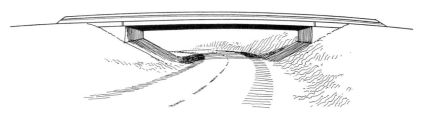

FIGURE 5-29 *Example of Type 1.*

**FIGURE 5-30** *Example of Type 2.*

FIGURE 5-30 *Example of Type 2.*

**FIGURE 5-31** *Example of Type 3.*

FIGURE 5-31 *Example of Type 3.*

There are three options:

**Type 1.** Carrying the parapet profile and as much deck overhang as feasible across the abutment to its end will increase the apparent length of the bridge. This idea works best for abutments no higher than one-third of the height of the end span. For abutments higher than that the high end wall dominates and offsets the effect.

**Type 2.** Carrying the parapet profile down the end wall corner, will make the abutment appear to frame the opening.

**Type 3.** Simply ending the parapet profile at the abutment end wall, which is simplest but will shorten the apparent length of the bridge.

The choice between alternatives should be based on the designer's design intention for the structure and should be influenced by the amount of slab overhang on the superstructure and the height of the abutment face. Type 1 works best for small-to-medium abutments, but is difficult to pull off for higher abutments. With high abutments the designer is trying to de-emphasize, by visual technique alone, two objects which make up two-thirds of the structure. Finally, as the height gets small (pedestal abutments), the differences between them disappear.

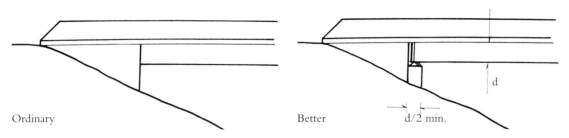

Ordinary                                    Better        d/2 min.

*If Bearings are a Major Structural Element,*
*Consider Leaving Bearings Exposed*

FIGURE 5-32 *Suggestions for bearings at abutments.*

Bearings at abutments can be exposed or hidden behind a "cheek" wall. This decision often produces passionate debate. Many feel that they should always be hidden because hiding the bearing simplifies the overall appearance of the structure and leaves the eye free to concentrate on the pier or other features. However, an outspoken minority feel they should be exposed because the increment of additional length will make the bridge seem thinner and demonstrate how the superstructure is supported. The author's opinion is that the question should be answered by the nature of the girder abutment joint: When the girder is acting integrally with the abutment, as in jointless bridges and abutment-restrained girders, the joint should be hidden. Otherwise, the bearing should be exposed.

*Make Beam Seat Width of at Least One-half the Girder Depth*

Narrow beam seats will seem visually too small to support the weight of the girders.

*Recess the Beam Seat Under the Girder*
*to the Same Plane as the Fascia Girder*

If the area of abutment under the girder is recessed to the same plane as the girder, the apparent height of the abutment will be reduced.

*Design Abutments Which Adjoin Retaining Walls*
*as a Continuation of the Retaining Walls*

Structures often occur in proximity to retaining walls. The wall should blend into the abutment without abrupt changes in pattern or configuration.

## Walls

Retaining wall shape is determined, to a large degree, by its placement in the highway environment, which determines its height at each point and therefore its overall shape as seen by drivers and other viewers. Full discussion of the factors involved was provided in the section, Abutment and Retaining Wall Placement, in Chapter Four. By following that discussion, a continuously curved plan and top profile, without jogs or offsets, should have been achieved. How to trim the wall at the top is a key decision.

*If Natural Surfaces will be Visible Above the Wall,*
*End it Without a Coping or Cap*

The wall will seem more a part of the landscape if there is no cap to create a line between the two.

*If Other Structures, Roadways, or Buildings will be Visible the Wall*
*Should be Topped with a Cap or Coping Which is Consistent*
*with the Adjoining Element*

Parapets, railings, and fencing installed on retaining walls should follow the same guidelines as for the same elements on bridges. If there are bridges near or adjacent to the wall, the parapet, railing, and fencing details should match.

*Use a Cast-in-place Cap with Precast Retaining Wall Units*
*to Achieve a Smoothly Curved Top Profile and to End*
*the Geometric Pattern of the Units*

Retaining walls made of proprietary, repetitive, precast elements have characteristic geometric patterns resulting from the form of the individual elements. As before, the most important thing is to provide a smoothly curved alignment and top profile.

Precast concrete crib walls, walls using larger precast planting boxes, and gabion walls offer another type of alternative. A smoothly curved alignment (within the restrictions of the unit size) is again a requirement. However, the dimension of the units usually prevents a smoothly curved top profile. On the other hand, the open nature of the construction offers possibilities for plant growth that can convert one of these walls into a kind of hanging garden. In fact, they should only be used where this kind of planting can be achieved. Then the top can be stepped back in a logical pattern related to the topography, and each step can be made a platform for further planting.

Retaining walls offer large surfaces which need to be visually organized. Otherwise the appearance will be the result of the vagaries of the construction process. Good appearance will be unlikely and entirely coincidental. An infinite number of possibilities exist which are hard to generalize about. For further discussion of wall treatments, see the section, Surfaces, Textures, and Ornamentation, later in this chapter.

FIGURE 5-33 *Color is an intrinsic part of a structure which together with the background affects our perception of the bridge.*

## COLOR

While the strongest determinants of the visual impression of a bridge are the shapes of its major elements, the surfaces of those shapes can, through color or texture, alter our perceptions of them. Because of the size of bridges and the distances at which they are usually first seen, color is a very important influence on how well the shape is perceived. A bridge which is very similar in color to its background will not be seen as clearly as one whose color contrasts with its background. Thus, color can be a very effective way to enhance and enrich a structural form.

Pattern and texture are other characteristics of surfaces which affect people's impression of a structure. Traditional materials such as brick and stone have their own characteristic pattern. However, when considering a use of pattern and/or texture, it's important to understand the color implications first. Color will influence the impression *before* pattern and texture. At the distances where color is first seen pattern and texture will have an effect, but only as modifiers of color. For example, when seen at a distance, concrete with a surface formed by narrow grooves will appear as a darker shade of the natural concrete color. The impression of a darker shade is produced by the minishadows created by the grooves—But the grooves themselves will not be identifiable.

For these reasons we will focus first on an exploration of color, and then move in the next section to patterns, textures, and ornament.

## The Role of Color

Color is like appearance itself—It is an intrinsic part of people's perception of an object. Color will influence their reaction to that object. That influence will occur whether or not the designer seeks to control the color.

Bridges are part of a larger visual scene, all parts of which have a color. The other colors of the scene are almost always beyond the control of the engineer. The bridge itself will have colors, even if they are simply the natural colors of the materials selected for structural reasons. Those colors will become part of the scene to which the bridge is added.

The impression created by the bridge and the emotions evoked by it will be influenced by all of these colors as they are seen together. The bridge will be seen against the other colors of the visual field, and the impression viewers form will be influenced by those colors. As we shall see, the impact a color makes—indeed, what hue and value we perceive the color to be—is affected by the other colors with which it is seen. It is important for engineers to understand these relationships in order to correctly anticipate the effect of their decisions about color.

Structural materials have a characteristic color and surface finish. Concrete and A–588 (weathering) steel have characteristic colors in their natural states. With respect to each of the surfaces of the structure, a decision must be made whether to leave the structural material as is, or to add some additional color, texture, pattern, or other surface material. Keep in mind that a decision to leave a structural material in its natural state is a decision about color whatever other criteria or considerations may have motivated it.

Two major points:

1.  The application of color or texture is not *necessary* for the creation of a good-looking bridge. Appropriately shaped structural materials in their natural state can do that on their own, except perhaps the rare case where the entire background is the same color as the materials of the bridge. Color and texture are bonuses, sources of enrichment and interest which can enhance a good structural design.

2.  Conversely, the application of color or texture is not *sufficient* to make up for an ugly structural form. There are other bridges painted red-orange, but it is the Golden Gate Bridge which has captured our imagination. Color can be used to influence our perception of shape, and thereby improve the appearance of an ordinary bridge, but it can never entirely compensate for poor decisions made about the basic shapes. Perhaps the best that can be done with color on an ugly bridge is to paint it the same color as its background, in the hope that it will be harder to see!

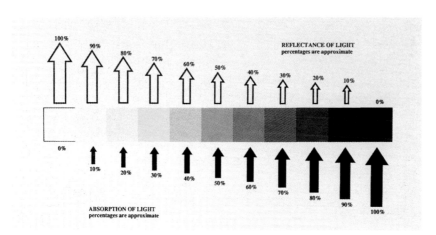

FIGURE 5-34 *The Gray Spectrum.*

## Color Basics

Using color requires an understanding of light, how colors work together, and how people see color. The use of color then becomes a result of knowledge and awareness rather than intuition alone. There's a bonus as well in the effort to learn more about color: as knowledge increases, intuition becomes more effective. Let's start with some definitions.

*Value* is the overall lightness or darkness of a surface. It is determined by the amount of absorption of all of the light striking the surface. It is usually measured by comparison to tones of gray which absorb varying percentages of light. Values can be judged by squinting at the view. In the limited light our eyes can no longer recognize hue but can recognize value.

*Hue* (red, yellow, blue) is determined by which wavelengths of light are absorbed/reflected by a material.

Hue relationships can most easily be understood by curving the visible spectrum into a circle, with red placed next to violet, creating a color wheel.[1] The most common version of this approach names red, yellow, and blue as *primary hues,* hues which can not be mixed from other hues. The primary hues lie about 120 degrees apart on the color circle (Figure 5-35).

*The secondary hues* are mixtures of the primary hues on either side of themselves: orange = red + yellow; green = yellow + blue; violet = blue

FIGURE 5-35 *The Color Wheel.*

+ red. A large number of *intermediary hues* between primary and secondary hues can be mixed, depending on the proportions of primary hues used.

Hues at 180 degrees from each other on the color wheel are called *complementary hues.* Red/green, yellow/violet, and blue/orange are complementary hues. Each intermediate hue also has its own complement. Placing complementary hues adjacent to each other creates the strongest reactions and the greatest contrasts of any color combinations.

*Intensity* is the relative degree of purity of a color. There are several other terms also used for this color characteristic: purity, saturation, strength, chroma, and brightness/dullness. *Tints* of a hue may be made by mixing it with white. *Shades* of a hue may be made with mixing it with black. Tints and shades reduce intensity. Hues can also be reduced in intensity by mixing them with their complement, which will eventually produce a dark gray or black.

Three-dimensional color wheels are available which relate all colors[2] according to hue and intensity. The wheels place low-intensity colors like tan and beige into a clear relationship with the pure colors. They are important tools in learning to judge the hue components of natural colors.

*Temperature* is a color characteristic which produces psychological and, to some extent, physical sensations of warmth or coolness. Red, orange, and yellow are considered the *warm hues.* Green, blue, and violet are considered the *cool hues.* At the boundaries between green and yellow and between violet and red are intermediate hues which seem either warm or cool, depending on their backgrounds.

## The Characteristics of Backgrounds

As was discussed in Chapter Two, the daylight in each part of the country has its own characteristics, some obvious, some subtle. Light is the starting point for decisions about color.

Locations with stronger, brighter light will create strong shadows and allow darker colors to be perceived. Lighter colors may seem washed out. Weaker light results in fuzzier shadows with less contrast. Colors must be clearer and lighter for the *hue* to be perceived.

The colors of the site constitute the background against which the bridge will be seen. The value(s) and hue(s) of the background will be present over a much larger area of the visual field than the area of the structure. It is important to understand what they are.

Most background colors in nature are not pure colors but low-intensity shades of one or more pure colors. For example, tan and beige are combinations of black and white with red and yellow. The rules governing the harmony of these colors with other hues will be the same as for their base colors. It is important to be able to pick out the base color in order to judge the relation of the background to proposed new colors.

Begin with the important viewpoints identified earlier. From those locations look at the values and hues of the background against which the bridge will be placed. Take color photos. Don't forget seasonal changes. If there will be snow on the ground for five months, get some wintertime shots, too.

Color photos are a valuable tool, and should be used extensively. However, some caution needs to be exercised. Many color films do not show every color to its true intensity and temperature. Shoot an experimental roll of the type of film you expect to use. Then compare the results to the actual scene viewed in similar light conditions. The comparison will give an indication if any mental corrections are necessary.

It's important to see what colors really *are* there as opposed to what colors you think are *supposed* to be there. Many people tend to feel colors should follow preconceived rules. Trees are green. Green, to many people, is the green that came in their elementary school crayon box. However, a copper beech tree is not green, it is purple, and hundreds of shades of green are necessary to depict all of the trees native to the United States.

Different parts of the country have different characteristic backgrounds, generally dominated by the vegetation, or lack thereof. In the Northeast, Mid-Atlantic, Southeast, and Midwest the background will be multiple shades of green in spring and summer, briefly oranges and yellows in the fall, and brown and gray in the winter (Figure 5-40, page 163). Across the southwest and west the background will be the sage green, brown and gray of desert vegetation and topography. In the Northwest the dominant color is usually the dark green of the coniferous forest. In California it is a few months of spring green followed by months of golden brown.

In most of the country there are well-defined seasons. The choice of colors should usually be based on the longest period of similar colors, usually spring-summer.

The general statements above may or may not apply to a specific site. Judgments about a specific bridge only can be made based on the conditions at the site. To reiterate, take photos from the important viewpoints. Try to get the background colors as accurate as you can, and use them in making judgments about color. Understand the position of the bridge in the visual field from the various viewpoints. How much of the field does it occupy? The larger the proportion of the visual field that it occupies the less influence the background color will have on the final result.

If the bridge or its immediate environs are lit, nighttime conditions should be considered. These can include the exaggeration of shadows and textures, depending on the location of the light source or sources, and changes in apparent color caused by the color effect of different types of lighting. For example, mercury vapor and metal halide lighting will bring out blues and greens, while reds and oranges become dulled and grayish; high-pressure sodium lighting will bring out reds and oranges, while blues and greens will become dulled and grayish.

The orientation of the bridge should also be considered. Colors will appear brighter on south-facing surfaces and, for half the day, on east- and west-facing surfaces. They will also fade faster on these surfaces.

Because signs have characteristic, strong colors, the presence of a sign on a bridge must influence the color selection, which is another good reason to leave signs off bridges.

## Picking Colors

In picking colors for bridges the designer's choices must focus on picking the color(s) of the bridge that will best combine with the background to evoke his design intent.

The first decision, of course, is determining what type of effect is desired as part of the design intent.

### Determine a Design Intent for the Color Choices

There are a number of effects which can be achieved with color:

- To make a bridge blend in or disappear against the background, either to avoid drawing attention from a more important object, or to prevent the visual cacophony of too many different colors in the visual field. Many highway bridge elements are not intended to be the focus of a given area. As background structures, their colors are better kept simple and subdued.

- To make the bridge contrast with its background, to bring the bridge out as a feature, a source of excitement, pride, or orientation. Many highway environments are spread out and monotonous. A bridge can be a feature that adds a moment of pleasure to a journey.

- To provide variety and interest, perhaps as part of a larger theme in, say, an urban commercial area with an overall urban design plan.

- To provide a symbol of an institution, town, or historic district, as has the Sunshine Skyway in the Tampa Bay area.

- To emphasize the structural shape itself by giving it a color which contrasts strongly with its background. The brilliant red-orange of the Golden Gate Bridge seen against the beige Marin hills is a familiar example.

- To display and underline the workings of the structure by using different colors for different parts of a structure. The Victorians carried this to an effective extreme in their iron structures, right down to a different color for the bolt heads.

Color can be an effective method to reach these goals in a way which does not compromise the structural form or add undue cost. Not all of these goals are mutually exclusive, and several can, in fact, be effectively applied in combination.

Different color combinations (bridge plus background) can evoke different emotional effects. Contrasts in hue, value, and intensity will help determine the mood evoked. Strong contrasts, especially in the values and intensities used, will tend to be more stimulating and exciting; weak contrasts will impart a more soothing, quiet effect.

Once a design intention is determined, the designer can move on to value and hue considerations. Since value comparisons dominate our initial impression, it is critical that the desired value combination be determined first.

### Settle on a Desired Value Scheme

The balance of light against dark is the first decision to make. Most natural backgrounds tend toward the middle range, medium values will help the structure blend in. Much lighter or darker values will be necessary to make the structure stand out.

**FIGURE 5-36** *An example of the medium-value differences typical of many areas of the country, particularly on hazy or overcast days; even the dark-gray shadow on the girder contains discernible detail.*

**FIGURE 5-37** *An example of strong value contrasts; in the clear mountain air and the strong Colorado sun even the light-colored abutment concrete is seen as black within the shadowed area.*

*Evaluate the Effect of Background Colors on Potential Hue Schemes*

If the desire is to blend the structure into the scene, colors should be used which are similar to the background colors. One question to be decided is which part of the background should the structure blend into. The structures in Figure 5-44 (page 164), photographed during painting, interacts with its background in two different ways. The closer, silver-gray structure takes on the color of the sky and seems to be pulled up into the sky; the rear structure, because of its value and hue, seems a part of the land and seems to visually connect the two hillsides.

If the desire is to have the structure stand out against its background a problem emerges. Because the area of the structure is a relatively small part of the visual field, the most effective tool in giving presence to the structure will be a strong contrast of hue and/or value. The use of colors which are complementary to the background colors will have the most striking effect. (Figure 5-40, page 163), stands out because its bright red orange is a near complement to the green hillside.) Using one or two colors which are neighbors of the complementary color is also effective.

## Coatings and Colorings

Most bridge-building agencies have settled policy toward the coating or coloring of structural materials based on cost and maintenance considerations. Since both concrete and A588 steel are reasonably durable in most situations, the policy frequently is to not coat either one. This will establish the colors of the major structural elements without any input from the designer. However, if these colors do not match the design intention, the designer must decide if the bridge can be made to match the design intention through the application of color to selected details. If that is not possible, the designer should appeal for an exception to the no-coating policy.

If the agency is open to, but does not require, coating or coloring of the structural materials, a decision must still be made on whether that is desirable on aesthetic grounds. Uncoated, uncolored concrete and A588 steel have characteristic colors that lend themselves to certain natural backgrounds. Leaving them alone may be the best choice. Only if the agency *requires* coating can the following step be skipped.

*Evaluate the Effect of the Natural Colors of the Structural Materials*

What is the effect of the natural color of the structural materials against the relevant backgrounds? What are the visual/emotional effects that are likely to be evoked? Do those match the intention of the designer?

*A588 steel's black/brown color will dominate all other colors in the structure.* The material starts as a medium brown but over a ten-year period reaches a permanent black/brown. There are even hints of purple in the final hue. The exact final color depends on local atmospheric conditions.

This aggressive color strongly affects all other colors used in the structure. The dominance is a result of both the strong hue and the dark value. That is fine if the design intention calls for a strong black/brown color; in other circumstances it may be necessary to temper the effects of the steel color. While there are several possibilities for dealing with the problem it is complicated by the fact that the steel color is a moving target. It starts out a rich reddish brown but gradually loses hue as it approaches black.

One solution is to provide an area of intense color on some other part of the structure. This could be applied as a "racing stripe" on the parapet, on specific areas of the piers or abutments, or on a railing or pedestrian screen. The effect will be to lessen the intensity of the steel hue and value. Red, violet, or blue would tend to make the structure stand out against most backgrounds, with the possible exception of a blue seen against the sky or water. If the intention is to make the structure blend in, neutrals of similar hue to the background and of a medium to dark value could be used in the same way.

A serious problem with A588 steel is that runoff from it stains everything below it for years until the surface stabilizes. By then concrete piers will be streaked almost as dark as the steel. Either the runoff must be caught and directed away from concrete surfaces, or the concrete must be coated.

One technique sometimes used to address this problem is to paint the section of the girder above the pier a color intended to match the natural steel color. The match never works beyond the first few weeks. The paint fades

**FIGURE 5-38** *Using a colored inset to add a strip of bright color to a concrete structure.*

while the weathering steel darkens. The contrast is soon apparent and visually breaks the girder up into sections, making it appear shorter, deeper and discontinuous. Other solutions should be sought.

*Concrete's light gray-tan color will contrast with most backgrounds, and the structure will stand out.* Most people consider concrete's natural color acceptable, if bland. One problem is the lightly mottled appearance caused by slight differences in the batches and/or imperfections in the forms. Also, the color is not memorable, and does little to add interest or life to the structure.

Here again, insets or details of stronger, brighter colors can help add life to the structure by attracting attention while the concrete becomes the background frame.

If the owner allows or requires coating the structural materials and/or details, the designer must move on to picking specific colors of hues and values that will accomplish the design intention.

### *Pick Values and Hues in Relation to the Backgrounds the Bridge will be Seen Against When Viewed from the Important Viewpoints*

If the goal is to have the bridge blend in, the bridge value should be similar to the background value; bridge hues should be similar or close to color wheel neighbors of the dominant background colors. If the goal is to have the bridge stand out, the bridge value should be much lighter or darker than the background value; the hue should be a complementary color or a near-color-wheel neighbor of a complementary of the dominant background colors.

The next steps must be made using the actual hues and values. Words won't do. There are too many varieties of green for "use green" to be of much help. Begin to experiment with rough studies made with color photographs of the site as the background. Use colored markers or pencils.[3] Don't worry about details. It is the large areas of color that will create the effect. If CAD is available, a three-dimensional model of the structure can be placed against a scanned photo and colors manipulated with graphic design software.

- *When picking colors remember that public reaction is more positive to brighter, clearer colors (blue, red, orange, green) and less positive to silver, gray, brown, and black.* William Zuk surveyed the reactions of thousands of drivers to the same bridge painted different colors.[4] A clear preference emerged for the stronger colors. In their book, *Color for Architecture,*[5] Porter and Mikellides show that the people whom we presumably design for have long desired more and better color in their built environments.

- *Pick colors in relation to the colors of other nearby structures.* When groups of closely spaced structures are involved, they will be seen one after each other in quick succession. The colors for each should be picked in relation to the others. This does not mean that they all have to be the same, but that they all have some discernible relationship. For example, one might conceive of a series of bridges on an urban freeway being painted in a series of colors which gradually shift through the color spectrum of the various shades of red, and have that group followed by another group which shifts through the various shades of blue.

- *Take care when picking greens to blend into a natural background.* There are many shades of green within the foliage of a single tree, and they change constantly with light and wind conditions. Picking a single green which will look good against a group of different types of trees is difficult. The presence of an interstate guide sign with its artificial, reflective color compounds the problem. Good color photos and visits to the site under varied light conditions can help.

- *Light colors result in stronger shadows, making any design which depends on contrasting shadows more effective.* A dark-colored surface is already absorbing most of the incident light, so the effect of a shadow is less pronounced.

- *Be aware that light-colored surfaces will reflect colored light onto nearby surfaces.* This will be especially noticeable on surfaces which are in shadow and not receiving much direct light. For example, the soffit of a deck next to a bright red girder web will have a red tinge. This can be a bonus for structures with pedestrians using the space below. Conversely, dark-colored surfaces will reflect very little light onto nearby surfaces, making them seem dark as well.

- *Avoid complementary colors on the same structure.* While complementary colors can work well to establish a contrast with the background, it is risky to use them in the same structure. They will disturb the unity of the structure. Better to use similar colors within the same or nearby structures.

There are significant differences in the application of color to concrete as opposed to steel. With steel bridges a wide variety of paint colors are available and colors can be picked to fit a color intention. Quality control is relatively easy to achieve, and the need for periodic repainting for maintenance reasons means that the color will be periodically renewed (though perhaps not in an unusual color or pattern). None of these factors apply to concrete. There are three possible approaches to coloring concrete:

- Integrally colored concrete is the most durable, but the colors available tend to be limited, and generally are the siennas, golds, and umbers of the earthtone family. Uniformity requires careful quality control, and can be difficult to achieve.

- Staining concrete is another possibility, though the range of pigments is still limited, and it produces a mottled effect. This technique is really only useful when the mottled effect is desirable.
- External coatings are the most promising approach to coloring concrete and can be quite durable if correctly applied. They have an additional advantage in not requiring as much quality in the finish as it comes from the form. The likely degree of maintenance is a major consideration. Textured or colored concrete in locations subject to vehicular impact is a particular problem, as it is almost impossible to repair it to match the original.

### If Color is Desired in Concrete to Provide Uniformity or Add Interest, Consider a Coating in an Earthtone

A basic problem with all concrete color technique is that the basic pigments are not durable. Since it is not necessary for maintenance reasons to recoat concrete, that means that the material will continue to exist in its faded condition. The earthtones and blues tend to last the longest; reds go the quickest. Color on the south side of the bridge will fade noticeably quicker than color on the north side. Lighter colors will lose less to fading, and chipping or flaking will not be as noticeable.

### Use Inserts of Other Materials for Bright Color Accents

Where strong, permanent colors are desired as part of a surface design in concrete, a better approach is inlays of material with permanent, characteris-

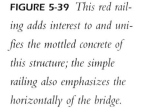

FIGURE 5-39 *This red railing adds interest to and unifies the mottled concrete of this structure; the simple railing also emphasizes the horizontally of the bridge.*

tic colors. Examples are terracotta, tile and glazed ceramic tile. These are available in a wide variety of colors, and have centuries of a successful history of exterior use in architecture.

As an example, one might conceive of working a decorative pattern built around the colors of a university into a parapet of a nearby bridge. If a color covers only a small portion of any one element of the bridge, and it is clearly incorporated into a decorative pattern independent of the structural form of the bridge, significantly more latitude is available in the choice of colors. This can be a tricky business, however. Large-scale full-color drawings are necessary to judge the effect, and professional advice may be necessary. For example, an artist might be asked to design an inset of colored tile for a parapet or retaining wall.

### Consider the Presence of a Sign When Making Color Selection

The green color of the national standard guide sign is *not* found in nature. Trying to find colors that harmonize with it results in clear colors which look artificial also, so that *no* part of the structure relates well to the background.

The rear of the sign and its mounting structure should be painted a color compatible with the bridge itself.

### Select Retaining Wall Color as a Function of the Size of the Wall in the Visual Field and Color of Nearby Structures

Small walls seen primarily against natural features should probably use colors which blend with nearby natural colors. Walls in a primarily man-made environment or adjoining other structures should borrow colors from those

**FIGURE 5-40** *Ridge Road over I-70 near Frederick, Maryland, photographed in the late afternoon in October, looking from the west. At this time of day the colors are bright and the shadows strong.*

**FIGURE 5-41** *Ridge Road over I-70 near Frederick, Maryland, photographed in the late afternoon looking from the east. All of the east-facing surfaces are shaded and the bridge is seen as a practically colorless silhouette.*

FIGURE 5-42 *This pattern creates random shadows at every sun angle.*

FIGURE 5-43 *A vertical pattern of closely spaced ribs hides drainage stains and construction irregularities.*

structures. Walls are truly background structures, and rarely deserve the contrast in hue or value that would draw attention to them.

### *Select Noise Wall Color as a Function of the Natural Background*

Noise walls are usually seen against a background of planting. Colors should be compatible with the seasonal variation of such backgrounds.

### *To Make Pedestrian Screens, Sign Structures, and Light Poles Less Obvious Use a Light Gray/Aluminum Color if the Element is Seen Primarily Against the Sky*

This color tends to pick up the sky color; dark neutrals of a hue similar to the hillside or black will work better for an element seen against a hillside.

### *Use a Formal Color-matching System to Specify the Colors Picked*

After the decisions are made and the colors picked, one important step remains: ensuring that the actual colors finally applied match the colors picked. There are important differences between the way colors are created by colored pencils, art markers, photographs, computer screens, color printers, and paint manufacturers. One medium's "green" is not the same as another's. One way to integrate these different versions is to use a color matching system, such as the Pantone system.[6] This system matches colors to uniform color samples, which are identified by number.

The best approach is to require the preparation on site of a sample panel, using the same substrate and field application techniques that will occur in the final structure. The sample can then be compared to the colors picked, and adjustments made.

FIGURE 5-44 *Photographed half-way through a repainting, the Maury River Bridge in Virginia demonstrates the interaction of color and background: the aluminum-colored span takes on the sky color and seems part of the sky, while the brown span emulates the colors of the topography and clearly ties together the two hillsides.*

# SURFACE PATTERNS, TEXTURE, AND ORNAMENTATION

Once color is determined pattern and surfacing materials can be studied. As with color the two major goals of pattern/texture/ornament in a bridge should be:

- To differentiate the various parts of the structure's lines and thereby clarify it.
- To create a desired emotional response in the viewer.

Pattern and texture are difficult to perceive by people traveling at highway speeds. Only large and distinct patterns will be understood. As the elements of a uniform pattern become smaller they are not seen as individual elements but as components of a texture. Textures will be seen primarily as color modifiers.

Texture does become more important at street and pedestrian speeds. People have the time to see the more subtle features—the mortar lines in brick surfaces, for example, and even reach out and touch surfaces that are inviting. Even at this level, however, the color of the surface and its relation to surrounding colors must be understood independent of the texture.

Concrete, whether used as a girder or wall, can be patterned in many ways, limited only by the imagination of the designer and the size of the budget.

A pattern can be as simple as a pattern of incisions based around standard form panel dimensions and concrete lifts. Possibilities beyond that include raised or recessed panels, ribs, and indentations.

Traditional materials such as brick and stone have their own characteristic patterns and textures. They also have associations which we carry with us because of their use in architecture. A particular type and color of brick, for example, may remind us of the buildings of a certain town. To the extent that these associations are widely shared in a community the use of that material may carry a message to the larger population that associates the bridge with a certain historical period or social values associated with that period. For example, using concrete patterned to look like the stone of the state capitol building can give a nearby bridge a sense of dignity because of its association with the capitol.

## Concrete Patterns and Textures

Concrete offers many possibilities for the imposition of various types of pattern through form liners, custom formwork, and other devices. The keys to success are:

- *Making sure that the pattern is subordinated to and contributes to the overall design features and proportions of the structure itself.*
- *Making the pattern large enough to be read at highway distances when the pattern will be seen primarily from the roadway.*

To a certain extent, the designer has no choice but to create some level of pattern in large concrete surfaces. The form joints and construction joints of the concrete will create a pattern, whether the designer recognizes it or not. The result is likely to be much improved if the designer at least controls these patterns through design, rather then leave them to the vagaries of the construction process.

One point is clear: Studying the pattern on elevation drawings is misleading if the wall will be seen primarily from a moving car. The wall will actually be seen as if it were on a vertical scroll unwinding in the peripheral vision. The impression created will bear little relation to what can be gleaned from the elevation drawing.

### Organize Retaining Wall Surfaces

- *Recognize and organize the expansion, contraction, and construction joints.* Drain holes at the base of the wall should be installed in a consistent and logical relationship to the surface pattern and, if possible, be hidden in the wall pattern.
- *Pattern lines should parallel the grade of the lower roadway, or be horizontal or vertical.* Lines which are close to but not identical to the roadway geometry and other features will be particularly noticeable and jarring. Continuous horizontal lines should be either level or follow the major lines of the roadway. Horizontal lines must be carefully controlled, as any irregularities will be immediately obvious. Textures created by repeated linear elements (such as ribs) are more successful if primarily made up of vertical elements because construction control is not so critical.
- *Control frequency of repeating patterns.* Patterns which repeat abruptly and continuously at intervals of about one-quarter second to one second at the prevailing speed (20 to 75 feet at 50 MPH) will be annoying and quickly become monotonous (the "telephone pole" effect). Patterns at shorter intervals will become a textural blur. Longer patterns (200 feet +) will be seen as adding variety, unless they are repeated too often without change.
- *Create patterns consisting of elements which are large enough to be seen at highway speeds.* (Minimum dimension of about 4 inches.)
- *Elongate object designs horizontally to compensate for perspective foreshortening.*

*When Working with Walls Made up of Repetitive Precast Units,*
*Develop a Consistent Strategy for Dealing with the Wall Pattern*

Walls made up of repetitive precast units have specific visual characteristics. The units themselves will create a unique pattern which is large enough to be read in the highway environment. The patterns often end in jagged hexagonal or cruciform edges.

This pattern can be made more noticeable by creating protrusions, recesses, or exaggerated edges in the precast units. Or, it can be somewhat concealed by overlaying regular patterns created by form liners.

A difficulty comes from having to provide for alternative bidding by manufacturers with different unit shapes. A design predicated on a hexagonal unit may be a different thing entirely if applied to a cruciform unit. If alternate bidders must be accommodated, the challenge will be to develop a design which applies equally well to all potential bidders. Alternatively, if a specific appearance is particularly important, bids should be restricted to manufacturers with compatible units.

- *Develop and apply a consistent method of completing the pattern at its ends.* In the section on Walls (page 147), a poured-in-place concrete caps is suggested to provide a smooth ending at the top. A similar strategy should be followed at the ends. The joint with a cast-in-place wall should be a simple vertical element which clearly ends the pattern of the precast elements and allows another pattern to begin. A joint which is a reciprocal shape to the precast elements usually looks like a poor attempt at imitation.

- *Where precast unit walls adjoin poured walls, care must be taken that the pattern and color of the poured wall is compatible with those of the precast wall.*

**FIGURE 5-45** *The cast-in-place beam seat seems to cradle the girders, while the precast units continue almost seamlessly around the corner.*

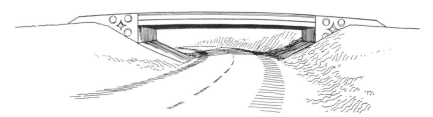

That does not mean that the cast-in-place wall should be scored to imitate the precast walls—the result will not be convincing. Better to contrast a larger pattern, taking care that the colors are compatible.

- *Abutments which are a combination of precast proprietary retaining wall elements and cast-in-place sections present a special problem.* The joint between the two prevents the wall from being seen as a simple continuation of the abutment.

- *For transitions between precast retaining wall sections and a cast-in-place retaining wall or abutment use a simple cast-in-place vertical feature at a logical location (perhaps at the expansion joint).* Surface treatment of abutments should be consistent with parapet treatments and pier design. For most structures the only abutment surfaces clearly visible will be the sidewalls. Facewalls are too foreshortened and usually too shadowed to be worth special treatment. Exceptions are unusually wide structures, skewed structures and bridges crossing city streets or pedestrian areas.

### *Developing Surface Treatments for Abutments*

When developing abutment surface treatments:

- *Layout plan and elevation of entire abutment and any adjoining retaining wall at one time.*

- *Recognize and organize expansion, contraction, and construction joints.*

- *All lines should bear some obvious relation to the main lines of the structure.*

#### *Any Feature Placed on the Abutment Should Help Unify the Structure, and not Make the Abutment Appear as a Separate Element*

For medium-to-high abutments an opportunity exists to draw attention to the abutment. The designer must decide whether to do that, and why. An inappropriate feature on the abutment can distract attention from the structure as a whole.

The guidelines for surface patterns and textures for retaining walls apply to noise walls, too. In particular, the use of panelized systems with a prominent post every 12 or so feet creates an unfortunate repetition of closely spaced verticals.

*Visually De-emphasize the Posts of Panelized Noise Walls*

This can be achieved by providing horizontal lines within the panels themselves and by painting the posts the same color as the wall panels.

*Use a Cap Pattern and Multiple Small Steps to Visually De-emphasize the Steps in the Top Profile of Panelized Noise Walls*

A combination of having steps always occur in the same small dimension (6 to 12 inches) and having a cap feature of a somewhat larger dimension will create the illusion of a continuous smooth top profile.

*Select Form Liners Which Support the Design Intention and are Consistent with Nearby Features*

Rubber and plastic form liners are an economical way to achieve interest and texture.

What clues does the immediate area offer? Brick buildings? Fieldstone walls? Woods? What will coordinate with other nearby highway structures? Surfaces can be chosen which blend in or contrast, whichever fits the overall concept.

- *In the highway environment use form liners which are abstract or random patterns with elements large enough to be recognizable.* Long lengths of retaining wall or noise wall next to a roadway are seen with so much perspective foreshortening that the repetitive pattern of the liner becomes obvious. It is a large-scale version of the boredom created in a large room with walls covered by wallpaper with a small repeating pattern. Random and abstract patterns hide the repetition better. They also are

FIGURE 5-47 *The pattern repetition for this long wall is clear to the driver.*

more consistent with the random textures in nature (tree bark, rock outcrops) which are frequently the background.

- *Form liners which seek to imitate brick or stone are unconvincing unless special care is taken.* Only if the effort is made to individually and differentially color each of the individual "stones" or "bricks" and to hide the joints between panels can the effect work. The best result is gained when the form liner itself is a mold taken from an actual masonry wall.

- *Form liners or surface treatments which attempt to imitate random wood boarding and similarly small-scale detail are wasted at highway speeds, but may be applicable in areas where pedestrians circulate.* Surfaces in pedestrian environments offer a wider set of possibilities because pedestrians are close enough, and moving slowly enough, to appreciate them. Decisions about them should be made based on the prior development of an aesthetic concept for the area. What is the predominant use of the area? Waiting for a bus? Walking to school? Sitting in the sun? How can the highway contribute to that use? Or protect itself? Is the highway intended to be friendly or unfriendly? For example, a surface can be created by fracturing protruding vertical concrete ribs with a hammer which produces myriad sharp edges. Such a surface would be a bad choice adjacent to a tot lot, but might be a good choice to in another area to discourage loitering.

Surface treatments which break down the concrete surface (e.g. bush-hammering, acid wash) are not generally successful in highway environments. They can not be read at highway speeds, and the surface becomes more porous and more susceptible to dirt and deterioration.

## Nonstructural Facing Materials

Nonstructural facing materials, such as brick, stone, and precast panels, can be used to provide color or texture on surfaces.

### Use Traditional Masonry Materials in Ways Consistent with Their Structural Capabilities and Historic Use

Masonry materials find their most logical application for facing of abutments and retaining walls, circumstances where they have been used structurally for centuries. They are not convincing as part of a span unless they are formed into a structural arch, consistent with their historic use. If they are used as part of a parapet, they need to be detailed in such a manner that the support provided by the girder below is clearly demonstrated.

Random fieldstone with large units (greater than 18 inches) appears to work best of the various facing materials, since its size and texture make it visible in the highway environment. Precast concrete panels can work well. The major concerns are surface color and texture and panel joints. Brick, with its mortar pattern, is on the small side for highway uses, but can still add interest. It is more appropriate to a pedestrian environment.

*Construct Sizable Sample Panels On-site to View Under Various Light Conditions Before a Final Decision is Made*

Color selection is even more critical with masonry materials, since the possibility of a future change is remote. Brick must be handled especially carefully, as the range of color choices is high, and the possibilities for an inappropriate choice multiply. With brick and stone, mortar color must also be considered.

## Ornamentation

Historical structures, especially those located in a city center or other important spot, were often elaborated with decorative railings and detail. The beginning and end of a bridge were often recognized with pylons or statuary. These features added interest and visually recognized the symbolic role of the structure and its position within the larger urban context. Citizens often feel that unadorned modern structures insufficiently recognize these needs.

The goal of the modern engineer should be to develop strength from the shape of the structure, and let that structural shape produce the aesthetic impact on its own. However, ornament can be used to articulate and emphasize the structural shape. This function can often be achieved by appropriately shaping structural details. For example, stiffeners on steel girders can be arranged to create a natural emphasis on the bearing point in a way that might be called ornamental, and still serve their structural function. Indeed, many of the classical systems of architectural ornamentation had their beginning in the elaboration of structural elements.

**FIGURE 5-48** *The Starruca Viaduct, an excellent example of large stone masonry from the nineteenth century.*

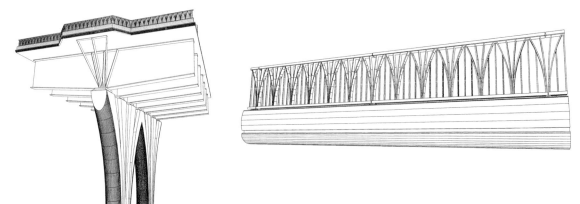

FIGURE 5-49 *The web stiffeners and overlook supports focus attention on the point of force transfer. The steel railing reflects the shapes of the pier.*

However, ornamentation and nonstructural surface materials can disguise, detract from, or destroy the structural form. This was the general practice in late-nineteenth-century architecture, and was the reason that the first modern architects looked to nineteenth-century engineering as an example of functional clarity and pure form.

Ornamentation can add additional levels of interest and richness. It is best when restricted to those locations with a commensurate level of importance and exposure. The critical criterion is to make sure that the ornamentation emphasizes, rather than camouflages, the structural form.

### Shape Structural Features to Call Attention to Points of Stress and Stress Transfer, and to Emphasize Structural Form

The stiffeners on the structure above create a pattern which focuses the eye on the point of stress transfer, and emphasizes structural form.

### Use Railing Details and Other Details Which Complement the Shapes of Major Structural Features

The structure will appear more unified if the details are clearly similar in shape to the major features.

## SIGNING, LIGHTING, AND LANDSCAPING

While these elements are not, strictly speaking, part of the bridge itself, they can have major impact on the structure's appearance.

## Signing

There are two types of signs on structures. The first and most common is where the bridge itself is used as a support for a sign serving the underpass-

FIGURE 5-50 *Lighting and landscaping can be successfully integrated into a structural design.*

ing roadway. The second is when a sign structure is erected on a bridge to serve the bridge's own roadway, which is often necessary on long viaducts and ramps.

In both types the sign usually blocks and/or complicates the lines of the bridge itself. The result is rarely attractive. Thus the most desirable option is to keep signing off of structures. It doesn't do any good to create an attractive bridge design and than saddle it with an ugly sign or sign bridge. The first goal should be to seek an alternative location for signs away from a structure. This will inevitably mean more specialized structures for the signs themselves. These structures should be simple and cleanly designed, relying on a few large members rather than truss work. A simple, attractive sign structure even 300 feet *before* a bridge is preferable to a sign *on* the bridge itself.

However, there will be locations where placing a sign on a bridge is unavoidable. Let us start with signs mounted on bridges for the benefit of the underpassing roadway.

### When a Bridge-Mounted Sign is Required for the Under Roadway, Sign(s) Should be Fit into the Overall Design

There are situations where the highway layout is so constrained that the only reasonable location for a sign is closer than 300 feet. In those cases, the driver's view through the sign bridge should be checked. If the sign bridge effectively blocks the view of the roadway bridge, the sign might as well be on the bridge.

Align the top of the sign with the top of the parapet, and align the bottom of the sign with the bottom of the superstructure. This may require a nonstandard arrangement of the message.

Where more than one sign is on a bridge, all of the vertical dimensions of the signs should be the same.

### Keep Sign Bridges on Structures Simple

When a sign structure must be mounted on a bridge structure, the connection should be made so that the sign structure looks like it belongs there, not like a slapped-on afterthought. Design connections sign structures on bridges as a logical extension of the structural members bridge itself.

## Lighting

There are two areas of concern here. The first, and more common, is the mounting of roadway lighting on a bridge. The second is mounting of fixtures under a bridge to light the underpassing roadway.

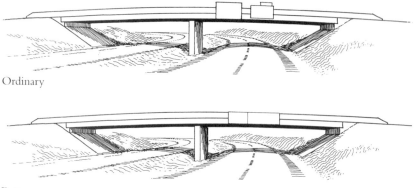

Ordinary

Better

FIGURE 5-53 *Sign structures on bridges should be coordinated with the structure by, for example, being placed on a pier.*

Usually the pattern of roadway lighting depends on a regular, even spacing of poles. The pattern frequently is started some distance from the bridge, and the poles end up at odd locations on the bridge, placed wherever the pattern happened to fall. However, roadway lighting is not that precise.

### For Short Bridges, Space Adjoining Roadway Lighting Off the Bridge

Small adjustments in spacing can be made without appreciably affecting light levels. Such adjustments should be made to bring the poles into a better visual relationship to the bridge.

### If Lighting on the Bridge Can't be Avoided, Place Roadway Lighting Poles in Some Relationship to the Structure

Lighting poles should be positioned so as to coordinate with the overall design. An example of this would be placing a pole over pier.

### Mount Lighting Poles on a Widened Area in the Parapet

The support element design needs to be as continuous as possible with the parapet itself and consistent with any railing posts, grooves, or recesses and

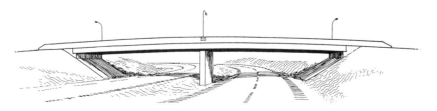

FIGURE 5-54 *Lighting supports should be organized around structural features.*

**FIGURE 5-55** *The support area for the light mounted on the bridge is continuous with the parapet; however, an improvement would have been to place it over the pier.*

construction joints of the parapet. The design goal should be to maintain the horizontal line of the parapet with as little interruption as possible.

### *Mount Lights Under Structures in Some Relationship to the Structural Features, so They Emphasize the Structural Form*

For example, placing lights between every third stringer of a girder bridge would not only light the roadway below, but light every third space between the girders, creating a rhythmic interval of light across the "ceiling" of the space underneath the bridge.

Light fixtures mounted under a bridge to light the underneath roadway offer a special opportunity to make the bridge a nighttime feature. In this case, the area beneath the bridge usually becomes the brightest part of the night visual field, creating a "lighted portal" effect.

### *Take into Account Special Lighting Needs*

There are specific instances where, because of the size of the bridge itself, its location in the community or the environment, or its symbolic importance, the bridge itself deserves lighting. There are two basic approaches in this situation:

- *To simply floodlight the bridge.* This will not replicate daytime appearance, since the shadow areas and the color effects will be unavoidably different. However, it does come closest to giving a complete picture of the bridge.

- *To outline significant features of the bridge in lights, or otherwise light only significant portions of the bridge.* This probably works best when it is designed to create a pattern which is essentially an abstraction of the basic structural form. An example is lighting the cables of a cable-stayed bridge.

Both of these techniques require a great deal of specialized expertise and experience. Designers interested in feature lighting should consult with lighting design consultants. The impact on the community and the community's reaction should also be considered.

## Landscaping

Landscaping should be an enhancement of an already attractive structure. It should not be relied on to cover up an embarrassment or hide some unfortunate detail. Conversely, it should not be allowed to grow up to hide some important feature which is crucial to the visual form of the bridge. Landscaping can be a more economical and effective way to add richness and interest to a design than special surface finishes or materials. For example, a large, plain concrete abutment can be effectively enhanced by well-chosen landscaping around it.

The application of landscape concerns, such as environmental suitability, topography, and existing vegetation, is part of the site analysis and conceptual development process for the bridge as a whole. That process will, in addition to producing a design intention for the bridge, produce a consistent design intention for adjacent landscaping. The landscaping concepts developed for a larger project should recognize the design intention for the structures on that route.

FIGURE 5-56 *Seasonal mass planting creates a colorful foreground for this North Carolina structure.*

FIGURE 5-57 *Blending of landscape patterns with the background results in a pleasing uninterrupted vista.*

### In Rural Areas Use Landscaping to Emphasize the Continuity of the Space Through the Bridge

Where the basic design intention of the bridge is to ensure the maximum openness of the space under the bridge and an unobstructed view through the bridge, landscape planting can help achieve this effect. One way this could be achieved would be to establish a recognizable pattern of planting which starts before the bridge, continues right through it (with a minimal interruption directly underneath), and continues for some distance beyond.

### Use "Landscape" Material for Slope Protection

Slope protection is both a landscaping job and a structural job. However, if concrete is used the structural aspects are emphasized and the slope protection appears to be part of the bridge, blurring the distinction between structure and ground and making the bridge appear larger and heavier. Slope protection should be performed by a landscaping material, such as riprap, placed so it looks like part of the landscape. Riprap has the advantage that natural plants will tend to colonize in it and blur the edge with the vegetation.

Use only enough slope protection to cover the area beneath the bridge where plants cannot grow. Drainage channels from the bridge should be accommodated with separate riprap channels or piping. Dark-colored stone is better for riprap, since it will attract less attention.

If concrete must be used, try to achieve a random pattern in the surface. Patterns pressed into newly placed concrete can give a good appearance at minimum cost and break up the flat surface of conventional concrete for paving. Colors should be different and darker than the structure colors.

FIGURE 5-58 *Slope paving carried to an extreme: these armored slopes seem part of the structure, adding two large visual masses which weigh down an otherwise graceful bridge.*

FIGURE 5-59 *Riprap allows plants to blur the edge of the slope paving and blend into the landscape; riprap does a better job of slope protection as well, replacing undermined concrete slabs in this example.*

## In More-Urban Areas Use Landscaping to Relieve and Contrast with the Hard-edged Elements in the Visual Field

The buildup of many different structural features in urban areas—bridges, retaining walls, and noise walls—often becomes overwhelming. Landscaping can give back some green to drivers and road users. As Figure 2-40 (page 56) shows, small auxiliary walls can be placed in front of major walls or abutments to create level planting areas.

In locations where a bridge adjoins a community or group of buildings, landscaping can be an indispensable element in mediating the differences in material and scale. Here, the goal is probably best served by intensifying planting patterns and species already existing in the community, in order to emphasize the continuity of the community environment.

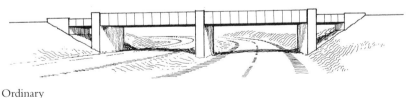

Ordinary

FIGURE 5-60 *Seen as a landscaping material, riprap slope paving maintains the continuity of the landscape through the structure.*

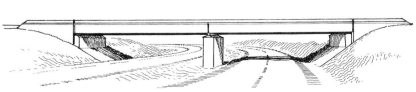

Better

*Pick Landscaping Colors and Shapes in Relation to Those of the Bridge*

Landscaping creates its own shape and colors. These must be related to the shapes and colors of the bridge. This means that the landscape architect should be part of the design team as the bridge concept is developed.

Even though highway landscaping generally works best and is most easily maintained when the materials and patterns replicate the existing natural vegetation in the immediate area, there will always be locations where contrasting plantings are desired in order to accentuate or emphasize a particular bridge location or structural form. These can be very legitimate, in the same way that it is legitimate to paint a bridge a contrasting color in a forest, as long as it is consistent with the design intention of the structure itself and the design theme of the highway involved.

1   Lambert, Patricia, 1991. *Controlling Color.* New York, NY: Design Press/McGraw–Hill, Inc.

2   op. cit.

3   The standard assortment of colored pencils and markers found in office or technical supply store won't do, either. They are too restricted as to shade and hue, and don't correctly represent the colors found in nature. Shop at an art supply store. Look for Berol Prismacolor pencils and markers and AD art markers or their equivalents.

4   Zuk, William, 1974. "Public Response to Bridge Colors," *Transportation Research Record.* Washington, DC: Transportation Research Board, vol. 507.

5   Porter, Tom and Mikellides, Bryon, 1976. *Color for Architecture.* New York, NY: Van Nostrand Reinhold.

6   Pantone, Color Matching Systems, Pantone®, Inc., 55 Knickerbocker Road, Moonachie, NJ.

chapter *six*

# PUTTING IT ALL TOGETHER: TYPICAL BRIDGES

*"The greatest glory in the art of building is to have a good sense of what is appropriate. For to build is a matter of necessity; to build conveniently is the product of both necessity and utility; but to build something praised by the munificent, yet not rejected by the frugal, is the province of an artist of experience, wisdom, and thoughtful deliberation."*

—LEON BATTISTA ALBERTI,
ON THE ART OF BUILDING, 1486

Chapters Four and Five developed a design language for the various bridge elements in the order of their importance as Determinants of Appearance. The components of the language are a series of guidelines for the design of the individual elements which will help to produce high quality appearance in bridges. Chapter Three discussed the process of bridge design, beginning with the development of a design intention for each bridge. This chapter shows how to put all of these ideas together, using typical bridge sites as examples.

Developing a design for an actual bridge site will follow a similar pattern to the typical sites discussed in this chapter, but an actual site will have specific features which may lead to a different result than the examples given here. The designer must be aware of these differences and follow where they lead. Mere imitation of the examples given here will not lead automatically to success, and may do just the opposite. After all, it is that exceptional match of need and solution which provides most satisfaction in life, in bridge design as in many other areas of endeavor.

FIGURE 6-1 *A well-designed highway overpass; it would be improved if the top of the pier did not interrupt the line of the girder's bottom flange.*

The discussion of each typical bridge type begins with the development of a design intention as described in Chapter Three, then the discussion illustrates the application of the Determinants of Appearance.

## HIGHWAY OVER HIGHWAY

This section focuses on the typical highway overcrossing of one to four spans, where both ends of the structure can be seen at one time. Longer structures are classified as ramps and viaducts and are discussed in Interchange Ramps and Viaducts, later in this chapter.

### Developing a Design Intention

#### Physical Requirements

The site requirements are largely determined by the geometry and horizontal and vertical clearance zones of the undercrossing roadways. Occasionally overlooked is the desirability of providing sight distance through the structure to objects that may lie beyond, such as a ramp nose or traffic signal.

Utilities associated with either the undercrossing or overcrossing are sometimes a consideration. Geotechnical considerations affecting potential foundations must also be understood.

The typical requirements will result in structures of from one to four spans with spans in the range of 50 to 200 feet.

#### Visual Environment

Overcrossings associated with freeways and major highways will typically be most affected by the environment created by the highway itself, its slopes, landscaping, retaining walls, and noise walls. In rural and suburban areas this environment is typically wide open with extensive horizontal vistas. The predominant influence will be the landscaping/cover of the ground surface and any retaining or noise wall in the scene. The structure will most often be seen against a background of sky.

In very mountainous areas and urban areas the mountainsides, walls, and any visible buildings will limit the vistas. Then the background will be heavily influenced by the materials of the mountainside and any vertical surfaces.

Highway bridges are most frequently seen from the undercrossing roadway. Because of the way people see things when moving at highway speeds, bridge crossings over freeways and high-speed arterials are seen best when they are still distant. The closest point at which such a bridge will "register" to a motorist is 300 to 500 feet. At any point closer, the motorist is focusing beyond the bridge, and the bridge itself is a blur in his peripheral vision. Because such overcrossings are seen by people who are moving along predictable paths, at predictable speeds, it is easier to predict what people will see at each point and to control what their perception will be.

Overcrossings of arterial streets are viewed from more varied locations. An understanding of the surrounding uses will indicate the important viewpoints. The designer should be aware of places where people congregate, such as the entrance of a nearby shopping center, or the stands of a nearby baseball diamond.

### Nearby and Associated Uses

Overcrossings associated with arterial streets are often close to existing or planned land uses, such as retail or residential areas, with associated buildings. The buildings become part of the backdrop for the structure. Their visual effect on the structure, and its effect on them, must be considered. Sometimes the structure will be considered an important feature in, say, a shopping district, and nearby building owners will want attention paid to its compatibility with existing buildings.

Often structures in this situation must provide for pedestrian use as well. The nature of this use, children going to and from school, for example, should be considered. In that example, clear visibility to all parts of the pedestrian walkway will be important.

### Symbolic Functions

Most highway overcrossings are subordinate parts of larger transportation facilities. Their symbolic role, to the extent that they have one, is to be seen as enabling a clear and safe passage. The message should be one of free and continuous movement.

Occasionally the position of a structure within a town or neighborhood may lead to a requirement that the structure be seen as a gateway or acknowledge nearby architectural styles.

### Boundaries

Since the whole structure can typically be seen at a glance, it is important to set boundaries that are logical and obvious. The structure and its abutments, including any attached retaining walls, should be seen as one unit out to the end of the parapets. Guardrails are seen as more site features than structural features, but their connection to the parapet will be apparent and should be done as a clear and simple transition.

### The Design Intention

At 300 to 500 feet the only parts clearly visible are the features of the elevation. This means that the following elevation features will determine the visual impression created by the bridge:

- the fascia of the superstructure;
- the parapet fascia;
- the end elevation of the pier;
- side walls of the abutments;
- the voids between these elements;
- the method of ending the parapet features.

Exceptions exist for bridges on a severe skew, very wide bridges, or bridges crossing a sharply curved or steeply sloped roadway. In these cases, portions of the abutment face or the pier may become important components of the visual field, unless they are in shadow. Sharply curved, highly superelevated bridges or bridges seen from the uphill direction of a steeply sloped roadway may expose their undersides to view. These situations need to be analyzed on a case-by-case basis, using perspective views taken from viewer locations on the undercrossing roadway. If pedestrians use the undercrossing street, the appearance of the underside will be important.

Most highway overcrossings are relatively short and are easily encompassed at one glance. Usually they are experienced as relatively minor elements along a much longer path. The view through them to the path beyond is almost always critical. It is important that they be kept simple, with all parts in clear relationship to one another.

When designing a highway-over-a-highway crossing, keep things simple; open up views through the structure and give the bridge an overall appearance of unity.

- *Develop apparent thinness in structural members.*
- *Provide generous vista through the structure.*
- *Choose shapes from the same family. Faceted piers should be used with faceted parapet design; rounded pier designs with rounded parapets.*
- *Use a minimum number of different materials, different colors, and different textures.*
- *Always use a given material, color, or texture the same way.*

Highway overcrossings often come in groups, for example, all of the bridges on a section of freeway, or all of the bridges in an interchange. Since multiple bridges will be seen in quick succession, it is necessary to consider their relation to each other, so that the result is not a visual hodgepodge. (See the discussion of Design Themes in Chapter Three.)

## Determinants of Appearance

### Geometry

The geometry of a highway overcrossing is largely determined by the needs of the intersecting roadways. However, there may be room for adjustments, and these should be investigated.

The structure will generally look better if it is on a vertical crest curve. This can often be accomplished without lengthening the structure, but may require slightly higher piers. However, sag vertical curves and horizontal

**FIGURE 6-2** *The crest curve creates a slight arch which most people find attractive; it also appears to open up the view through the bridge.*

**FIGURE 6-3** *The thin girder permitted by this abutment-restrained design in Tennessee minimizes the apparent weight of the structure.*

**FIGURE 6-4** *The parallel edges and relative depth of this girder make this a heavier and less open-looking bridge than the bridge in Figure 6-3.*

curves can be acceptable if they are long enough. Make sure any alignment curves are at least half as long as the structure. Otherwise, the structure will look like it has a kink in it, creating a visual problem which cannot be resolved by later decisions.

### Superstructure Type

Since the elevation view is very important in the appearance of this type of structure, the proportion and relative slenderness of the girder will have a major effect in forming people's impression of the structure. Relative slenderness should be sought when picking superstructure type. Haunched girders can create an impression of slenderness and also tell a story about how the structure works, adding an element of interest.

Steel and concrete rigid frames were popular for highway overcrossings in the early days of freeway building, when span lengths were generally shorter. They looked good because the proportion of leg to span was in balance. In recent years, however, longer spans have thrown the balance off and, in most current structures, it is hard to give the legs a visually convincing length. However, structures with delta-frame center supports and slanted legs are possible and can provide a structure with greater-than-usual memorability. Figure 4-14 (page 98) shows that delta frames can work for highway overcrossings.

Arch structures are rarely used for highway overcrossings because the spans are too short for an arch to be economical and the vertical clearance is usually not sufficient to offer a reasonable span-to-rise ratio.

## Pier Placement and Abutment Placement

Since these bridges will be seen all at once, and since the placement of the abutment strongly influences the placement of the piers and vice-versa, it is best to consider pier and abutment placement at the same time.

The pattern of the undercrossing roadways sets the possibilities for pier placement. The most common situations are:

1. No pier at all (one-span structure).
2. The median of an undercrossing dual roadway (two-span structure).
3. Both outer edges of the undercrossing roadway (three-span structure).
4. The median of an undercrossing dual roadway and both outer edges of the undercrossing roadways (four-span structure).

All of these solutions establish a basic symmetry for the structure which must be respected in all further decisions. (The symmetry will be weakened if the structure is highly skewed, on a continuous vertical grade, or if the dual roadways are of substantially different widths.) Each solution also has implications for the apparent openness of the structure.

The views through the structure must be considered. Ramp splits, weaving and merging areas, and traffic control devices are important to safety and should not be blocked from view. A scenic focal point (a distant building or mountain, for example; see Figure 5-37, page 157), represents a rare opportunity to create an event on the journey, which should be recognized wherever possible.

With both ends of the bridge in view at the same time and with so few other elements in the structure, the placement and resulting proportions of

FIGURE 6-5 *Two of the possibilities for pier placement, showing the basic symmetry that results.*

FIGURE 6-6 *The right abutment is much larger than the left, worsening the effect of the vertical grade and giving the bridge an unbalanced appearance.*

the abutments will be critical to the visual impression. The key guidelines were given in Chapter Four. The most important is to relate abutment height to clearance at the roadway edge and to girder depth.

Skewed bridges have characteristics of their own which require special consideration. Two guidelines which ease the problem are to select superstructure types that allow large overhangs and narrow piers (Figure 6-7), and to move abutments to the tops of embankments and place at right angles to the overcrossing roadway. (Figure 4-61, page 131).

### Superstructure Shape, Parapets, and Railings

Highway overcrossings have so few elements that the fascia girder and parapet become major factors in forming the visual impression. Small differences in proportion and detail can be critical, so it is important to design the parapet–girder combination together. The goal is to emphasize apparent thinness and horizontally to fit in with the dominant horizontal dimension of the

**FIGURE 6-8** *The parapet overhang creates a horizontal shadow line which reduces the apparent thickness of the parapet girder combination, while the exposed beam seat allows the structure to appear longer as well as thinner.*

**FIGURE 6-9** *The smooth transition in girder depth help this bridge appear longer, thinner, and unified.*

FIGURE 6-10 *The series of Wisconsin overpasses in Figures 6-10, 6-11, and 6-12, shows how a haunch gives an otherwise ordinary overpass some visual distinction, opens up the view, and improves safety by eliminating the shoulder piers. The initial type was this four-span structure.*

FIGURE 6-11 *Perhaps in an effort to deal with a slightly longer span this haunch was added. However, the haunch seems too small and provides little visual benefit.*

FIGURE 6-12 *Then the realization came that the haunch provided the possibility of eliminating the shoulder piers, which greatly improved the safety and appearance of the structure at little or no additional cost.*

FIGURE 6-13 *This structure from Colorado shows that haunches can be done with precast concrete as well. The piers are unfortunately heavy for this graceful superstructure.*

typical highway environment. Application of the guidelines from Chapter Four will result in a girder-parapet combination with a pronounced horizontality and a thin appearance.

Since highway overcrossings are seen at one glance, any abrupt changes in girder depth will be jarringly obvious. Constant or smoothly varying depth will make the structure more unified. It will also make the structure appear to be longer, and therefore thinner. Structural continuity is a big help here, since it keeps everything visually continuous as well.

FIGURE 6-14 *This frame's legs are too short.*

Haunched girders express the forces in the structure, and will provide an important point of interest which reinforces the basic symmetry of the structure. Haunches may allow for shorter approaches if the structural depth is reduced at the clearance point. If a haunch is not feasible, the structure will depend primarily on the proportions of the girder, particularly its relative thinness, as compared to the other features of the structure for its interest.

Shaping rigid frames and delta frames is difficult at the relatively low heights of most highway overcrossings and requires exploration. Much depends on the relative lengths, vertical clearance, and shape of the side slopes. Written guidelines can be misleading. Better to make sketches of multiple shapes, as seen from the important viewpoints. Then pick the one that seems most graceful.

### Pier Shape

The basic goal of design for highway overcrossings is an appearance of a clear and safe passage through the structure with a clear view to what lies beyond. The pier should not distract or detract from these goals, but should do its job of support as simply as possible. The most likely distraction is the end elevation of the pier cap. Chapter Five provides guidelines for pier designs.

Since these bridges have so few visual elements the proportions of each to the other takes on great importance. The goal here is a balance between the apparent mass of the superstructure and the size of the pier. Piers that are too thin will look spindly and piers that are too thick will look squat.

The side view of the far-side pier of a skewed structure (and a long-span multispan structure) is more visible than the side of the center pier of a two-span bridge. Thus pier design becomes more important on skewed bridges.

FIGURE 6-15 *The pier cap, and particularly its end elevation, adds a complication and a distraction; this pier would have been improved if the first column had been moved out slightly and the sloped face extended up to the girder, thereby eliminating the pier cap end.*

FIGURE 6-16 *The skew makes this pier more visible than the usual highway overcrossing pier.*

### Abutment Shape

Because the abutment and parapet are such major elements, and because both ends of the bridge can usually be seen at once, the decision about how to shape the abutment has a major impact on the appearance of highway overcrossings. Figure 5-37 (page 157) is a good example. The slope of the abutment face can be a major influence on the appearance of the structure. Bearings are a major structural element, and if left exposed will make the structure look longer and thinner. The end of the parapet profile and pedestrian screen at the abutment are also important considerations. The guidelines in Chapter Five should be followed.

### Color

The opportunities for making an impact with color on highway overcrossings depend on the features seen in elevation: the fascia girder, parapet face, railings, pedestrian screen, abutment faces, and end elevations of any piers. Because highway overcrossings are somewhat self-contained a bold color or pattern can make a major impact, producing a more memorable structure than the size of the structure would normally allow. Because highway overcrossings are often seen in quick succession in groups, designers can use color, pattern, and/or texture to provide a theme that ties the group together.

With conventional steel girders, the necessity of painting the girder makes a color choice necessary and offers a "free" opportunity to add interest. With A588 steel and concrete surfaces, the application of color can be avoided, but the combination of light gray and dark brown may not suit the surroundings, the desires of the community, or the designer's intention.

The application of carefully placed areas of color on the major surfaces is a good way to add interest even if most of the surfaces are uncoated or as a complement to coated surfaces. A "racing stripe," inset in the parapet and coated, is one frequently used technique. The bright-red stripe on the bridge in Figure 5-38 (page 159) makes it a memorable event, while reducing the apparent depth of the parapet. Insetting materials such as glazed tile are other possibilities. The use of color on a railing or pedestrian screen is a good way to add interest and make these elements something more than utilitarian extras.

By dividing a girder horizontally into several areas of different but compatible colors, the girder can be made to seem thinner. This works best when a horizontal stiffner is present to provide a logical division line (Figure 6-52, page 231).

Because the entire bridge is seen at a glance, it is important that all color decisions are considered at the same time and coordinated. Figure 1-25 (page 25) shows a pedestrian screen of one color on a bridge painted with a different color scheme. The orange of the screen is the complementary color of the blue of the girder. Complementary colors will always draw attention and create visual tension. That is acceptable if anticipated and desired, but is difficult to make work within a single structure. A near-complementary color (red or yellow) for the pedestrian screen might have worked better.

### Surface Texture and Ornamentation

When the undercrossing roadway is a high-speed roadway, the effectiveness of patterns is limited unless the units are large. Any detail less than 4 inches in size will be missed. The faces of the parapet and the higher abutments offer opportunities to add interest through the addition of patterns. These can be abstract or representational and can be repetitive or singular. Chapter Five illustrates several examples.

Any pattern must be kept within, and consistent with, the geometry of the structural feature of which it is a part. If a pattern bears no relation to structural features it will divide the structure into visually separate but physically connected objects. Because highway overcrossings are seen at one glance the dichotomy will be noticed and seem jarring (Figure 5-46, page 168).

Traditional masonry materials are often considered for abutment faces and piers either to recall nearby historic buildings or to establish consistency with associated natural features. These can be satisfying features as long as they

FIGURE 6-17 *The pattern on the abutment makes it seem an independent element, not a part of the design of the whole structure.*

are used in ways consistent with their inherent structural capacities and historical uses. That means restricting their use to pier or wall facings. Using such materials as a girder facing puts heavy masonry in the air with no visible means of support. People don't understand how it can work and become uncomfortable.

For structures over high-speed roadways, larger masonry units are necessary to maintain some sense of texture and differentiation (see Figure 3-13, page 78). Smaller units blur into a single surface color.

Structures over streets and arterial roadways offer more scope for smaller-scaled textures and materials. If pedestrians are present, the use of interesting materials at fingertip range will enrich and enhance their experience and will be appreciated.

### Signing, Lighting, and Landscaping

Highway overcrossings are often called on to serve double duty as sign bridges. The visual result is almost always unfortunate for all the reasons outlined in Chapter Five. It is particularly a problem for highway overcrossings because these bridges can be seen at a glance and the presence of the sign is immediately obvious. Also, the sign covers a large portion of the total structure, and is usually placed without regard to the basic symmetry of the bridge or the size of the sign relative to structural features.

The best solution is to find another location for the sign—on an elegant sign structure separate from the highway overcrossing, for example. Rarely are the rules for sign placement so inelastic that the highway overcrossing offers

**FIGURE 6-18** *There are many other options for the location of this sign away from the structure.*

the only possible location. Even 300 feet upstream is enough of a separation to provide an effective view of the bridge.

The second-best solution is to design the sign panel to fit the features of the bridge as described in Chapter Five. The effort is particularly worthwhile for highway overcrossings.

If a sign will be present, it will have a large influence the view of the structure, and should be considered in any color choices that are made.

Lighting can also have a major effect on the appearance of a highway overcrossing. Typical highway lighting poles are twice as high as typical overcrossings and represent sizeable physical features when compared with the bridge itself. If placed without a clear relationship to the structural features of the bridge, they can seem very much out of place. The rules outlined in Chapter Five are particularly important.

Because highway overcrossings are relatively short, it usually should be possible to adjust the spacing of fixtures for an overcrossing roadway so that a pole location coincides with a central pier location. Other poles will then have a symmetrical relationship consistent with the basic symmetry of the bridge.

When the overcrossing roadway is a street with pedestrian sidewalks, there is sometimes a desire to provide more numerous fixtures at a lower height, often with ornamental features. It is even more important that these be lined up with basic structural features, because they will establish a dominant visual spacing which will make anything not in alignment with them seem out of place. Such fixtures can indeed establish a memorable appearance for the structure both day and night.

The lighting of the undercrossing roadway is generally not a concern in most highway situations unless the overcrossing roadway is very wide. However, if pedestrians are present, the lighting of the undercrossing roadway is very important. The basic rule is to arrange the fixtures in some consistent relationship to the major structural features, such as one fixture for every third girder. Lighting the surfaces of the structure, such as an abutment wall or the underside of a box girder, can make the area seem more attractive and secure than lighting the sidewalk only.

If the structure is serving as a gateway, it may be useful to light the structure itself. One approach is to light the elevation surfaces: the fascia girder, parapet, and abutment faces. Another is to light the underside of the superstructure and the abutment walls. That produces an arch of light and can give a very effective welcome. It is wasteful to do both together.

Landscaping can significantly enhance the appearance of highway overcrossings. The overcrossings are typically part of largely man-made environments that will be replanted, in any case. The structure is not so large as to overwhelm any landscaping that may be attempted. Since the structure can be seen all at once, the role of landscaping in the overall scene can be understood and appreciated.

Planting can be seen as a technique to "stretch" the structure and make it appear longer, and therefore thinner. Planting can also be used on the undercrossing roadway to lead the driver's eye through the structure and to emphasis the continuity of the scene (see Figures 2-40, page 56, and 5-60, page 180).

However, if a structure will be in a naturalized environment, it is very likely that the nearby plant material will grow to hide the abutment and/or piers. If that is a likely situation, then effort spent on enhancing the appearance of these features is wasted. Simplicity should be the goal.

## VALLEYS AND HIGHWAY CUTS

This section focuses on sites where the height of the structure is large relative to its length, a situation that frequently occurs in ravines, valleys, and highway cuts.

## Developing a Design Intention

### Physical Requirements

By definition, sites for this type of structure are physically demanding: high vertical clearances, steep and/or long slopes, often with environmentally sensitive features, and waterways. Determining site requirements involves complete review of the available environmental and geotechnical reports and

**FIGURE 6-19** *Haunches reflect the concentration of force and add interest to this Ontario girder bridge.*

interviews with representatives of other agencies with interests in the area. Avoidance of roadways, wetlands, and waterways may restrict pier location. Utilities may be a concern both as to pier location and as a requirement that the structure carry one or more utilities. There may be restrictions on the disposition of drainage from the structure which will affect the design.

### Visual Environment

The visual environment will be dominated by the nature of the slopes adjoining the structure. If they are natural they should be viewed and photographed. Tree cover, the extent and nature of rock outcroppings, and the steepness and shape of the slopes will all have a bearing on later decisions. There is no substitute for a personal investigation of the area.

If the slopes will be created by a highway project, their nature can be determined from the highway plans and replanting practices. For example, it may be possible to influence the slope design to create a shelf that would become the logical point for the placement of an arch abutment. A personal visit is still necessary to become familiar with the larger area and to determine from what areas and viewpoints the new bridge will be visible.

### Nearby and Associated Uses

The bridge itself will be insulated to some degree from immediately nearby uses by the adjoining slopes. However, because of its size, it will have a dominating effect on any nearby use area from which it is visible. A frequent situation is a bridge over a natural area, such as a park. The park users will see the bridge as a dominant landmark and it will influence all future enjoyment of the park. A high bridge near a town will become a dominant landmark for the town.

High bridges over highways, because of their position and size, will be a memorable event, a milepost by which people will measure their journeys.

*Symbolic Functions*

Because of their size and prominence, these bridges will often assume symbolic functions which should be anticipated. A high bridge crossing a highway near a town will be seen as the gateway to that town. A high bridge which is visible from the center of a town can become, for better or worse, the defining landmark for that town. A bridge over an important natural area will become a symbol of respect for that area if sensitively done or, if not, a symbol of carelessness.

*Boundaries*

The slopes that define these bridges set the boundaries. The size of the bridge usually dwarfs any associated highway elements, so the bridges can be effectively considered on their own.

*The Design Intention*

The first consideration is the position of likely observers. In the event the bridge is also spanning a roadway, particularly a bridge spanning a major highway cut, many of the observers will be in cars on the underroadway. However, the extended length and much greater height make this a much different situation than the ordinary highway overcrossing.

For this type of bridge there will be a number of important observer locations, some of which may be a mile or more away. While the designer can't cover them all, he or she at least should be aware of the most important, and should consider these viewpoints when decisions are made. When photos, drawings, and sketches are made, they should be taken from at least two or three of the most important viewpoints.

If the area under the bridge is used by pedestrians, or if the underside is exposed to motorists below the appearance of the underside will be important also. From any viewpoint, the major structural features of the bridge are likely to determine the visual impression.

When designing a bridge over a valley or highway cut, pay attention to the overall shape and color of the major structural members compared to their surroundings.

The key decisions will be:

- the shape of the basic horizontal and vertical geometry;
- superstructure type and shape;
- pier placement or, to look at it another way, the number and shape of the openings;
- shape of piers.

On bridges over valleys or ravines, the depth of the superstructure is generally not as critical, since the overall length is so great. Also, details of shaping the parapet and abutments will not be as critical, because these elements are a relatively smaller portion of the total bridge. However, general rules of simplicity and continuity of materials still apply.

## Determinants of Appearance

### Geometry

The bridge will look best from surrounding areas if it is straight or composed of a few long, continuous curves. Any consideration of geometry also needs to take into account the driver's view from the overcrossing roadway. This will also generally be best if the curves are long, continuous, and generous. In particular, placing two short vertical curves on either end of a bridge, with a tangent on the bridge in between, will produce a very uncomfortable view for the driver. This is usually done to avoid a sag vertical curve on the bridge. Sag vertical curves on bridges are a better choice and are visually acceptable if they are long enough.

FIGURE 6-20 *Long continuous curves create an attractive geometry.*

The creation of a drainage sump on a bridge is undesirable for maintenance reasons. Careful coordination with the highway designer will usually make it possible to move the actual low point off the bridge even though the balance of the curve extends well onto or across the structure.

The longer structures of this type may contain superelevation transitions, which should be checked for their visual effect on appearance of the parapet.

### Superstructure Type

Valleys and highway cuts present most of the opportunities for an arch or major rigid frame. The surroundings "contain" the visual thrust of the arch and frame legs, and there is enough vertical height to allow frame legs of a reasonable length. The choice of structural type should depend first on the structural economics of the required bridge. However, arch and frame forms offer a visual dynamism which may weigh in the balance at particularly prominent or important locations (Figure 3-16, page 83).

Girders are also a frequent solution to this type of bridge. Pier placement and girder shape then become the key elements in determining the visual impact.

The appearance of the underside may be important if the bridge is seen from below. The usual confusion of wind bracing and diaphragm bracing required by I-girders is a potential distraction because of the number of members, the number of different angles at which they are installed, and the visual competition they offer to the main lines of the structure (not to mention the additional roosts offered to birds).

FIGURE 6-21 *View of girder bracing and suspended utilities from below.*

Concrete or steel box structures, where the underside is completely enclosed, solve this problem, particularly if the steel is painted a light reflective color. Girder-type bridges can be satisfactory as long as the details of diaphragms and wind bracing are kept simple and consistent along the bridge and, if steel, they are painted a light color.

The choice between steel and concrete superstructure is a visual issue because the structural members are so important in creating the visual impression of this type of bridge. The color the bridge will have, as seen against its background, should be considered. Ordinary steel can be painted to suit the situation. If exposed, A588 steel is desired, the dark brown color will strongly affect the impact the bridge makes. The same is true for the light gray color of concrete. The effect that these colors will have in forming the impression of the bridge from the major viewpoints should be considered.

The shape of the valley may require large variations in span lengths and even changes to a different superstructure type. It is important to maintain continuity of structural form, material, and/or depth.

### Pier Placement

For all valley and highway cut bridges, developing pier and footing placement requires consideration of the overall shape of the valley or cut, of the clearance requirements of obstacles, and of the height of the bridge. Diagonal views from underside uses and nearby communities are usually important, and several piers are often visible from a given location. In order to prevent the view from degenerating into a wall or a forest of columns, the characteristics of groups of piers need to be considered. The guidelines in Chapter Four apply.

### Abutment Placement

Abutment location is generally determined by the shape of the side slopes. In this type of bridge the abutments are a small proportion of the total structure and have relatively little influence on the overall appearance. Best to keep them small (abutment height = adjoining girder depth, more or less) and simple.

### Superstructure Shape, Parapets, and Railings

The choices made about the superstructure shape will also have a dominant effect on the final impression made by the structure. Arch and rigid frame structures should be careful shaped using the guidelines in Chapter Four.

With girder bridges the spans will often vary in length over the bridge. It will often be necessary to change girder depth, provide haunches, or do both in a single bridge. It is important to keep structural depth constant or smoothly varied over the entire bridge.

Bracing details are often very visible for this type of structure, and have a much larger impact on the final appearance of the structure than can be predicted from elevation or section drawings.

Parapet details are less critical to the view from adjoining areas for this type of bridge, because parapets are such a small proportion of the total structure.

*FIGURE 6-22 By using long spans with a single column at each pier line, this Tennessee structure keeps diagonal views through the structure open.*

FIGURE 6-23 *The details of this Kentucky structure do a good job of indicating how the superstructure responds to the forces on it.*

FIGURE 6-24 *The effect of bracing on appearance is not always evident from an elevation drawing.*

### Pier Shape

Because of their size and the multiple locations from which they will be viewed, the piers will be major elements in forming the impression of the bridge. Since the piers will more than likely vary in height over the bridge length, the key is to come up with a family of pier shapes which relate well to each other when viewed as a group. The goal is to portray a smooth flow of forces along the girders and from the girders into the piers and to the valley floor. The guidelines for tall piers in Section 4.6 will generally apply.

The pier cap is a prominent element in the oblique view, and it will interrupt the visual lines of the structure unless it is minimized. Because of the length of the bridge this effect will be repetitive and obvious. This is particularly true if the end of the cap is near or at the same plane as the face of the parapet. Figure 6-20 (page 198) is a clear example of the potential prob-

FIGURE 6-25 *A simple but effective solution to a family of tall piers. A large deck overhang pays visual dividends here because it keeps the piers narrow and the girder in shadow.*

lem. Figure 6-25 shows a design which eliminates the pier cap end and maintains the flow of the girder line. The bridge in Figure 6-22 (page 200) does almost as well by rounding the end of the pier cap. See Chapter Five for other ideas for minimizing the pier cap end.

### Abutment Shape

Because of the small part they play in the appearance of these structures their abutments should be kept as simple as possible.

### Color

Color is the final important element in the success of these bridges. Structures across dramatic valleys deserve colors which are as bold as the structures themselves. The goal should be to contrast with the backgrounds with colors that enhance the background hues. A bright red-orange against a forested hillside is a classic combination. Figure 5-40 (page 163) shows an example of good color contrast. Sienna red against a brown western mountainside is another satisfying solution. By overlaying CAD-generated drawings, on color photos, many choices can be tested before a commitment is made to paint.

Bridges of concrete and A588 steel must live with the color of the structural material. Opportunities may exist to influence the impression made by that color by adding strongly colored smaller elements to the parapet face or girder, such as a painted stripe in the parapet face, or to add color to a railing or light posts.

Bridges in park lands or near other uses must take into account the nature of those uses and compatibility with them. It may not be as desirable to have a bold color on a bridge which is predominantly seen as part of the tree canopy or which is visible from the town square. In those cases, colors more compatible with the other colors seen from those viewpoints may be in order.

### Surface Texture and Ornamentation

Traditional brick and stone are generally not convincing when used as components of these bridges. These bridges are generally so much larger than the historic masonry structures which people are used to that the use of the materials is not credible.

If a masonry material is absolutely necessary, large block ashlar stone is the one material with some visual and historic credibility. Natural stone is generally not economical, but it can be simulated with high-quality form liners.

The details of the girders offer possibilities to add interest in ways that are consistent with the structure. The arrangement of stiffeners on steel structures can be ornamental as well as structural. The details of bearing seats and pier connections can also be shaped to provide interest and make a positive contribution to the overall structure. These details can be further accentuated by the use of paint or inset materials of contrasting colors.

### Signing, Lighting, and Landscaping

Sign structures are sometimes attached to the bridge for the benefit of the upper roadway. Such structures can be a distraction for these bridges. Better not to have them, but if they are absolutely necessary, it is important to smoothly integrate the connection of the support structure into the overall structure. The sign structure should seem like part of the original concept, not a bolted-on afterthought.

The presence of roadway lighting poles will provide a chain of light spots across the bridge which will heavily influence the appearance of the bridge at night. Lighting poles should be spaced in some easily understood relationship to the main structural members—for example, at a spacing which is a constant fraction of the pier spacing. If the bridge is or appears to be symmetrical, the light poles should be symmetrically placed. Their supports should be smoothly integrated into the parapet/railing design.

Landscaping will be dominated by the natural conditions of the adjoining slopes, and is generally not a major consideration for this type of bridge. Any planting should be aimed at restoring natural conditions to areas disturbed by construction.

**FIGURE 6-26** *With very simple elements this Tennessee structure conveys strength, continuity, and horizontality.*

## RIVERS AND TIDAL WATERWAYS

This section is aimed at bridges crossing larger water bodies. Small waterway crossings have much in common with highway overcrossings, which have already been discussed. While there obviously is a continuum of waterway sizes, this section focuses on sites where the water surface is a dominant feature in the visual scene.

## Developing a Design Intention

### Physical Requirements

The width, depth, navigational requirements, and bottom conditions of the waterway will be the overriding site conditions for this type of structure. The presence of a navigational channel will probably be the major consideration when setting the height and span of the largest span. The nature of the foundations required and their cost will largely determine the economical span range for the structure. Submerged utility lines may be a concern, and there may be a need to carry utility lines on the structure. Frequently there are railroads or roadways on the shore which must also be spanned. Roadways often intersect with the bridge at or near the shoreline, creating a need to gracefully widen the structure to accommodate intersecting ramps and streets.

These bridges typically have one or a few main spans. Bridges across wide waterways will have a series of repetitive approach spans which can be a much larger portion of the total bridge than the main spans.

*Visual Environment*

The visual environment is first established by the width of the waterway. Very wide waterways (wider than one mile) will themselves be the dominant aspect of the visual environment. For narrower waterways the nature of the shoreline will be more important in setting the visual environment. The range of shoreline uses can be very broad, including industrial, commercial, residential, developed park, or natural. At any given site one or two uses usually dominate. An example would be industrial uses on one side and a park on the other. The visual effect of the uses should be confirmed in the field with photographs. An industrial use may in fact be screened from view by riverbank vegetation, such that the actual visual environment is quite natural. The resulting information should be used to key decisions related to the visual environment.

*Nearby and Associated Uses*

Public shoreline open space, such as a riverfront park, fishing pier, or festival marketplace, will be very important in determining viewpoints and the nature of the design. Commercial or residential uses offering a number of potential overlooks will also be important considerations. Industrial uses offering no public access will require less consideration.

The placement of the structure within the overall fabric of the area will also be important. If it is at, near, or visible from a town center or other important location, then it will become a landmark of importance to the entire region.

These bridges are often called on to provide pedestrian and bicycle access, and access for fishing, all of which need to be anticipated from the beginning.

*Symbolic Functions*

If the bridge is at or visible from a town or neighborhood center, it will become both a landmark and the entrance gateway to the town or neighborhood. If done well, it may become the signature landmark for the town.

*Boundaries*

Sometimes these bridges end conveniently at the shoreline. More often the boundaries are not so clear. The project may extend across adjoining rail lines, roadways, and riverbank areas. A riverfront walk may adjoin the structure and require consideration as to detail and connection. There may be a desire, for example, to carry the same ornamental lighting on the bridge as is used on the river walk.

Anything that can be seen at one time from the important viewpoints should be considered part of the structure for design purposes. The goal should be to develop a consistent concept that carries across the entire length of the project.

### The Design Intention

The most important views of bridges over rivers and tidal waterways are usually oblique views from points along the shore. Particular locations can be identified which are likely to be the most-favored viewing points. For example, there are often areas along the shore dedicated to public docks or parks, where people are likely to congregate. A shoreline condominium development will have many observers on balconies. In the event there is a curve in the roadway approaching the bridge, drivers may also get a view of the bridge prior to crossing it. On waterways with a significant amount of recreational boat traffic, the view from the water should also be considered.

The point of contact with the shore can also be an important feature in forming the visual impression, particularly if there is pedestrian use or a shoreside roadway at that point.

Photographs should be taken from the most important viewpoints and used as the base for future sketches and renderings.

At the most likely oblique viewpoints, the following major features of the bridge are likely to determine the visual impression.

- The shape of the basic horizontal and vertical geometry.
- Structural type or types, and the transitions between different types or shapes.
- Pier shape, particularly as seen at an oblique angle with piers lining up one behind the other.
- Parapet and railing design.

Superstructure depth, exact pier and abutment placement, and abutment shape are generally of less concern for these structures.

Bridges of this type can be quite long and are usually seen in their entirety from the most important viewpoints. It is the whole of the bridge that will make the visual impression.

### When Designing a Bridge Across a River or Tidal Waterway, Aim for a Display of the Basic Geometry as a Sweep of Roadway "Ribbon"—One Unified Form

The goals at the shoreline should be focussed on the uses at that point. Pedestrian or park uses under the bridge, for example, may suggest a concern for the appearance of the underside. The need for access to a pedestrian walkway may impose a need for gradual slopes for a ramp or stairway.

## Determinants of Appearance

### Geometry

The topography near a river crossing is usually obvious. People can understand it easily by the shape of the waterline and the profile of the adjoining bluffs. People will judge the appearance of these bridges by how logically they fit the topography—in particular, whether they are aligned along the shortest apparent distance between shores.

Because these bridges can be quite long, and the whole bridge will be visible from many viewpoints, the horizontal and vertical geometry will be critical in forming its visual impression. The visual effect should be considered from the beginning in establishing the alignment. The goal is to construct both vertical and horizontal alignments from long continuous curves. The overall appearance should be one continuously flowing line.

Because of their length these bridges may well have horizontal curves. It is important to analyze the effect superelevation transitions have on parapet alignment.

### Superstructure Type

This type of structure often requires several different span lengths to address varying requirements at different points along the structure. The result

FIGURE 6-27 Both horizontal and vertical curves are present, but they blend into an uninterrupted flowing line.

FIGURE 6-28 *This South Carolina structure smoothly accommodates the different main span by simply deepening the same trapezoidal box used for the approach spans; the structure is so long that the piers still line up into a wall at this oblique angle, even with long spans and a simple pier design. A paired-column pier design similar to the one shown in Figure 6-25 (page 202) might have kept the structure more transparent.*

is often different superstructure types, sizes, or shapes at different points in the structure. It is not always easy to make a clear and simple transition between them, but doing so is critical to the visual success of the structure. The bridge should be a single unified concept; changes in structural type or depth to accommodate differing span conditions should be made smoothly; similar structural shapes, materials, and/or colors should be used to tie the structure together.

### Pier Placement

In the oblique views in which these bridges are usually seen, the piers will appear to line up behind each other. The number of piers becomes a significant visual parameter. The fewer piers, the less wall-like the bridge will appear when seen in the oblique view.

Determining the number of piers and pier spacing is typically seen as primarily an economic issue. Decisions are often made by considering superstructure and pier costs separately, considering each based on rules of thumb and experience from other bridges. This will produce misleading results. Superstructure costs and foundation costs should be considered together when developing optimum span lengths, as described in Chapter Four. Spans at the long end of the minimum range should be picked. The bridge in Figure 6-26 (page 204) has a graceful combination of river spans, but the land spans seem too short.

For arch and rigid-frame bridges the placement of the springing point should be on shore near the shoreline to give the structure a strong visual end point. See Chapter Four for additional guidelines.

### Abutment Placement

The shoreline is the obvious place for the abutments, which can be fine as long as they are not too high. More likely the presence of floodplain or shoreline land uses will require that the abutment be placed some distance from the shore. Then the placement will be a matter of accommodating those uses.

If there are no shoreside uses, the final consideration will be the desirable height and lengths of approach fills. In that case the structure will look best if the abutment has some clear relationship to topographic features. For example, locating the abutments at riverside bluffs usually makes sense economically and will be visually logical.

### Superstructure Shape

Accommodating the various spans required is the main design challenge of this type of structure. If all the spans can be accommodated with girders, the matter can be simplified. The structural depth can be kept constant or smoothly varied over the entire bridge. The tapered sidespans of the bridge in Figure 6-26 (page 204) gracefully accommodate the change in depth from main span to approach spans.

Haunched girders offer a visually logical way to accommodate longer spans while still keeping uniformity of depth with adjoining spans. The haunches visually punctuate the sweep of the bridge and draw attention to the longest span.

**FIGURE 6-29** *This Minnesota bridge allows for shoreline uses.*

**FIGURE 6-30** *The wide overhangs of Oregon's Alsea Bay Bridge create a shadow line which ties this structure together.*

**FIGURE 6-31** *These visually complex piers seem to hold down and break the smooth sweep of the girder.*

**FIGURE 6-32** *These piers in California appear as extensions of the curves of the girder.*

Deck overhangs are important for both the superstructure and the substructure. The deck overhang should be continuous throughout the structure as a way of emphasizing the visual continuity of the bridge. The shadow accentuates the continuity of the superstructure, and the overhang permits narrower, therefore less obtrusive, piers with fewer columns.

Parapet faces and railings will be important in establishing the visual impression of this type of structure. The parapet and any railings should be used to reinforce the horizontal continuity of the superstructure. Since small details will not register on bridges of this size the design should use large offsets, insets, or repetitive patterns which emphasize horizontal continuity. The simple railing design on the bridge in Figure 5-39 (page 162) emphasizes the horizontality of the structure.

### Pier Shape

In the oblique views in which these bridges are usually seen the piers will appear to line up behind each other. The more elements in each pier (columns, pier cap, etc.), and the more angles at which they are placed, the more confused the whole effect will be. If possible, use no more than two columns/piers at each pier line. If more columns are necessary for unusually wide structures, they should be paired.

When haunched girders are used at main channel spans, the main span piers will have a different shape than the flanking piers. Arch, truss, and rigid-frame structures may also require special pier shapes. Pier heights in these bridges sometimes vary dramatically as the bridge rises to meet marine clearance requirements. Since most or all of the piers are visible at once in the oblique view, it is important that these be a continuity of form and shape (Figure 5-22, page 143).

Just as for the bridges discussed in the previous section, the pier cap will be a prominent element in the oblique view, and will interrupt the visual lines of the structure unless it is minimized. The bridge in Figure 6-26 (page 204) deals with the problem by making the horizontal dimension of the pier cap end seem larger than the vertical dimension. See Chapter Five for ideas for minimizing the pier cap end.

A clear demarcation between superstructure and substructure at the bearings will help the structure seem to stand free and emphasize its horizontal continuity. Bearings and pier tops can be detailed to provide a visual demarcation as outlined in Chapters Four and Five. (*See* Figure 5-24, page 144.)

In marine construction, individually driven precast concrete cylindrical piles with precast caps have become very economical. The challenge is to find a way to meet the structure's visual goals with this economical technology. One concern is the number and batter of the piles. It is important to avoid mixing battered columns and vertical columns to avoid a confusion of angles with some columns leaning and some not.

### Abutment Shape

With this type of structure, the abutments should be shaped to respond to their immediate surroundings. If there are pedestrian uses, the abutment may be an important point of access to walkways on the bridge. Or, it may

FIGURE 6-33 *These piers, from the bridge in Figure 6-26 (page 204), develop the sense of strength appropriate to the long river spans they support; the same piers under the much shorter land spans, however, seem heavy.*

FIGURE 6-34 *The abutment and side spans on the Christopher Columbus Bridge, in Columbus, Ohio incorporates provisions for a riverwalk.*

be necessary to relate the design of an abutment into the design of a nearby river walk or the architecture of a nearby building.

If there are no nearby associated uses the abutment can be kept simple. Because of its relative size compared to the structure as a whole, it will have little effect on the appearance of the bridge.

### Color

Color should be used to reinforce the horizontal continuity of the structure. Similar elements, such as approach girders and arch stringers, should be painted the same color across the whole structure. Where steel and concrete girders are used together, the steel paint color should be selected to match the concrete. Bright color applied to a secondary element, such as a railing, can be used to visually pull together different structural types. The bridge in Figure 6-35, with its light-colored parapet, and the one in Figure 5-39 (page 162), with its distinctive railing color, show the effectiveness of using a colored horizontal element to unify a structure and emphasize its horizontal sweep.

When selecting colors, the apparent color of the water will be an important consideration over the wider waterways. Apparent water color is a function of the color of the water itself, which can vary by season depending on runoff and temperature, and sky color, which will also vary by day and season. Multiple observations over an extended period will be necessary to establish the dominant color or colors that should be used as a basis for the decision.

FIGURE 6-35 *The lights on this bridge are spaced to fit into the spans (six per span) and coordinated with the railing spacing as well.*

FIGURE 6-36 *Bridge light reflections on the water are an important part of the nighttime scene.*

### *Surface Treatment and Ornamentation*

Traditional brick and stone are generally not convincing when used as components of these bridges. The spans of these bridges are generally so much larger than historic masonry structures that the use of the materials is not credible. Stone or brick pier facing is one use of traditional materials that is consistent with historic uses of these materials.

Most of the bridge will be in view over the water at one time from many viewpoints. Drawing attention to points of interest along the structure can improve the appearance of these structures. Structural details can be specially designed to perform this function. Added color or detail at points of structural importance can contribute as well. If there is a pedestrian walkway on the structure, overlooks at key piers will punctuate the sweep of the structure and provide a pedestrian amenity.

Pedestrian walkways on river crossings must be made wide enough to be comfortable for two people to walk abreast or pass each other. Because of the length of these structures an otherwise adequate width can seem narrow. Six feet should be the minimum, with larger widths for walkways that are expected to get significant use and/or bicycle traffic. Patterns in the walkway surface should be used to break down the apparent length of the journey into manageable increments.

### *Signing, Lighting, and Landscaping*

Because of their length and the frequent presence of intersecting roadways at their ends, this type of structure is often called on to support sign structures. Integrating the sign structure with the superstructure and/or parapet design is the important factor.

Lighting is also often a consideration for this type of structure because of the length. Size, spacing, and style of the fixtures may have a significant impact on appearance, and should be considered in relation to the overall design intent for the bridge. The fixtures will produce reflections in the water that will magnify their impact at night. Pole spacing should coincide with or be an even multiple of the spans or the spacing of other structural features.

If the lighting is to continue along an adjoining roadway or river walk, a light fixture and pole spacing should be selected which fits the overall concept and detailing of the bridge as well.

Landscaping elements are too small to have much of an impact on the appearance of the overall bridge. However, landscaping may be a very important part of shoreline uses, and may affect the appearance of bridge elements on shore, particularly abutments.

See Chapter Five for more ideas on signing, lighting, and landscaping.

**FIGURE 6-37** *This viaduct visually organizes a complex scene and creates the "ceiling" of an outdoor "room."*

**FIGURE 6-37** *This viaduct visually organizes a complex scene and creates the "ceiling" of an outdoor "room."*

## INTERCHANGE RAMPS AND VIADUCTS

Simple diamond and cloverleaf interchanges usually have one structure or paired structures which are basically highway overcrossings and can be treated that way. More complex interchanges require multispan ramps. They form a separate category, with many features in common with viaducts.

### Developing a Design Intention

#### Physical Requirements

Ramps and viaducts typically have a complex set of requirements related to the intercrossing roadways, railroads, utilities, and land uses. Each of these will have horizontal and vertical clearance requirements, some of which may overlap or conflict. The first step is to locate all of the requirements on a plan and profile of the structure and see if any logical pattern presents itself. The challenge of the structure will be to develop an arrangement of piers and superstructure which creates an apparent visual order among the conflicting requirements.

#### Visual Environment

The visual environment for ramps is usually dominated by the highway interchange of which they are a part. The graded, landscaped slopes and other nearby bridges will set the backdrop against which the structure must make its impression. These environments are spread out, but visually complex, with curved roadways seeming to intersect in space in ways which may not be immediately obvious. Drivers have the problem of finding their way through the complexity, a stressful process which distracts from their ability to enjoy the experience.

Viaduct sites usually have a different kind of visual complexity. The undercrossing roadways, utilities, etc. are often at varying angles to each other and the structure. Even if the undercrossing facilities are on a street grid at right angles to the structure, there will be buildings, stands of trees, parking lots and vacant spaces of various sizes and shapes and at varying intervals.

Again, the challenge is to bring some apparent visual order to the complexity.

### Nearby and Associated Uses

For a ramp the nearby uses are mostly highway related. The need is for safety for off-the-road vehicles and sight distance to ramp terminals and the traffic ahead. Ramps sometimes become part of shopping malls, office parks, or even downtown development. Then buildings become part of the backdrop of the structure. Their uses, size, color, and materials should become a consideration in determining the appearance of the structure.

Viaducts are usually in and among other uses. The appearance of nearby buildings and natural areas, and the uses expected for the area under the structure, need to be considered in forming the design intention. Areas under viaducts are often used for pedestrian circulation, parking, park, even industrial and commercial uses. The underside of the viaduct then becomes the "ceiling" of a large outdoor "room." Its appearance and lighting become important considerations.

### Symbolic Functions

Ramps are usually seen as a functional feature of the larger interchange of which they are a part. It is difficult and unusual for them to have a symbolic function apart from the symbolism of the interchange itself. Major interchanges are sometimes seen as milestones along a freeway; as points of orientation or entrance. As the most prominent feature of the interchange, the ramp structures might be called on to demarcate the interchange or set some theme. Ways that can be done include picking an unusual structural type, parapet or abutment pattern, or color and using that feature on all of the structures of a given interchange.

In addition to this larger function, ramps can contribute to the attractiveness of interchanges by demonstrating the smooth and efficient flow of traffic.

The symbolism associated with viaducts is often negative. It was a viaduct that first earned the nickname, "the Chinese Wall." Viaducts can be seen as the dividers of communities and the attractors of vandalism and building vacancies. Avoiding these effects depends on maintaining clear sightlines through the structure in as many directions and from as many viewpoints as possible. It also depends on arranging piers in logical patterns which complement the pattern of the underlying facilities. It is important to avoid the creation of odd bits of land and hidden areas which cannot be reused and which become unattractive nuisances.

### Boundaries

Ramps should seem to blend into the geometry of the roadway they are carrying, to become an extension and continuation of that roadway. In that sense they should not have a clear boundary.

Because viaducts are generally long and close to other uses, it is often difficult to see the entire structure at one time. All that can be seen is a slice of the structure. Again, the structure does not appear to have boundaries.

However, the boundary assumed along a viaduct can have a significant effect on the visual quality of the result. Particularly important is the condition of the ground surface under the viaduct. If the boundary of the structure is assumed to be the bottom of the piers, then the ground surface will be left bare and unkempt, and the structure will attract the nuisances described above. The boundaries should be set at the edges of the ground plane of the nearest uses, and the whole surface area between those boundaries developed as part of the design of the structure. That may mean paving for parking, landscape or hardscape for park uses, or whatever is required to bring the underbridge area back into a productive use that complements its neighbors.

### The Design Intention

The viewpoints in complex interchanges are usually a multiplicity of locations along the intersecting roadways. The most important can be identified based on traffic volumes of the roadways from which the ramp will be visible or length of time a particular structure is in sight from a given roadway. If the ramp is among or near adjoining buildings, then points of visibility where people gather in or among the buildings should be located.

Viaducts, particularly in urban areas, will have an almost infinite number of viewpoints, many of which may involve pedestrian traffic in close proximity to the bridge. With this range of possibilities, it is hard to identify specific features of the bridge as being more important than others. Any and all features could be important depending on the circumstances.

However, with both ramps and viaducts, the following features will be important in all cases:

- the shapes created by the basic horizontal and vertical geometry;

- pier placement relative to underbridge area;

- structural type or types;

- the appearance of the underside.

The most powerful visual aspect of interchange ramps and viaducts is the sweep of the roadway geometry itself. It is the most important visual characteristic of the structure and must be enhanced to develop the visual strength necessary to overcome the surrounding visual cacophony. Ideally, it should be married with the superstructure, to produce a structural ribbon carrying the roadway over and under various obstructions.

The second most powerful visual tool will be establishing a strong and logical order of piers which complement the sizes and spacings of the underlying facilities.

When designing a ramp or viaduct:

- *strive to bring out the basic geometry of the structure,*

- *establish a visual order with the piers which complements the patterns of adjoining uses, and*

- *focus on few and consistently used materials, few and consistently used shapes, and continuous surfaces and shapes.*

Interchange ramps and viaducts in urbanized areas represent a special challenge since they often require the integration of bridges and retaining walls. They also require placement of lighting, signing, and even traffic signals on the bridge.

Since urban interchanges and viaducts are inherently confusing, the visual design goal should be to make the structure and appurtenances as simple as possible. Because of the need to focus attention on traffic signals and signs and because of the frequent presence of pedestrians, the design of the underside becomes even more important. Once again, simple details and shapes consistent with the overall structure and aligned along the outlines of the major structural elements help to create the impression of visual order.

FIGURE 6-38 *A good ramp structure in Nevada becomes a visual statement of the roadway geometry itself.*

FIGURE 6-39 *Torsionally stiff box girders in California allow thin central piers, making this an excellent structural type for complex interchanges.*

## Determinants of Appearance

### Roadway Geometry

Because of their length and their position, the geometry of these structures will be the most powerful element in forming people's visual impression. That shape will be visible from many of the important viewpoints. It is critical that the geometry produce an attractive overall shape, without dips and kinks. The horizontal and vertical alignments should be constructed from long continuous curves.

The geometry will also determine the nature of the structure alignment with undercrossing roadways and uses. It is important to investigate adjustments in the alignment which would make possible a more regular placement of piers or avoid the creation of leftover slivers of land.

### Superstructure Type

Girders are the most frequent form for ramps and viaducts. The spans are generally not long enough to require other types. Girders provide a ribbon of structure which fits the need for visual continuity. Relative slenderness should be sought when picking superstructure type, and curved girders should be used for curved roadways.

Because of the height and locations of these bridges, their undersides will often be prominent, particularly where pedestrians are involved. The designer should approach the features of the underside with the knowledge that they will be important factors in forming people's visual impression of the bridge. Concrete slab and box structures avoid visual clutter and provide a light-reflecting surface for the "ceiling" as well. Figure 6-37 (page 214) is a good example. Steel box structures can have similar qualities, particularly if they are painted a light color.

Precast I-girders and steel plate girders present more of a challenge because of the shadowed areas between the girders and the visually confusing and dirt-catching bracing required. Such bridges can be made acceptable with attention to the details and lighting and, in the case of steel, with a light paint color. See Chapter Four for a discussion of details.

Viaducts and ramps often have to contend with many conflicting geometries in undercrossing roadways, railroad tracks, and utilities. It can be a particular problem if the structure must cross a street grid or rail yard at an oblique angle. The transverse geometry created by pier caps at right angles to the ramp or viaduct itself imposes an additional geometry which may conflict with all of the others. The solution is often to arrange the pier caps at odd angles to the roadway geometry in an effort to mediate between the roadway and what it must cross. The visual result of this approach is always disastrous. What is already a visually complex situation becomes hopelessly confused as the pier caps interrupt the roadway geometry and disrupt any chance for the roadway to create an overriding order. The structural situation becomes more complex, too, as every girder and pier cap becomes a different length. Figure 4-43 (page 117) is an example of how bad the problem can get.

Integral pier caps are a potential solution. They are less obvious, and their geometry does not interfere with the roadway geometry. The flexibility in pier placement they provide can assist in dealing with conflicting underbridge conditions while allowing a uniform girder span. By keeping the girder depth constant and using an integral pier cap the viaduct in Figure 5-21 (page 143) spans a series of streets simply and cleanly. Box girders with interior pier caps are particularly successful in resolving these problems.

Keeping the parapet-girder-overhang edge condition uniform along the structure will reinforce the sweep of the roadway geometry, on which the visual success of the structure depends.

### Pier Placement

The placement of piers is a major opportunity to create a visual order which will organize a complex scene. A strong and logical pattern is the goal. Piers should be placed in a consistent relationship to undercrossing streets and other features so as to create a regular spacing or a smoothly varying progression of different spacings.

FIGURE 6-40 *Three different pier types create a sense of visual confusion.*

FIGURE 6-41 *The strong pattern of piers in California creates a strong visual order which can override confusion on the ground plane.*

Undercrossing roadways at differing angles will suggest piers skewed at different angles. This will result in a complete confusion of appearance from below. In this case piers should be placed so they are parallel to others in a series or radial to the overroadway.

The best approach is to plot all of the restrictions on pier placement on the plan view—roadways, pedestrian areas, utility crossings, buildings, and streams—then develop pier placements that satisfy the restrictions and still preserve a clearly organized layout.

Because the structure will often be seen from oblique angles the piers will often seem to line up one behind the other. There are two ways to alleviate this problem. The first is to extend span lengths, considering superstructure costs and foundation costs together to develop optimum span lengths. The second is to use wider overhangs in the superstructure to allow narrower piers. Both approaches open up spatial corridors through the structure, including the diagonal corridors often seen from important viewpoints.

### Abutment Placement

For ramp structures, the abutment placement should begin with the grading plan of the interchange as a whole. The slopes should be shaped to provide smoothly flowing landforms. Once that is accomplished, the abutments can be established. Abutment heights should be kept to a minimum to emphasize the horizontal continuity of the structure.

For viaducts, abutment placement will be a function of the location of the underlying facilities that are being spanned. Abutment placement should be approached using the same guidelines that are used for pier placement. The abutment should be seen as simply the last pier in the series.

### Superstructure Shape

Superstructure shape should be developed to emphasize the continuity and visual sweep of the structure. It is important to seek girder dimensions and details which emphasize apparent thinness and horizontality, and to keep structural depth constant or smoothly varied over the entire bridge.

Haunches can be used on a ramp or viaduct for a few unusually long spans. However, a long series of haunches tend to look disturbing unless the spans are more or less equal and the height above the base plane is similar from span to span.

Ramps and viaducts often require widening and splits in the bridge to accommodate ramps and acceleration lanes. Any structure involving individual girders requires the layout of girders in such a way as to logically accommodate the gradual change in width.

The parapet face can be shaped to emphasize the horizontal continuity of the structure by means of offsets to create shadow lines and other patterns. Railings and noise walls, if present, should be detailed with the same goal in mind.

**FIGURE 6-42** *Long span lengths and wide overhangs with narrow piers allow diagonal views through this structure in Switzerland.*

### Pier Shape

Because there will be so many piers, and because they will be visible from so many different viewpoints, it is important to minimize the number of elements and keep the shape simple. One way to do that is to use piers which eliminate or minimize the pier cap. This is particularly important when undercrossing streets cross at various angles, as the pier caps will be at conflicting angles with all but one of these undercrossing streets, thereby setting up a visual conflict.

Since the structure will be seen from many viewpoints it is important to design piers that create pleasing compositions when seen together. Keep the slopes and curves of adjoining piers consistent. If the structure gets higher or wider it will be necessary to provide a method of gracefully lengthening or widening the pier so that the series of piers looks good when seen together.

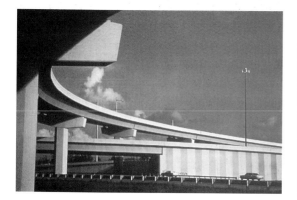

FIGURE 6-43 *The continuation of the parapet overhang on this ramp abutment extends the horizontal shadow line of the structure; the effect would have been improved if the lines of the girder had been extended by keeping the vertical pattern on the retaining wall below the level of the bottom flange of the girder.*

FIGURE 6-44 *Large overhangs emphasize horizontal continuity and minimize pier width. The notched piers create "fingers" which seem to barely touch the superstructure floating overhead. (Note how the girder smoothly deepens to provide a haunch for the longer span in the distance.)*

### Abutment Shape

Ramp abutments in landscaped interchanges will be relatively minor elements in the visual scene and should be kept simple, small, and shaped to emphasize the continuity of the ramp structure. If a ramp abutment ties into a retaining wall, it should be detailed to carry through the same pattern as the adjacent retaining wall.

Viaduct abutments will often be prominent elements from nearby viewpoints and should be compatible with surrounding features. If their are buildings or particular street features nearby, the abutment can be detailed to reflect them.

FIGURE 6-45 *Viaducts and ramps should split in a simple and clear manner.*

## Color

Color can be used to emphasize the continuity of these structures. Placing a strong color on the girder, railing, or some repetitive feature of the parapet will tie the whole structure together and give it a presence which will help the structure unify the overall scene.

## Surface Texture and Ornamentation

A continuous surface texture or pattern on the parapet face can also help unify these long structures.

Since the abutments are such small parts of most viaducts, textures or patterns on the abutments will not have much effect on the overall impression. Abutment patterns or textures can improve the impression the bridge makes in their immediate area. When abutments are part of retaining walls, texture and pattern can be effective in emphasizing the continuity of the structures.

## Signing, Lighting, and Landscaping

There are usually alternate locations for signs in interchanges. Every effort should be made to keep them off of ramp structures. The sign will always seem to interrupt the visual continuity of the structure.

If signs cannot be avoided, the size of signs for undercrossing roadways should be adjusted so that the vertical dimension stays below the parapet top. Sign structures on the ramp bridge should be integrated with the superstructure design.

FIGURE 6-46 *The lights correlate to the structural members, reinforcing an attractive pattern while providing illumination to the area below.*

FIGURE 6-47 *Use of the ground plane under this New York viaduct restores the connection between the uses on either side.*

Sign structures are often part of viaducts. The long length of the structure makes them unavoidable, both for the undercrossing roadways and the viaduct itself. Again, supports for sign structures on the viaduct should be integrated with the superstructure design. (*See* Signs on Bridges in Chapter Five, page 173.)

Lighting of the underside of urban interchange structures and viaducts is often important for reasons of function, as well as appearance. Lights should be placed to coordinate with the major structural elements and the traffic patterns below. By taking this approach the lighting can be made to make a positive contribution to the visual impression over and above merely providing light.

Supports for roadway lighting should avoid interrupting the overall sweep and continuity of the structure. Widenings, or "blisters," tacked onto the parapet can be distracting unless detailed with a smooth taper.

In interchange areas and along viaducts, it is sometimes possible to use higher, ground-mounted poles, which can be a preferable solution.

Landscaping can provide an important visual contribution to both ramp and viaduct structures. An interchange landscaping plan can emphasize the major forms of the interchange and the continuity of the roadways while screening out distractions. Such a plan will make traversing the interchange both a safer and more pleasant experience.

Landscaping and hardscaping areas under and near viaducts is an important way to knit back together again the uses on either side, making the space under the viaduct a neighborhood asset rather than a neighborhood nuisance.

## RAILROAD BRIDGES

This section concerns bridges carrying railroads. Bridges carrying highways over railroads are similar in many respects to highway overcrossings and viaducts. The ideas for such bridges can be derived from those sections of the book.

Bridges for transit lines represent a different category. The loads imposed by transit trains or cars, whether "heavy" rail or "light" rail, are substantially less than those imposed by railroads. The structural types and dimensions are similar to those used for highway construction. The visual guidelines developed in the other sections of this book, particularly the section on ramps and viaducts, apply to transit structures as well.

## Developing a Design Intention

### Physical Requirements

The railroad's alignment is typically less flexible than the highway's. The clearance requirements imposed by the railroad will be a controlling factor. If the structure is part of an existing railroad the need to keep the track(s) in service will impose construction staging requirements which will influence the type of structure and the methods of construction. On streets and arterials provisions for pedestrians are often requirements which create design problems and opportunities.

FIGURE 6-48 *The deck overhang helps this structure seem thin; the abutments are set back so that views through the structure are opened up.*

### Visual Environment

Railroads often abut industrial areas. Bridges there will be seen as just a part of a larger industrial complex. However, grade separations are also required in residential, commercial, agricultural, and wooded areas. In such areas the structure can be the largest feature of the street scene or neighborhood of which it is a part, and will attract the attention of people in the area. Its position as a visual focus needs to be recognized and understood.

### Nearby and Associated Uses

If there are nearby residential and commercial buildings they will become the backdrop for the structure. It will be necessary to consider the compatibility of the structure with the nearby buildings. If there are to be pedestrian uses through or around the structure their needs should be considered. The emphasis must be on clear visibility to all parts of the pedestrian walkway and a clean and pleasant environment under the structure.

An often-overlooked criterion is the need to provide clear lines of sight through the structure. Railroads can literally and figuratively divide communities, presenting a "Chinese wall" appearance. Extensive visibility through the structure along the connecting street can help to visually knit the community back together.

### Symbolic Functions

Railroads being the utilitarian facilities they are, the symbolic functions of these structures is usually limited. However, the position of a particular structure in a particular streetscape may give it symbolic importance.

For example, one could imagine a grade separation project on the main street of a small town that could become the symbol of reuniting a town formerly divided by an at-grade railroad line. It would be important to design the structure so that the functional division of the at-grade tracks is not replaced by an equally disruptive visual barrier.

Railroad passenger stations are not the entry points they once were. Now many have become the centerpieces of historical redevelopment areas. A bridge in the vicinity would become an important symbolic adjunct to their historical revival.

### Boundaries

Along the line of the railroad the boundaries of the project will most likely be the abutments of the structure. Along the line of the undercrossing street the boundary will depend on the extent to which the project is part of a larger streetscape or pedestrian environment. Then it will be important to continue the paving, lighting, and other items far enough to reestablish the visual as well as the physical connection through the structure.

### The Design Intention

The most important viewpoints for railroad bridges are typically associated with the undercrossing roadway. If that roadway is part of a freeway system or an arterial that carries only highway traffic, the important views of the structure will be no closer than 300 to 500 feet. At any point closer viewers will be looking through the structure to features beyond. The time available to appreciate the structure will be similarly limited depending on the point at which it first becomes visible and the speed of approach. For such structures the important visual features will be the large elements. Details smaller than about four inches will not be noticed.

Structures over arterial streets and roadways with pedestrian traffic can be seen at a leisurely pace and at fingertip distance. Decisions about details and materials will have more impact on the visual impression.

Bridges carrying railroads over highways create an entirely different visual impression than the typical highway structure. Because of the heavier railroad loads and the reluctance of railroads to use continuous structures, the superstructures become very deep and appear heavy. The design challenge is making these deep structures appear graceful.

The visually most important features are likely to be:

- superstructure characteristics, especially the depth-to-span ratio;

- pier and abutment design, especially the substructure/superstructure interface;

- superstructure details.

While there are some design tactics which can be used to give the structure additional grace, the inherent strength and weight of the structure must be recognized. The best impression is created when this strength is displayed, while at the same time the apparent length of the structure is maximized.

*When designing a railroad bridge, try to reduce the apparent depth and weight of the structure and extend its apparent length.* Unfortunately, the design of ordinary railroad bridges moves in just the opposite direction. Piers are extended vertically to hide the bearings, which also visually cuts the girder into shorter lengths and makes it appear deeper, while the vertical stiffeners visually shorten and deepen the girder even more.

## Determinants of Appearance

### Geometry

There is rarely much room to maneuver with the geometry of the railroad. Any flexibility that may be available will be with the alignment of the undercrossing street. That should be checked to see if it is possible to adjust the geometry to enlarge views through the structure or to create a more graceful transition with the roadway on either side of the bridge.

### Superstructure Type

The most usual type of structure for railroad bridges is a welded-steel-plate girder. In recent years there has been some use of posttensioned concrete and steel box girders as well. Truss bridges were frequent decades ago but are now rarely used except for spans beyond the range of this book. The decision is generally controlled by economics and the preferences of the railroad's engineering staff. Concrete may have some visual advantages because there is no need for stiffeners and the color is lighter than A588 steel. However, these differences are not compelling.

It is important not to interrupt the view of the girders with pilasters or cheek walls at the piers and abutments. If not interrupted, the girder will seem to be one horizontal unit with an apparent depth-to-span ratio for the whole unit which is thinner than the actual ratio for each individual girder.

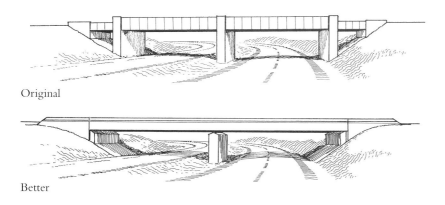

Original

Better

**FIGURE 6-50** *Placing the abutments back on the slope opens up the structure better than adding side spans.*

### Pier Placement and Abutment Placement

Because of the loads there is a natural desire to keep the spans as short as reasonable. For spans over one or two roadways this can mean simply placing piers at the points permitted by the undercrossing roadways. However, the spacing should appear logical and not produce variations in girder depth. Keeping the girder depth the same over the entire structure will make the bridge seem longer and therefore thinner.

Short spans over side slopes are a particular problem. If the girder is kept the same depth over the smaller span the short-span girder will look unreasonably heavy. If the short-span girder is made thinner a jump in girder profile will be created. In this case little is gained visually by the additional spans, as the heavy shoulder piers block most of any additional view through the structure. It is better to use instead an abutment placed as far from the edge of the shoulder as the budget will allow.

### Superstructure Shape

Railroad bridges present limited opportunities for influencing appearance, but the available ones should be explored. Girder dimensions and details can be used which emphasize apparent thinness and horizontality, and structural depth can be kept constant or smoothly varied over the entire bridge. For deck girder bridges a limited overhang may be available which can be enhanced to establish a horizontal shadow line which will make the bridge seem thinner.

When it comes to shape, railroad bridge girders are similar to Henry Ford's Model T. Model Ts came in one color: black. Railroad bridge girders come in one shape: rectangular. One variation available for a through girder is to round the upper corner of the girders. This is a worthwhile, if subtle, detail because it adds a touch of interest that would not be there if the gird-

**FIGURE 6-51** *This*
*through-girder bridge shows the advantages of exposed high bearings and variable stiffener spacing in making a bridge seem longer and thinner. By holding the constant depth girders up off the pier caps the bearings allow the horizontal lines to be seen, making the bridge seem longer and thinner. The signs over the opposing lanes disrupt this effect and would have been better placed elsewhere.*

er were just sliced off. Tapered or haunched girders are worth exploring if the railroad will permit continuous structures, or to provide visual continuity between long and short span girders.

Details of the stiffeners and bearings are the primary areas for making the girder appear to be thinner and more graceful. Use high bearings, pedestals, or chamfers at pier tops to visually attenuate the bearing point. High-bearing shoes with pin connections to the girders in particular can exaggerate the apparent length of the girder. They also make the girder appear lighter because the girder is supported by a feature which seems very small compared to the size of the girder. In order to take advantage of this possibility the shoes must be visible. In no case should pilasters be used to hide the bearing.

The pattern of stiffeners on steel fascia girders can be used to improve the appearance of the structure. Horizontal stiffeners can be used to visually subdivide the girder and make it appear thinner. This is another application of the visual illusion illustrated in Figure 2-15 (page 41). Vertical stiffeners can help if their spacing is allowed to vary according to the shear stress. This creates a pattern which varies horizontally (the stiffeners are closer together over the supports), which encourages our eyes to move horizontally, and therefore exaggerates the horizontal dimension of the girder.

Deck girders require a parapet and/or railing. The details of these features should be developed to enhance the horizontally of the structure, as shown in the structure in Figure 6-49.

### Pier Shape

Notwithstanding the techniques described above, the girder will still seem large and heavy. It is necessary that the pier seem to be clearly capable of supporting this weight. Any details should seem to reinforce the pier's weight-carrying ability. The emphasis should be on large simple shapes.

By its shape the pier can enhance the apparent length of the girder. A pronounced chamfer at the top of the pier will emphasize the continuity of the superstructure. It also reinforces the visual effect of high bearings.

A special situation exists where supports for electrical catenary must be carried on the bridge. If such a situation is unavoidable, the best approach is to widen the piers, and carry the catenary poles directly on the piers. Alternatively, the poles can be carried to the ground beside the piers. Any attempt to support the catenary on the structure itself will result in a hopelessly complex and heavy detail.

### Abutment Shape

The comments above about clearly being able to support the weight of the girder and enhancing the apparent length of the girder apply to the abutment as well. Other guidelines which help are to slope the face of the abutment outward to emphasize the separation between abutment and girder, to reduce the apparent height of the abutment, and make it appear to have a greater carrying capacity, since it appears wider on the bottom. Wing walls should be aligned parallel to the railroad and parapet and railings should be carried out to the ends of the wing walls. Bearings are a major structural element and should be left exposed. These actions will have the effect of making the bridge seem longer and therefore thinner.

### Color

Color can provide an inexpensive way to reduce a girder's apparent depth by dividing the girder horizontally into different areas of color. It helps if a

FIGURE 6-52 *The apparent depth of this railroad bridge is reduced by the band of contrasting color above the horizontal stiffener. The pier would be improved without the pier cap end, which is a visual distraction and is too thin to be structurally convincing under the massive girder.*

horizontal stiffener forms the line of division because it provides a visually logical location for the change (Figure 5-39, page 162).

### Surface Texture and Ornamentation

In areas where there are pedestrians or slowly moving traffic the use of patterns or texture on abutment walls can add interest. Any special patterns, textures, or materials should be complementary with nearby uses and buildings.

Historic railroad bridges often used the logo of the railroad company on the pier or painted on the girder. They demonstrated how visually helpful it was to break up these large areas of steel and concrete. Town logos, graphic designs inset in the concrete, small areas of bright color, and other devices can be used in the same way to add interest to these large and otherwise feature-less structures (*see* Figure 6-48, page 225).

### Signing, Lighting, and Landscaping

Signs are less of a problem on a railroad bridge than they are on a highway bridge. The bridge is deep and bulky to begin with, and the sign is less likely to project above the upper edge of the structure.

Lighting may be a necessary feature for the underbridge area and its approaches if there will be pedestrian uses.

Landscaping in the abutment area can be an effective way to reduce the apparent size of high abutments and should be seriously considered.

**FIGURE 6-53** *A pedestrian bridge which incorporates thinness, lightness, and a visual response to the concentration of forces.*

## PEDESTRIAN BRIDGES

The following discussion is aimed at freestanding pedestrian bridges. There are many other pedestrian bridges which are built to connect buildings or parts of buildings. These represent fascinating design problems because of their need to tie both physically and stylistically into the architecture of which they are a part. Such structures are not addressed in this discussion.

## Developing a Design Intention

### Physical Requirements

Span requirements are usually set by the clearance envelope of the undercrossing facility. Pedestrian approach requirements will be dominated by the regulations of the Americans with Disabilities Act (ADA), which sets ramp grades, widths, turning radii, and surface requirements. The nature of the crossing and its users may impose requirements for screens which prevent the dropping or throwing of objects on undercrossing vehicles.

### Visual Environment

Pedestrian crossings can occur in any type of environment: residential, commercial, industrial, and undeveloped. If the area is developed the facades of any nearby buildings will be important backgrounds. Often pedestrian structures are associated with school playgrounds, parks, or open space greenway systems where the background is formed by landscape features, trees, and grass.

The bridge will also be an important feature to persons on the undercrossing roadway, whether in vehicles or not. There may also be areas where people congregate in the surrounding neighborhood that should be investigated as potentially important viewpoints.

### Nearby and Associated Uses

Nearby land uses will determine the nature of typical users of the structure. Bridges near schools and sports facilities will be used by people in groups who may well be in a boisterous mood. The need for security screens should be recognized. Structures associated with a park or art museum, on the other hand, may have less need for such elements.

### Symbolic Function

Since pedestrian bridges are relatively lightweight structures one would think that they would not have the presence to carry a major symbolic burden. However, there are many cases where a pedestrian bridge has been called on to do precisely that. For example a nearby institution or sponsor, such as a corporation or museum, has often used a pedestrian bridge to make a statement about its activities and values. Design engineers have used the opportunity to exhibit innovative structural concepts. Even in less-significant situations the bridges are often very important to the life of a neighborhood, the residents of which value the symbol of safe connection provided by the structure.

It is important to recognize all of these potential concerns and incorporate them in the design intent of the structure.

### Boundaries

The structure cannot be considered independent of the pedestrian system that feeds into it. There are too many pedestrian bridges that are bypassed by their intended users because the ramps/stairs look too steep or because the approaches and/or structure seem too far off their intended direction of travel. Pedestrians are a contrary lot. They will seek the apparent shortest route between two points. A successful pedestrian bridge must look like it is that route.

The trick is to design the structure so that it either occupies or seems to occupy that shortest line between the two points. Grading, landscaping, and fencing can be used with pathways and the structure itself to create the impression that the structure is indeed the quickest and easiest way to get where people are going. The view should at all times present an easily traversed path which is secure, interesting, inviting, and the most direct route to the intended destination. That means that all of these associated features must be considered part of the bridge project. They must be designed and built at the same time.

### The Design Intention

Pedestrian bridges are a unique opportunity to develop light and graceful structures. They look best when the superstructures are kept very slender, and the lines of the structure flow continuously over the supports and into the ramp or stair sections. Since stairs are inherently discontinuous features, real design ingenuity is required to integrate them smoothly into the balance of the structure. Ramps are much more easily accommodated.

When designing a pedestrian bridge, it's important to:

• create the best pedestrian route,

• conceive the span and ramps/stairs together as one continuous structure,

- strive for lightness and continuity, and

- incorporate the symbolic aspirations of the community and/or sponsor.

Pedestrian bridges are the place to let the imagination run free.[1]

## Determinants of Appearance

### Geometry

Because of the typically lightweight structure of the bridge, the geometry of the pathway will dominate the shape of the structure. Even with all of the requirements of the ADA and the need to present to users the appearance of a direct and efficient path there is more flexibility in the design of the pathway geometry than there is with roadways. The pathway geometry should be considered an aspect of the design of the whole structure. It should be developed as part of the superstructure development.

The structure will look best if the geometry flows with continuous gentle curves. If the space available imposes straight line elements, then at least the connections between them should be curved. It is particularly important that vertical crest connections be long and continuous vertical curves. A kink in the vertical alignment will be annoying to both users and observers.

With pedestrian bridges there is also the possibility of varying the width of the walkway. This can be done to accommodate the superstructure concept, to tie into branching pathways at the end of the structure, to provide an overlook opportunity on the structure, or just to enhance the visual interest of the bridge.

FIGURE 6-54 *The asymmetry of the bridge responds to the asymmetrical wall of the ravine, creating a memorable scene for users and neighbors.*

FIGURE 6-55 *The railing of this pedestrian bridge has elements that reflect the triangles of the truss.*

FIGURE 6-56 *A suspension pedestrian bridge gives the lightest appearance, yet makes the strongest visual statement*

### Superstructure Type

Girders, trusses, arches, rigid frames, cable-stayed, and suspension bridges have all been used for pedestrian bridges in the span ranges which are the subject of this book. Relative slenderness should be sought when picking superstructure type. Continuity of structural form, material, and/or depth should be maintained.

Girders are the most simple and straightforward, but can appear too heavy for their load, particularly if used in a deck configuration. The design of the parapet/railing/screen then becomes very important in establishing the impression created by the structure.

Trusses can be detailed to be light and graceful in appearance. One technique is to use a Warren configuration with no verticals and with all of the diagonals at the same angle. Trusses have the advantage that the pedestrian screen can be incorporated within the structural envelope, without requiring additional posts and fittings. Standardized, predesigned truss structures can be a very economical choice. Structures of this type are offered by a number of manufacturers. If well detailed they can offer the same visual advantages as custom designed structures.

If the site offers slopes or rock outcroppings that are natural places to found an arch or rigid frame then these can be appropriate types of structures. At less robust sites tied arches or combinations of full and half arches can be used. Another option is to use the abutment/ramp/stairs as opportunities to create massive elements that will contain a true arch or rigid frame. If the arch can be kept flat enough it is possible to place the pathway directly on the upper surface of the arch rib.

Arches have an appealing gateway appearance that may be particularly appropriate in some situations. The arch pedestrian bridge in Figure 2-11 (page 38) uses the arch itself as the walkway.

Cable-stayed and suspension bridges offer the lightest possible appearance and the most flexibility in the horizontal geometry. They can be structures of exhilarating grace.

However, such structures require talented and sophisticated design and knowledgeable contractors. It can be difficult to integrate the design of a pedestrian screen without losing the appearance of lightness. Finally, the height of the towers may not be appropriate at some locations.

### Pier Placement

Pier placement will be determined by the needs of the undercrossing facility and the nature of the superstructure. Since these structures tend to be visually light in weight and thin they do not present the same sense of visual obstruction as other structures. This gives the designer more flexibility in locating the piers, and in particular to place piers in logical relation to topographic features.

### Abutment Placement

The abutments can be very important visual features for this type of bridge. The visual impression is sometimes dependent on the contrast between a light and airy structure and a massive abutment or approach ramp.

Because of the light weight of the superstructure, it is even more important than usual to keep the abutments far enough back from the edges of pavement to maintain clear views through the structure for any undercrossing roadways. Otherwise there will be a visual question: Why crowd the roadway edge with the abutments when a few more feet of apparently inexpensive superstructure would solve the problem?

### Superstructure Shape

Since the goal is to present an appearance of lightness and thinness, it is necessary to shape the superstructure in ways that achieve that end. It is important to seek dimensions and details which emphasize apparent thinness and horizontally, and to keep structural depth constant or smoothly varied over the entire bridge.

To keep the bridge light in appearance concrete parapets should be avoided, unless the parapet is also the supporting girder. Use a full-height railing or pedestrian screen instead.

Deck overhangs will be smaller on a pedestrian bridge, but can still have a significant influence in making the structure seem light and thin.

The railing/screen design will have a major impact on the impression created by the bridge. There are two reasonable approaches.

The first is to keep the design as simple as possible, with the emphasis on horizontality. This approach is more compatible with arch and cable-supported structures. These superstructure types have strong shapes of their own with much intrinsic interest. Figure 6-56 shows a good example. Elaborately detailed railing/screens can distract from the structural shape and diminish its appeal.

The second approach is to elaborate the screen design with details that become decorative motifs responding to the surrounding areas and/or the symbolic intentions of the structure. Since girder and truss structures can seem bland, elaborately detailed railings can add interest that would otherwise be missing. With truss structures it is important for the details to be consistent with the basically triangular geometry of the truss. Figure 6-55 shows how this can look.

Because the users are in such close contact with the pathway the details of drainage can have more of an impact than on roadway structures. A roadway usually has a curb and gutter arrangement which accepts drainage and debris and carries them away. Even if some leftovers remain they are seen as part of the street, not the sidewalk. On a pedestrian bridge water and debris must be handled on the walkway surface. They often get trapped in pockets along the intersection between pathway and parapet, making the walk unattractive and perhaps impassable with ordinary shoes. Positive methods of handling drainage and debris must be provided.

Leaving the edge open is the best way to get rid of both drainage and debris. If the edge must be closed a small gutter should be provided next to the parapet/railing, with enough outlets to avoid overflows.

### Pier Shape

The piers also should present an appearance of lightness and thinness. This quality can be emphasized by chamfering the top of the pier and using

**FIGURE 6-57** *This branched pier recalls the shapes of natural forms, and seems quite appropriate for this light-weight structure.*

**FIGURE 6-58** *This abutment provides in an integrated manner for both ramp and stairs.*

high bearings to visually disconnect the pier from the superstructure.

The piers are also an opportunity to create shapes that add interest to the structure. This will be especially true and necessary for the towers of cable-supported bridges. The shapes must be consistent with the pier's load-carrying requirements, but that does not require them to be bland.

### Abutment Shape

The abutment can be a very important visual foil for the superstructure. If the superstructure is a true arch, the abutment must provide the visual weight to convincingly contain the thrust of the arch. If the superstructure is a girder or truss the abutment must support them in such a way that they seem to lightly touch down. For cable structures the visual focus will be on the towers, and the abutments should be kept small and simple so as not to compete.

The abutment is often required to serve as a stairway or ramp, or both. If these requirements are gracefully integrated the result will be a visually successful structure.

FIGURE 6-59 *The lighting of this structure is made part of the ornamentation of the tower.*

### Color

Color is one economical way to add presence to a pedestrian bridge so that it can carry a symbolic design intention. The color selected needs to have a specific symbolic and/or compatible relationship to the area and/or sponsor. One example would be using the colors of a nearby university for a structure used primarily by its students. Another would be selecting a color that is the complementary color to the dominant color of background woodlands.

By simply making the bridge an unusual visual event in an otherwise unnoticeable series of structures color can convert the bridge into a neighborhood symbol. People will remember and remark on "the red bridge."

### Surface Texture and Ornamentation

Surface texture is a valuable way to add interest to and enhance the user's passage across the structure. Here the previously stated rules about large-scale

detail are reversed. Pedestrian users will more enjoy smaller features, particularly if they are amenable to touch.

Ornamentation will be more likely to be appreciated at pedestrian speeds and distances, also. The elaboration of railing designs discussed above is a type of ornamentation. Logos of towns or sponsoring institutions or abstract patterns are other possibilities. Lighting fixtures and posts can be ornamental in themselves, even when not lit. The fixture design should have a clear relationship to the design of piers and towers, so that the bridge looks like it was designed all at once, and the fixtures don't appear to be afterthoughts.

### Signing, Lighting, and Landscaping

In one of the few exceptions about signs on structures, signs can be successfully integrated into the design of truss pedestrian bridges. The structure provides a depth which is of the same order of magnitude as the sign panel's vertical dimension. Also, the structure itself looks a bit like the familiar sign bridge.

Other types of pedestrian superstructures are not as hospitable to signs. Arch and cable-supported structures are particularly incompatible with signs. If a sign absolutely must be accommodated at a particular location then that may be a presumptive reason to select a truss design there.

Lighting is a very important feature of pedestrian bridges, for both security and visual reasons. Unless the whole area is lit by high-mast fixtures normal roadway lighting will be too uneven to be comfortable for pedestrians.

Separate fixtures specifically designed to light the walkway both on and off the bridge should be provided.

In designing this arrangement it is necessary to avoid glare for both walkway users and drivers on the undercrossing roadway. Sharp cut-off fixtures should be used. The type of light source used (mercury vapor, high pressure sodium, etc.) should be selected to complement the materials and colors used in the structure.

Landscaping can be a valuable adjunct to pedestrian structures. It can be helpful in directing users toward the desired route, in providing additional interest and pleasure for users, and in complementing driver's views of the structure.

---

1   For inspiration, see the book on Jorg Schlaich's pedestrian bridges: Oster, Hans Jochen et al., 1994. Fussgangerbrucken, Jorg Schlaich und Rudolph Bergermann Katalog zur Ausstellung an der ETH Zurich. Zurich, Switzerland: Institut fur Baustatik und Konstruktion.

chapter *seven*

# MAKING IT HAPPEN: RELATED CONSIDERATIONS

*"When the design philosophy from top management to the actual design team is one that encourages beautiful structural design, the end result can be an aesthetically pleasing structure that is also economical."*

—JAMES E. ROBERTS,
AMERICAN BRIDGE ENGINEER,
FROM ESTHETICS IN CONCRETE BRIDGE DESIGN.[1]

The dreary appearance of many everyday bridges is not due to a lack of good intentions among designers. Most engineers do believe that concern for appearance should be an integral part of their work, but improvement may be beyond their powers as individual engineers. Engineers respond to the priorities of their clients—governmental highway departments, toll authorities, public works departments, and transit agencies—who may or may not have made appearance a priority. Their elected officials and their public may not have given clear direction that appearance is important. Their engineering education may not have given them the wherewithal to respond. This chapter addresses these issues.

## THE ROLE OF BRIDGE-BUILDING ORGANIZATIONS

### The Aesthetic Responsibilities of Engineer/Managers

Governmental highway departments, toll authorities, public works departments, and transit agencies are the key decision makers when it comes to the

FIGURE 7-1 *The result of a policy of apathy and neglect.*

FIGURE 7-2 *The result of a policy of knowledge and concern.*

quality of America's bridges. They set the standards, select the designers, and pay for the results. Each of these agencies has an aesthetic policy, whether it realizes it or not. Just as every bridge produces an aesthetic impact, each agency's bridges, taken together, enunciate that agency's aesthetic policy. It may be a policy of apathy or ignorance, but it has its effect nevertheless. The relevant issue about an aesthetic policy is not whether it exists, but the quality of the bridges it produces.

A number of bridge-building agencies have made appearance an integral consideration in their bridge building. It is an integral part of their planning, preliminary design, final design, construction and maintenance. Concern for aesthetics becomes a routine part of job descriptions, consulting contracts, standard details, and employee and consultant evaluation. These agencies face all of the same time, money, and political constraints as any other, yet they are able to build bridges that are attractive assets in their communities. Most of the better examples in this book are not special structures built in special circumstances; they are typical products of these agencies, built to the same high standards as all of that agency's bridges.

Perhaps an individual engineer working as an employee or consultant cannot expect to change an agency's aesthetic policy, though he or she should certainly take advantage of opportunities to exert influence. On the other hand, engineer/managers running an agency can improve an agency's aesthetic policy, and should do so.

Engineer/managers usually cite one or more of the following reasons why they don't try to improve their agency's aesthetic policy. Let's examine each one.

1. *The bridges will cost more.*
   Not necessarily true, as we saw in earlier chapters.

2. *The bridge design will cost more.*
   Again, not necessarily true, once a training and transition period takes place.

3. *With our production schedule and/or manpower levels we can't afford the time to train and revise procedures.*
   There is an unavoidable cost in time and money to retrain and install new procedures and standards. However, if this is an insurmountable obstacle, one must ask if the agency intends to *ever* make *any* improvements for *any* reason. Most agencies have some budget allowance for staff development and procedural improvement. If these resources were focused on aesthetics for a short period, much could be accomplished without little disruption to established budgets and schedules.

4. *The public/governor/legislature mayor/council doesn't care about better-looking bridges.*
   They probably don't *know* that they can have better-looking bridges. They've been numbed by mediocrity. Any active bridge-building agency will have had recent instances where the appearance of a bridge has become controversial. These instances prove that people care. Good appearance is part of the value they expect to get for their tax money.

Engineer/managers in public agencies have a professional responsibility to the public to bring the best practice of the profession into their agencies.

**FIGURE 7-3** *Routine excellence in North Carolina.*

For the same reason that they recommend the adoption of new materials or improved construction techniques when they believe them to be cost-effective, engineer/managers should recommend the best aesthetic policies for their agencies.

There are easy to find examples where excellent aesthetic policies have been established within all of the usual constraints of budget and politics for any engineer/manager to say it can't be done. Again, one can cite organizations as different as the California Department of Transportation, the Tennessee Department of Transportation, the Ontario Ministry of Transport, and the Washington D.C. Metro who have done exactly that.

Americans want full value for their tax money. They want not *just* bridges, but *beautiful* bridges. It is up to engineer/managers to find ways to satisfy that desire.

## Improving an Agency's Aesthetic Policy

There are four steps in accomplishing this:

1. Establish aesthetic quality as an explicit goal of the agency.
2. Upgrade the skill of engineers and consultants.
3. Remove bureaucratic barriers.
4. Review standard details and procedures.

### Establish Improved Aesthetic Quality as a Goal

An agency usually gets what it asks for. In order to get better-looking bridges an agency must ask for them. The first action is to announce improved aesthetic quality as an explicit agency goal. The second is to make improved aesthetic quality an explicit criterion for every bridge under design. The announcements should make clear that the improvement is to be made within the agency's current cost structure.

The announcements must be communicated in an effective way, then reinforced through seminars, conferences, and newsletters. Aesthetic quality needs to become an integral part of employee recognition. Consulting contracts, evaluations, and procedures need to incorporate aesthetic concerns.

### Improve Skills

Training programs need to be established which improve the aesthetic abilities of agency design engineers and consultants working for the agency. This step is key, for it is out of the efforts of engineers working on specific bridges that guidelines, details, and, eventually, policies will evolve. Seminars, in-house mini-competitions, and case studies of recent agency bridges can all be valuable teaching tools.

### Remove Bureaucratic Barriers

The typical methods of organization within an engineering agency impose barriers to aesthetic improvement. For example, the design of a bridge is sometimes broken down sequentially among different groups of engineers. One group may do the preliminary design. A second group may do the final design. A third group will review it. All will make some changes during this process. A fourth group of engineers may develop some of the details, such as parapet designs, which may be applied years later to bridges which were not even conceived at the time the details were developed.

As a result, it is difficult for a unified concept to emerge, and the result is often a visual hodgepodge. The solution is to place more of the total design of each structure in the control of one person or group, including the ability to modify standard details if the situation calls for it.

Problems often arise even before the design of the bridge itself begins. The position and alignment geometry of a bridge is usually determined beforehand by a highway engineering division. Often this geometry is treated as fixed for the purpose of bridge design. However, there are often small changes in the vertical and horizontal alignment that would make major improvements in the appearance of the bridge at no significant detriment to the highway design. Because of the split between highway and bridge design functions, bridge engineers are not able to obtain these changes. The placement of signs on bridge structures is often handled the same way, without an opportunity for alternate locations to be found.

**FIGURE 7-4** *Nobody cared what this bridge looks like, and the result shows it.*

Bridge design procedures should be changed to give bridge designers an opportunity to feed back to the highway designers and others and obtain needed changes.

### Review Standard Details

Perhaps the single biggest impediment to improved aesthetic policy is the inertia created by inappropriate standard details. Since small- and medium-span bridges are so numerous, many agencies view their design as a process of assembling standard details. Standard pier shapes, parapet profiles, and standard abutments essentially establish the appearance of an average highway overcrossing no matter what else the designer might do. There is some obvious economy in this approach. However, it does not relieve anybody of responsibility for the appearance of the resulting bridge.

The basic truth is this: a standard detail can save money regardless of whether it is attractive or ugly. Why not make it an attractive one? Why grind out mediocrity when, for the same price, you can grind out beauty?

An appearance criterion must first be applied to the standard details. Do they produce attractive bridges? Then it must be applied to the use of the details for each specific bridge. Are the details appropriately applied to this particular bridge, or should they be modified or disregarded?

There are many agencies which use standard details to achieve excellent performance, reasonable cost, and outstanding appearance, *all at the same time.* They do it by developing attractive details to start with, then allowing their designers the flexibility to apply them at the appropriate place.

**FIGURE 7-5** *California bridges such as this one benefit from the application of standard pier shapes and other standard details.*

California has approached this problem by developing a series of standard attractive pier shapes for use with their typical concrete box girder bridge. The series provides for variety—rounded versus faceted designs, for example—but it is limited to a manageable number of variations. Knowing that designs will almost always come from one of these standard shapes, contractors and form rental companies feel safe in investing in the specialized forms required. Since these forms can be written off against many jobs, their cost ceases to be a factor in deciding which shape to use. The result is bridges that are both attractive and economical.

An agency should take a comprehensive review of the effect on appearance of all of its standard details. Then each can be revised to contribute to the overall aesthetic concept that the agency is seeking to develop and to give designers more flexibility. While the functional aspects of standard details must be respected, their appearance should be reconsidered for each bridge to make sure they fit that bridge's design concept.

# EDUCATING ELECTED OFFICIALS AND THE PUBLIC

## Good Appearance and the Public Purse

Americans have not been clear concerning their desire to have visually attractive public works. Calls for better-looking structures have often been overwhelmed by calls for economy, leaving politicians and public works officials indifferent or actually hostile to concerns about aesthetics.

The basic problem is a general perception that improved appearance will automatically cost more. The experience from states such as California, Tennessee, and Washington, and the Province of Ontario proves that this perception is mistaken. Excellent appearance can be achieved with cost-effective design. These agencies do it routinely. Engineers, user groups, contractor groups, elected officials, and the public need to be educated to this fact. Engineers should be spreading the word to elected officials that quality appearance does not have to cost more.

Groups interested in scenic quality and urban design are potential allies in this effort. These groups are often squelched on the basis that "mere aesthetics" should not rank with matters such as education and public safety in the competition for tax dollars. If good appearance need not cost more, then it is no longer a budget issue. That puts these people in a stronger position to request a higher level of performance from public works agencies.

## Competitions

Occasionally a bridge comes along where the problems of structural conditions, public exposure, and/or environmental impact seem to exceed the capabilities of the usual designs. In Switzerland, Germany, and France such situations are often resolved by holding design competitions. In these competitions appearance is made an explicit criterion along with performance and cost. The competition attracts outstanding engineers who develop designs that are often much better than would usually be seen. Because of that fact, and because the community can get involved in picking from alternatives, the competition often successfully resolves stubborn controversies.

The designs also have influence beyond the competition. They are imitated at other sites in subsequent projects, and thus influence the development of the profession. Because appearance is an explicit criterion, competitions have been instrumental in sensitizing engineers to aesthetics and to raising the general level of bridge appearance in those countries.

FIGURE 7-6 *Recent European competition bridge.*

In the United States competitions are unfortunately rare. Most U.S. agencies resolve controversial bridge projects by a time-consuming process. They review successive alternative designs until one is found that the public will support. However, in 1988 Maryland faced a controversial bridge replacement at the Severn River in Annapolis, and decided to resolve it by holding a design competition.

The site is important to Maryland for a number of scenic and symbolic reasons. The bridge forms the eastern gateway to Maryland's capital, Annapolis. Annapolis is an historic city with many fine examples of Georgian and Victorian architecture. The bridge's western approaches lie on the grounds of the Naval Academy. At the crest of the hill beginning the eastern approach there is a stunning view of the Naval Academy and the skyline of Annapolis. The eastern end of the bridge adjoins Jonas Green State Park, which is a community center for fishing, boating, and picnicking. The Severn itself is a scenic tidal river, whose mouth at the Chesapeake Bay is within sight of the bridge. The river is a premier site for recreational sailing, and its shoreline and bluffs are occupied by many fine homes.

The prize was simple: The winning design firm would be contracted to perform the final design for the bridge. In addition, $25,000 in prize money would be awarded. In view of the state's desire to select the bridge design by competition, the Federal Highway Administration agreed to accept the winning concept and not require alternate designs.

The competition began with advertisements in the engineering press and local newspapers in January and February of 1989. The ads invited qualified engineering firms to submit letters of interest outlining their qualifications and previous work of note. Twenty-one letters of interest were received. Based on these credentials six firms were chosen as finalists.

The finalists were each asked to prepare a preliminary design for the bridge. Design criteria were defined by a written Program and Rules. The design had to be prepared in sufficient detail to allow definitive decisions about the sizes of the major structural components of the bridge, and to allow preparation of a realistic cost estimate. Each finalist was paid a fee of $20,000 to prepare its entry. Five of the six finalists submitted their designs. All of the drawings and other materials were identified by code letters only.

A 14-member jury was formed, made up of prominent engineers, an architect, a sculptor and a landscape architect, representatives of the Anne Arundel County and Annapolis governments, interested state agencies, and community groups. The jury was advised by two review panels consisting of experts in bridge engineering and construction. The jury selected the winner (Figure 1-24, page 21), ranked the other proposals, and awarded the prize money. Based on the jury's recommendation the State Highway Administration awarded the contract for the final design to the winning firm, which immediately began work.

The initial public reaction to the selection was almost all positive. Because of the broad-based membership of the jury all of the relevant elected officials felt able to support the selection. When critical statements were received at a later date from a few narrowly focused groups the elected officials' consensus remained firm. When the critics brought suit, the court ruled that the process met all necessary legal requirements.

The competition was successful in achieving a better-looking bridge which resolved the controversy at the site. Because cost was an explicit criterion, the cost of the bridge was comparable to similar bridges in Maryland. The bridge was completed in 1994 to general acclaim, even by many who had originally opposed the proposal. It remains to be seen whether the bridge will influence the design of future bridges.

FIGURE 7-7 *The new Naval Academy Bridge over the Severn River at Annapolis, the result of a competition that resolved a major local controversy.*

## Engineering Education and Aesthetics

School is the natural place to lay the foundation for aesthetic skill. However, in the struggle for a place in the curriculum, aesthetics may not seem as necessary as strength of materials and partial differential equations. On the other hand, the public holds the engineering profession responsible for its decisions—all of them—including the ones that affect appearance. When measured by the number of people affected, aesthetic decisions can be very serious indeed. How shall this responsibility be discharged if no basis for this decision-making is developed in the schools?

Some schools are beginning to respond to public criticism of the narrow base of engineering education by enlarging the place of the humanities in the curriculum, and by providing "Introduction to Engineering" courses which bring forth all of the varied aspects of the engineer's role. Consideration of aesthetics has a natural and indispensable place in both of these efforts.

Other schools have had success by introducing aesthetic considerations in senior-level design courses. A typical bridge is assigned as a design project. Sometimes the local highway agency supplies data on a project current in their program. This lends realism to the project, allowing students to view the site in the field, and to take advantage of traffic, geological, and drainage data that the agency has assembled.

The students are asked to develop a design for the entire bridge. Consulting engineers and contractors participate as advisors. The students often work in groups, in a minicompetition format, with the final designs reviewed by a jury of faculty, agency staff, and consulting engineers. Aesthetics is a consideration along with structural effectiveness, economy, and constructability.

During the project students are exposed to and learn about the entire range of issues present in actual bridge projects, including aesthetics. The excitement generated by the intergroup competition makes the whole experience additionally effective.

1   Roberts, James E., 1990. *Esthetics in Concrete Bridge Design.* Detroit, MI: American Concrete Institute. Editors Watson, Steward C., and Hurd, M.K.

# conclusion

# THE ENGINEER AS STRUCTURAL ARTIST

*"The real cycle you're working on is a cycle called yourself. The machine that appears to be 'out there' and the person that appears to be 'in here' are not two separate things. They grow toward Quality or fall away from Quality together."*

—ROBERT M. PIRSIG, AMERICAN AUTHOR,
FROM ZEN AND THE ART
OF MOTORCYCLE MAINTENANCE

Engineers are the professionals who our society has given the responsibility of designing bridges. Our society asks that their bridges perform well, cost no more than necessary, and look good. They want structures that are assets to their communities, in every sense of that word.

Those facts impose on us, as engineers, the responsibility to learn how to make structures attractive. Other professionals have contributions to make, but it is our responsibility and cannot be delegated. Aesthetics must take its place along side of performance and economy as a criterion of bridge design. The achievement of aesthetic quality must take its place along side the achievement of performance and economy as skills of bridge engineers. Aesthetics is not any more important than the other two, but should not be any less important, either.

Aesthetic awareness will give each individual engineer the potential to create structural art. Engineers such as John Roebling and Gustave Eiffel in earlier times, and Robert Maillart, Christian Menn, Jean Muller, and others of our own time have given us inspiring examples of this art. Any engineer with any bridge can aspire to these standards. While he or she may not always

**FIGURE C-1** *Structural art at Glade Creek in West Virginia; the pier responds to the forces on it while providing a massive contrast to the spidery truss.*

attain them, the experience and the product will be better for the effort.

Unfortunately, the achievement of structural art cannot be guaranteed simply from the application of these guidelines. The guidelines can help the designer avoid the worst errors, provide a standard of basic quality, and point him or her in the right direction. However, the achievement of great art is beyond prescription. It depends on a unique confluence of the problem, the resources, and the sensibility of the designer.

We have reviewed some techniques designers can use to help develop their sensibility. But, in the end, the result will depend on judgments and ideas the designer must find within. Judgments and ideas that are honed by looking at, thinking about, and designing the best possible bridges.

# ILLUSTRATION CREDITS

## CHAPTER ONE

Figure 1-1: Photograph courtesy of J. Wayman Williams.

Figure 1-2: *Bridge Aesthetics Around the World*. (1991 by Transportation Research Board, National Research Council. Reprinted by permission.

Figure 1-3: Eric Hyne, Illustrator, based on photographs by Fritz Leonhardt.

Figure 1-4: Eric Hyne, Illustrator, based on photographs by Fritz Leonhardt.

Figure 1-5: Eric Hyne, Illustrator, based on photographs by Fritz Leonhardt.

Figure 1-9: *Bridge Aesthetics Around the World*. (1991 by Transportation Research Board, National Research Council. Reprinted by permission.

Figure 1-11: Photograph courtesy of Portland Cement Association, Skokie, IL.

Figure 1-12: *Bridge Aesthetics Around the World*. (1991 by Transportation Research Board, National Research Council. Reprinted by permission.

Figure 1-13: Photograph courtesy of Vic Anderson, Delcan Corporation, Toronto, Canada.

Figure 1-14: I-181 over State Route 1, Kingsport, Sullivan County, TN. Photograph courtesy of Tennessee Department of Transportation, Nashville, TN. Designer and Photographer: George Hornal.

Figure 1-16: Photograph courtesy of Mancia/Bodmer, FBM Studio.

Figure 1-17: Billington, David, 1979. *Robert Maillart's Bridges, The Art of Engineering*. Princeton, NJ: Princeton University Press. Reprinted by permission.

Figure 1-18: Photograph courtesy of Mancia/Bodmer, FBM Studio.

Figure 1-19: Billington, David, 1979. *Robert Maillart's Bridges, The Art of Engineering*. Princeton, NJ: Princeton University Press. Reprinted by permission.

Figure 1-20: Billington, David, 1990. *Robert Maillart and the Art of Reinforced Concrete*. Architectural History Foundation and Massachusetts Institute of Technology. Reprinted by permission of MIT Press.

Figure 1-21: Photograph courtesy of Mancia/Bodmer, FBM Studio.

Figure 1-22: Photograph courtesy of Jon Wallsgrove.

Figure 1-23: Benevolo, Leonardo, 1971. *History of Modern Architecture.* Cambridge, MA: MIT Press. Reprinted by permission.

Figure 1-24: Photograph courtesy of J. Wayman Williams.

Figure 1-25: Photograph courtesy of J. Wayman Williams.

Figure 1-27: Photograph courtesy of Juan Jose Arenas de Pablo.

## CHAPTER TWO

Figure 2-1: Photograph courtesy of David P. Billington.

Figure 2-2: Route 1369 over the Watauga River, Washington County, TN. Photograph courtesy of Tennessee Department of Transportation, Nashville, TN. Designer and Photographer: George Hornal.

Figure 2-3: Made available for the National Steel Bridge Alliance/ American Institute of Steel Construction promotional purposes.

Figure 2-4: Photograph courtesy of California Department of Transportation, Sacramento, CA.

Figure 2-6: Photograph courtesy of Solomon R. Guggenheim Foundation, New York.

Figure 2-7: Photograph courtesy of Fritz Leonhardt.

Figure 2-8: Photographer: Michael Freeman. Courtesy of Fruitlands Museums, Harvard, MA.

Figure 2-9: Arenal Bridge, Cordoba. Designer/Photographer: Julio Martinez-Calzon.

Figure 2-10: Drawing by Alicia Buchwalter, based on sketches by the author.

Figure 2-11: Photograph courtesy of David P. Billington.

Figure 2-14: Eric Hyne, Illustrator, based on sketches by the author.

Figure 2-15: Drawing by Alicia Buchwalter, based on sketches by the author.

Figure 2-17: Drawing by Alicia Buchwalter, based on sketches by the author.

Figure 2-18: Eric Hyne, Illustrator, based on sketches by the author.

Figure 2-20: Photograph courtesy of Hed Grouni and Ontario Ministry of Transportation.

Figure 2-21: Photograph courtesy of Portland Cement Association, Skokie, IL.

Figure 2-22: Eric Hyne, Illustrator, based on sketches by the author.

Figure 2-23: Drawing by Alicia Buchwalter, based on sketches by the author.

Figure 2-24: Photograph courtesy of Portland Cement Association, Skokie, IL.

Figure 2-25: Photograph courtesy of Maryland State Highway Administration, Baltimore, MD. Maryland route 213 over Sassafras River. Designer: Envirodyne Engineers, Inc.

Figure 2-26: Photograph courtesy of Maryland State Highway Administration, Baltimore, MD. Maryland route 213 over Sassafras River. Designer: Envirodyne Engineers, Inc.

Figure 2-27: *Bridge Aesthetics Around the World.* (1991 by Transportation Research Board, National Research Council. Reprinted by permission.

Figure 2-28: Made available for the National Steel Bridge Alliance/ American Institute of Steel Construction promotional purposes.

Figure 2-29: Drawing by Alicia Buchwalter, based on sketches by the author.

Figure 2-30: Designer and CAD simulation by Short Elliot Hendrickson/HDR Engineering. Photographer: Neil D. Kveberg, Minnesota Department of Transportation.

Figure 2-31: Photograph courtesy of Fritz Leonhardt.

Figure 2-32: Photograph courtesy of David P. Billington.

Figure 2-33: Photograph courtesy of Steve Ladish.

Figure 2-35: Photograph courtesy of Portland Cement Association, Skokie, IL.

Figure 2-36: Photograph courtesy of Portland Cement Association, Skokie, IL.

Figure 2-38: Melrose Interchange, Nashville, TN. Photograph courtesy of Tennessee Department of Transportation, Nashville, TN. Designer and Photographer: George Hornal.

Figure 2-40: Sleater-Kinney Road Bridge, Interstate 5 Olympia, WA. Washington State DOT Bridge & Structures office, Olympia, WA. Designer/Photographer: R. Ralph Mays, Architect, Olympia, WA.

Figure 2-41: Photograph courtesy of Portland Cement Association, Skokie, IL.

Figure 2-42: Photograph courtesy of J. Wayman Williams.

## CHAPTER THREE

Figure 3-1: Eric Hyne, Illustrator, based on sketches by the author.

Figure 3-2: Photograph courtesy of Fritz Leonhardt.

Figure 3-3: Made available for the National Steel Bridge Alliance/American Institute of Steel Construction promotional purposes.

Figure 3-5: Photograph courtesy of Conrad Bridges.

Figure 3-6: Drawings courtesy of HDR Engineering, Folsom, CA.

Figure 3-7: Drawings courtesy of HDR Engineering, Folsom, CA.

Figure 3-8: CAD simulation by Viscom, Sacramento, CA.

Figure 3-9: Catalogue for the ETH exhibition on Jorg Schlaich. FuBgangerbruckern by Jorg Schlaich and Rudolph Bergermann. Photographer: Ackermann und Partner, Munchen.

Figure 3-10: Eric Hyne, Illustrator, based on sketches by the author.

Figure 3-11: Photograph courtesy of Maryland State Highway Administration, Baltimore, MD. US route 50 over US route 301. Designer: Maryland State Highway Administration. Photographer: Marvin Blimline.

Figure 3-12: Photograph courtesy of Maryland State Highway Administration, Baltimore, MD. I-97/I-595 connector. Designer: Whitney, Bailey, Cox, & Magnani. Photographer: Marvin Blimline.

Figure 3-14: Drawing by Miguel Rosales.

Figure 3-15: Photograph courtesy of J. Wayman Williams.

Figure 3-16: Photograph courtesy of Portland Cement Association, Skokie, IL.

## CHAPTER FOUR

Figure 4-1: Made available for the National Steel Bridge Alliance/American Institute of Steel Construction promotional purposes.

Figure 4-2: Photograph courtesy of California Department of Transportation, Sacramento, CA.

Figure 4-4: Drawing by Alicia Buchwalter, based on sketches by the author.

Figure 4-6: Made available for the National Steel Bridge Alliance/American Institute of Steel Construction promotional purposes.

Figure 4-7: Photograph courtesy of Portland Cement Association, Skokie, IL.

Figure 4-8: Drawing by Alicia Buchwalter, based on sketches by the author.

Figure 4-10: Made available for the National Steel Bridge Alliance/ American Institute of Steel Construction promotional purposes.

Figure 4-11: Drawing by Alicia Buchwalter, based on sketches by the author.

Figure 4-12: Eric Hyne, Illustrator, based on sketches by the author.

Figure 4-13: Eric Hyne, Illustrator, based on sketches by the author.

Figure 4-15: Eric Hyne, Illustrator, based on sketches by the author.

Figure 4-16: Photograph courtesy of Maryland State Highway Administration, Baltimore, MD. Blooming Rose Road over I-68. Designer: Ewell, Baumhardt & Associates. Photographer: Marvin Blimline.

Figure 4-17: Drawing by Alicia Buchwalter, based on sketches by the author.

Figure 4-18: Eric Hyne, Illustrator, based on sketches by the author.

Figure 4-19: Eric Hyne, Illustrator, based on sketches by the author.

Figure 4-20: Eric Hyne, Illustrator, based on sketches by the author.

Figure 4-21: Eric Hyne, Illustrator, based on sketches by the author.

Figure 4-22: Drawing by Alicia Buchwalter, based on sketches by the author.

Figure 4-23: Photograph courtesy of J. Wayman Williams.

Figure 4-24: Photograph courtesy of Hed Grouni and Ontario Ministry of Transportation.

Figure 4-25: Photograph courtesy of David P. Billington.

Figure 4-26: Eric Hyne, Illustrator, based on sketches by the author.

Figure 4-27: Eric Hyne, Illustrator, based on sketches by the author.

Figure 4-28: Eric Hyne, Illustrator, based on sketches by the author.

Figure 4-29: Eric Hyne, Illustrator, based on sketches by the author.

Figure 4-30: Eric Hyne, Illustrator, based on sketches by the author.

Figure 4-31: Eric Hyne, Illustrator, based on sketches by the author.

Figure 4-32: Eric Hyne, Illustrator, based on sketches by the author.

Figure 4-33: Photograph courtesy of Maryland State Highway Administration, Baltimore, MD. I-97 North under Maryland route 3. Designer: Hayes, Seay, Mattern, & Mattern. Photographer: Marvin Blimline.

Figure 4-34: Photograph courtesy of Stewart Watson.

Figure 4-35: Eric Hyne, Illustrator, based on sketches by the author.

Figure 4-38: Photographs courtesy of North Carolina Department of Transportation, Raleigh, NC.

Figure 4-40: Eric Hyne, Illustrator, based on sketches by the author.

Figure 4-41: *Bridge Aesthetics Around the World.* (1991 by Transportation Research Board, National Research Council. Reprinted by permission.

Figure 4-42: Eric Hyne, Illustrator, based on sketches by the author.

Figure 4-43: Photograph courtesy of John Minor.

Figure 4-44: Photograph courtesy of J. Wayman Williams.

Figure 4-45: Photograph courtesy of Maryland State Highway Administration, Baltimore, MD. Old Montgomery Road over I-95. Designer: Green Associates. Photographer: M. A. Zulkowski.

Figure 4-46: Eric Hyne, Illustrator, based on sketches by the author.

Figure 4-48: Eric Hyne, Illustrator, based on sketches by the author.

Figure 4-49: Eric Hyne, Illustrator, based on sketches by the author.

Figure 4-50: Eric Hyne, Illustrator, based on sketches by the author.

Figure 4-51: Eric Hyne, Illustrator, based on sketches by the author.

Figure 4-52: Eric Hyne, Illustrator, based on sketches by the author.

Figure 4-53: Photograph courtesy of Portland Cement Association, Skokie, IL.

Figure 4-54: Eric Hyne, Illustrator, based on sketches by the author.

Figure 4-55: Eric Hyne, Illustrator, based on sketches by the author.

Figure 4-56: Eric Hyne, Illustrator, based on sketches by the author.

Figure 4-57: Eric Hyne, Illustrator, based on sketches by the author.

Figure 4-58: Drawing by Alicia Buchwalter, based on sketches by the author.

Figure 4-59: Eric Hyne, Illustrator, based on sketches by the author.

Figure 4-61: Photograph courtesy of Stewart Watson.

## CHAPTER FIVE

Figure 5-1: Drawing by Alicia Buchwalter, based on sketches by the author.

Figure 5-2: Eric Hyne, Illustrator, based on sketches by the author.

Figure 5-3: Eric Hyne, Illustrator, based on sketches by the author.

Figure 5-4: Eric Hyne, Illustrator, based on sketches by the author.

Figure 5-5: Eric Hyne, Illustrator, based on sketches by the author.

Figure 5-6: Eric Hyne, Illustrator, based on sketches by the author.

Figure 5-7: Made available for the National Steel Bridge Alliance/American Institute of Steel Construction promotional purposes.

Figure 5-8: Eric Hyne, Illustrator, based on sketches by the author.

Figure 5-9: Eric Hyne, Illustrator, based on sketches by the author.

Figure 5-10: Drawing by Alicia Buchwalter, based on sketches by the author.

Figure 5-11: Eric Hyne, Illustrator, based on sketches by the author.

Figure 5-12: Eric Hyne, Illustrator, based on sketches by the author.

Figure 5-13: Drawing by Alicia Buchwalter, based on sketches by the author.

Figure 5-14: Eric Hyne, Illustrator, based on sketches by the author.

Figure 5-15: Eric Hyne, Illustrator, based on sketches by the author.

Figure 5-16: Eric Hyne, Illustrator, based on sketches by the author.

Figure 5-17: Eric Hyne, Illustrator, based on sketches by the author.

Figure 5-18: Eric Hyne, Illustrator, based on sketches by the author.

Figure 5-19: Made available for the National Steel Bridge Alliance/ American Institute of Steel Construction promotional purposes.

Figure 5-20: Photograph courtesy of California Department of Transportation, Sacramento, CA.

Figure 5-23: Photograph courtesy of Portland Cement Association, Skokie, IL.

Figure 5-24: *Bridge Aesthetics Around the World.* (1991 by Transportation Research Board, National Research Council. Reprinted by permission.

Figure 5-25: Eric Hyne, Illustrator, based on sketches by the author.

Figure 5-26: Eric Hyne, Illustrator, based on sketches by the author.

Figure 5-27: Eric Hyne, Illustrator, based on sketches by the author.

Figure 5-28: Eric Hyne, Illustrator, based on sketches by the author.

Figure 5-29: Eric Hyne, Illustrator, based on sketches by the author.

Figure 5-30: Eric Hyne, Illustrator, based on sketches by the author.

Figure 5-31: Eric Hyne, Illustrator, based on sketches by the author.

Figure 5-32: Eric Hyne, Illustrator, based on sketches by the author.

Figure 5-33: Photograph courtesy of Maryland State Highway Administration, Baltimore, MD. Looking North (Orange), Looking South (Green). Designer: Envirodyne Engineers, Inc. Photographer: Marvin Blimline.

Figure 5-34: "Controlling Color" ( Patricia Lambert, 1991 Design Press.

Figure 5-35: "Controlling Color" ( Patricia Lambert, 1991 Design Press.

Figure 5-36: Photograph courtesy of Stewart Watson.

Figure 5-38: Harrison Pike over I-181, Kingsport, TN. Photograph courtesy of Tennessee Department of Transportation, Nashville, TN. Designer and Photographer: George Hornal.

Figure 5-46: Eric Hyne, Illustrator, based on sketches by the author.

Figure 5-49: Drawing by Alicia Buchwalter, based on sketches by the author.

Figure 5-50: Photograph courtesy of Portland Cement Association, Skokie, IL.

Figure 5-51: Photograph courtesy of California Department of Transportation, Sacramento, CA.

Figure 5-52: Eric Hyne, Illustrator, based on sketches by the author.

Figure 5-54: Eric Hyne, Illustrator, based on sketches by the author.

Figure 5-56: Photographs courtesy of North Carolina Department of Transportation, Raleigh, NC.

Figure 5-57: Eric Hyne, Illustrator, based on sketches by the author.

Figure 5-58: Photograph courtesy of Stewart Watson.

Figure 5-59: Photograph courtesy of Maryland State Highway Administration, Baltimore, MD. Maryland route 175 EB over Patapsco River. Designer: Green Associates.

Figure 5-60: Eric Hyne, Illustrator, based on sketches by the author.

## CHAPTER SIX

Figure 6-3: Granby Road over I-181, Kingsport, TN. Photograph courtesy of Tennessee Department of Transportation, Nashville, TN. Designer and Photographer: George Hornal.

Figure 6-4: Photograph courtesy of Portland Cement Association, Skokie, IL.

Figure 6-5: Photograph courtesy of Portland Cement Association, Skokie, IL.

Figure 6-10: Photograph courtesy of David P. Billington.

Figure 6-11: Photograph courtesy of David P. Billington.

Figure 6-12: Photograph courtesy of David P. Billington.

Figure 6-13: Photograph courtesy of J. Wayman Williams.

Figure 6-19: Photograph courtesy of Vic Anderson, Delcan Corporation, Toronto, Canada.

Figure 6-20: Photograph courtesy of Portland Cement Association, Skokie, IL.

Figure 6-22: State Route 62 over White Creek, Morgan County, TN. Photograph courtesy of Tennessee Department of Transportation, Nashville, TN. Designer and Photographer: George Hornal.

Figure 6-23: Photograph courtesy of Portland Cement Association, Skokie, IL.

Figure 6-25: Photograph courtesy of Portland Cement Association, Skokie, IL.

Figure 6-26: State Route 20 over the Tennessee River, Perry County, TN. Photograph courtesy of Tennessee Department of Transportation, Nashville, TN. Designer and Photographer: George Hornal.

Figure 6-27: *Bridge Aesthetics Around the World*. (1991 by Transportation Research Board, National Research Council. Reprinted by permission.

Figure 6-28: Photograph courtesy of Portland Cement Association, Skokie, IL.

Figure 6-30: Photograph courtesy of Portland Cement Association, Skokie, IL.

Figure 6-31: Photograph courtesy of Portland Cement Association, Skokie, IL.

Figure 6-32: Photograph courtesy of Portland Cement Association, Skokie, IL.

Figure 6-33: State Route 20 over the Tennessee River, Perry County, TN. Photograph courtesy of Tennessee Department of Transportation, Nashville, TN. Designer and Photographer: George Hornal.

Figure 6-35: Photograph courtesy of Portland Cement Association, Skokie, IL.

Figure 6-36: Photograph courtesy of Portland Cement Association, Skokie, IL.

Figure 6-37: Photograph courtesy of Fritz Leonhardt.

Figure 6-38: Photograph courtesy of Portland Cement Association, Skokie, IL.

Figure 6-39: Photograph courtesy of California Department of Transportation, Sacramento, CA.

Figure 6-40: Photograph courtesy of Portland Cement Association, Skokie, IL.

Figure 6-41: Photograph courtesy of Portland Cement Association, Skokie, IL.

Figure 6-42: Photograph courtesy of David P. Billington.

Figure 6-43: Made available for the National Steel Bridge Alliance/ American Institute of Steel Construction promotional purposes.

Figure 6-44: Photograph courtesy of Portland Cement Association, Skokie, IL.

Figure 6-45: State Route 386 over I-65, 2-Mile Pike and CSX RR. Photograph courtesy of Tennessee Department of Transportation, Nashville, TN. Designer and Photographer: George Hornal.

Figure 6-46: Photograph courtesy of Paolo Rosselli, Milano.

Figure 6-48: Made available for the National Steel Bridge Alliance/ American Institute of Steel Construction promotional purposes.

Figure 6-49: Photograph courtesy of Portland Cement Association, Skokie, IL.

Figure 6-50: Eric Hyne, Illustrator, based on sketches by the author.

Figure 6-52: Made available for the National Steel Bridge Alliance/ American Institute of Steel Construction promotional purposes.

Figure 6-53: Photograph courtesy of California Department of Transportation, Sacramento, CA.

Figure 6-54: *Bridge Aesthetics Around the World*. (1991 by Transportation Research Board, National Research Council. Reprinted by permission.

Figure 6-55: Made available for the National Steel Bridge Alliance/ American Institute of Steel Construction promotional purposes.

Figure 6-56: Catalogue for the ETH exhibition on Jorg Schaich. FuBgangerbruckern by Jorg Schlaich and Rudolph Bergermann. Photographer: Rudolf Menk, Betonverlag: Dusseldorf.

Figure 6-57: Catalogue for the ETH exhibition on Jorg Schaich. FuBgangerbruckern by Jorg Schlaich and Rudolph Bergermann. Photographer: Gert Elsner, Stuttgart.

Figure 6-58: Photograph courtesy of Portland Cement Association, Skokie, IL.

Figure 6-59: Photograph courtesy of Portland Cement Association, Skokie, IL.

## CHAPTER SEVEN

Figure 7–3: Photograph courtesy of Portland Cement Association, Skokie, IL.

Figure 7–6: Photograph courtesy of Flint & Neill Partnership, Dissing + Weitling Arkitektfirma A/S, Ramboll A/S, and Terence O'Rourke plc.

Figure 7–7: Photograph courtesy of Maryland State Highway Administration, Baltimore, MD. U.S. Naval Academy Bridge over the Severn River at Annapolis, the result of a completion that resolved a local controversy (nighttime view). Photographer: Jill Marie Blimline.

## CONCLUSION

Figure C–1: Photograph courtesy of Steve Ladish.

*ALL OTHER PHOTOGRAPHS AND DRAWINGS ARE BY THE AUTHOR.

# INDEX